ARABIAN DESTINY

ARABIAN DESTINY

The Complete Autobiography

EDWARD HENDERSON

MOTIVATE
PUBLISHING

Published by **Motivate Publishing**

Dubai: PO Box 2331, Dubai, UAE
Tel: (+971 4) 282 4060, fax: (+971 4) 282 7898
email: books@motivate.ae www.booksarabia.com

Office 508, Building No 8, Dubai Media City, Dubai, UAE
Tel: (+971 4) 390 3550, fax: (+971 4) 390 4845

Abu Dhabi: PO Box 43072, Abu Dhabi, UAE
Tel: (+971 2) 677 2005, fax: (+971 2) 677 0124

London: Acre House, 11/15 William Road, London NW1 3ER
email. motivateuk@motivate.ae

Directors: Obaid Humaid Al Tayer and Ian Fairservice

First published by Motivate in 1999
Reprinted 2002, 2010

ISBN: 978 1 86063 029 3

British Library Cataloguing-in-Publication Data. A catalogue record for this book is available from the British Library.

Author's notes

In spelling names I have tended to keep with modern practice. I have not used accents to differentiate Arab letters which have no English equivalent. Many names are customarily written in English omitting the Arabic definite article. For example Al Sharjah is now commonly written Sharjah in place of Ash Shariqah, also I have Al Hasa for Al Asha, and Buraimi for Al Buraimi.

Printed by Rashid Printers & Stationers, Ajman, UAE

Contents

Dedication

I dedicate this book to His Highness Shaikh Zayed bin Sultan Al Nahyan as an expression of my gratitude for his friendship and encouragement over so many years.

Preface

by His Excellency Ahmed Khalifa Al Suaidi

Edward Henderson came to the Trucial Coast in 1948 in the service of Petroleum Development Trucial Coast. Later he entered the British Foreign Service (1956-74) and he ended his career in the service as the first British Ambassador to independent Qatar. From 1976 until his death he was a member of the Centre for Documentation and Research in Abu Dhabi.

The new, unabridged book covers in detail the years 1948-56 and then brings the story up to date with the discovery of oil and its consequences. These years were the best ones both for the Arabs and Britain and it was not until 1971 that the British decided to leave peacefully. As a result, Edward Henderson, both in the search for oil and as a diplomat, did not feel any of the pull of dual loyalty which often confronted British officers during the 19th century. Thus it was natural that Edward Henderson was able to befriend and work with the shaikhs of the Emirates and also with the people; he had a close friendship with His Highness Shaikh Zayed bin Sultan Al Nahyan. His academic achievements in the Centre for Documentation and Research and his lectures in the United States (1982-3) enlightening the American public were much appreciated by His Highness Shaikh Zayed, as well as by academic scholars. I am sure that scholars and diplomats among others will find these memoirs useful and fascinating.

Foreword

by Jack Briggs, Commandant of Police, Dubai, 1965-75

My dear friend Edward Henderson passed away in April 1995, two years after I wrote the foreword to the last edition of his memoirs, entitled *A Strange Eventful History*. The entire manuscript has since come into the hands of the publishers, who decided with Edward's widow, Jocelyn (who remains living in Abu Dhabi through the kindness of Sheikh Zayed), that it should be published in an unexpurgated version, containing as it does 35 per cent more text than the previous edition. This new book provides a more personal account of Edward's life and gives us a valuable insight into the fabric of UAE society and its recent, eventful past. I am delighted that the whole book has now come into publication, and I am sure that Edward would have been extremely proud to see this. *Arabian Destiny* appears with the original dedication to his friend, Sheikh Zayed.

I came to the Gulf the year after Edward Henderson joined Petroleum Development Trucial Coast, an international British run company, and knew him since soon after I arrived. I was first in Bahrain, a comparatively sophisticated place compared to where Edward was then serving. Bahrain was the centre of all activity in the Gulf and a place which every expatriate in the area visited from time to time. The numbers were so small that every expatriate Britisher either knew, or knew of, all the others. But I really got to know him well after he joined the British Foreign Service. I had more contact with him then and we had a common link in that we had both served in Palestine. I soon became aware of the very high regard in which he was held by so many Gulf Arabs, from the Rulers themselves down to vehicle drivers.

After this book was first published I was living in England and had been invited to have lunch with an old friend, Easa Saleh Al Gurg, now H.E., the U.A.E. Ambassador to the United Kingdom. When he heard that I had not read Edward's book he took me to the nearest bookshop and bought a copy, which he gave to me and which I read and enjoyed. Although I took no part in the events Edward relates, I was aware of nearly all of them, simply as an interested bystander, and I was amazed by his modesty about the role which he played in the affairs of those days. But I was almost irritated by the way he set out, in three pages, the events of his life leading up to his time in the Gulf, including more than five years of the Second World War. Circumstances had prescribed for me a very easy war, but I had lived through all the major events of the Second World War and I was still aware of when and where these took place. And here, in Edward's book, I found Dunkirk; the expulsion of the Vichy French from Syria (where the last cavalry charge of the British Army took place); the Special Air Service; the Western Desert; 7th Armoured Division at the Salerno Bridgehead; a Normandy landing on D-Day itself, again with the 7th Armoured; and all the battles right through to Hamburg and VE-Day, all covered in just a few lines, with not even a hint of the significance of being part of these momentous events, each one of which was enough for any man's lifetime.

This same unpretentious style is used throughout the book, and it behoves those who read it to remember this in assessing the achievements of Edward Henderson in the Gulf. I am very proud to have known Edward, to have been considered as a friend by him and to have been asked to write a preface to this new edition of his memoirs.

Foreword to the 1988 and 1993 editions: *This Strange Eventful History*

by the late Sir David Roberts

Edward Henderson's fascinating book tells two important political stories; and a lot more besides.

First, there is the story of how the Sultan of Muscat was enabled to establish a united state of Muscat and Oman with oil reserves to propel its primitive economy into take-off and to play a vital role in the security of the Arabian Peninsula. For centuries the authority of the Sultan of Muscat over the interior of his country had been precarious, since it was disputed by the Ibadhi Imams. The whole history of Oman is characterised by a series of Imamates in Ibadhi tradition with a number of intervening years without an Imam when the state was still regarded as viable.

The capital was always in the interior until 1748. When the present dynasty drove out the Persians in the middle of the 18th century they put the capital on the coast in Muscat and kept it there. This succeeded under strong Sultans but not under the strongest of all, Saiyid Said (1807-56), because of his preoccupation with empire building in Africa. The interior became more and more independent. In the 19th century there were short periods of union and longer periods of partial disunion. In 1913 the interior based on the highland area revolted and only the British saved the Sultan. In 1921 a curious agreement was made at Sib by which the interior became semiautonomous. (Petroleum Development Trucial Coast [PDTC] had a concession with the Sultan before the Second World War; but the problem was that the Sultan and his government had very little authority inland and he and his ministers and officials were not allowed to visit it.) Under a sort of *modus vivendi* the Imam's people had Muscat passports, paid customs on entry of goods and could go to the Muscat appeal court. Otherwise they were virtually independent.

In the 1950s an Ibadhi Imam, supported by money and arms from Saudi Arabia, attempted to assert complete independence of the Sultan. Edward Henderson, representing Petroleum Development Trucial Coast, intrigued with the shaikhs of one of the leading tribes (the Duru) and in effect persuaded them to acknowledge the Sultan's rule and thus create the minimum of stability required before a company would incur the expense and risk of drilling for oil. He succeeded in the teeth of the Sultan's refusal to support his operations, indeed his actual veto against any operations. As a result the Sultan's authority was established (although only after some spectacular operations by the SAS) and oil was found. Throughout this period Henderson acted as an independent agent to promote what he believed to be British and Omani interests. He was proved right.

The second story, also set in the 1950s, is the capture and the pacification of Buraimi, the name loosely applied to a large oasis in the north of Oman which is an equivalent of Crewe Junction to the communications of the desert and lies amid rich oilfields. An armed Saudi band, with the support of an American oil company eager for new concessions, had taken control of Buraimi in breach of a Standstill Agreement between the British Government, acting on behalf of the Sultan of Muscat, and the Ruler of Abu Dhabi. A British expedition of Trucial

Oman Levies captured Buraimi and removed the Saudis and their supporters. Henderson accompanied the expedition as Political Officer charged to prevent bloodshed. This succeeded and a further step was taken towards the security of this strategic area. The author was very modest indeed about his own doings, but I know from British and Arab participants that he played a conspicuous part in these important events.

So steeped was he in the tradition of the area that he wrote exactly like a Bedu telling a tale in a *majlis* or round a fire in the desert. But he also conveyed a vast quantity of information about tribal customs and history which anyone who has had to deal with that part of the world will recognise as of inestimable value. Those of us who served in the Gulf always knew that the Gulf Arabs and their ways of doings things were an intricate speciality within the wider speciality of the Arab World. A diplomat might speak excellent Arabic and have deep experience of the Levant or Egypt or the Maghreb, but he would need at least six months before he could comport himself in a *majlis* or at an Arab feast and even longer before he could arbitrate with confidence between two contending Rulers in a dispute over land or water. When I was Ambassador to the United Arab Emirates in Abu Dhabi from 1977-81 I always told any visiting British official or businessman that if he wished to apply himself seriously to Abu Dhabi he must first carry in his head the family tree of the Al Nahyan family; otherwise he would simply not understand the personalities or their motives for action. Edward has captured not only the detail of this world but the authentic flavour of the Arabs of the area. I would urge any young diplomat or businessman who aspired to work effectively in the area to read this book slowly and at leisure; and to dip back into it from time to time.

I first knew Edward when I was Political Agent in the Trucial States, based in Dubai from 1966-8; and he used to visit us from Bahrain, where he was on the Political Resident's staff. It was quickly clear to me that I could learn from an hour's talk with him what it would take me weeks and some luck to find out for myself. He could walk in unannounced, just as the Bedu do in their curiously democratic way, to the *majlis* of any Ruler the length of the Gulf, a privilege enjoyed by few Britons indeed. My great friend and mentor, the late Geoffrey Arthur, held the same view of Edward as I did.

I heartily commend this book by a valued friend and colleague of many years' standing. We can all learn from a man who quietly belongs to the long tradition of British explorers of the Arabian Peninsula, and who could truthfully say, "I have done the State some service; and they know it."

Introduction

There have been dramatic changes throughout the world over the last 20 to 30 years, but has any one of them been as startling and remarkable in its effects as those which took place in the country which is now the United Arab Emirates and in the neighbouring Sultanate of Oman? Our first reaction must be 'Thank God it all happened'. That is the heartfelt sentiment which runs through this story.

Much has been written of the economic, social and material advances that have been so quickly made in those states, but do we yet have a picture of what it felt like to the people of these countries (and to any one who was involved with them right through this time up to the present)? The changes in the Gulf were entirely different from those which took place elsewhere in the world.

We have seen the astonishingly quick development of 'new towns' in Europe and America, but these places were built in a 'developed' country; services were available, so were materials, machinery, engineers, workers and all the necessary communication networks. Anyone can build a new town if he has a big bank balance, but supposing he has no bank, nowhere for imported engineers, managers, skilled tradesmen, doctors, nurses and so on to live, and only a tiny labour force with no skilled workers at all to draw on.

In the shaikhdoms as late as the 1950s there were no medical services, no port to land machinery and equipment, no electricity, bridges or roads. Add to this one of the fiercest summer climates in the world and you have what we are inclined to call 'a problem'. Imagine a population explosion in Abu Dhabi shaikhdom from (say) 40,000 in 1960 to over half a million by 1984, and more than double that for the whole country in less than 25 years. This vastly increased population now has every modern facility to be found in any top-standard-of-living country in the world; here you have something you can safely call an achievement.

I lived inside this turmoil, always amazed, always slightly unbelieving; yet it is all true and it has happened and the people of the shaikhdoms are naturally very happy that this is so. Both the nationals and the expatriates had to work very hard to find and produce the oil which made it all possible, and then work even harder to achieve all this development so quickly and so well.

Part of the story I found most exciting, all of it fascinating, as I lived through it and saw and heard it all happening. I hope also to give some idea of how the people of the area emerged after suffering the hardship of a terrible economic depression and how they all worked to turn the riches from underground, which annoyingly we never actually see, into a new reality above ground and into happiness for their children. Credit for all this must go to the people who carried out the work, to the experts from abroad who brought in the necessary technical expertise, and above all to the leaders whose inspiration made it all possible.

The Buraimi *Falaj* System

(underground water-canal system)

Key:

Falaj

Areas already cleaned

Underground crossings (tunnels)

The author prepared this map of *aflaj* (plural of *falaj*) and their springs in 1955, when he was supervising their cleaning. A frame was drawn around palm plantations to determine their boundaries, while houses (not appearing on the map), were on the fringes of those plantations.

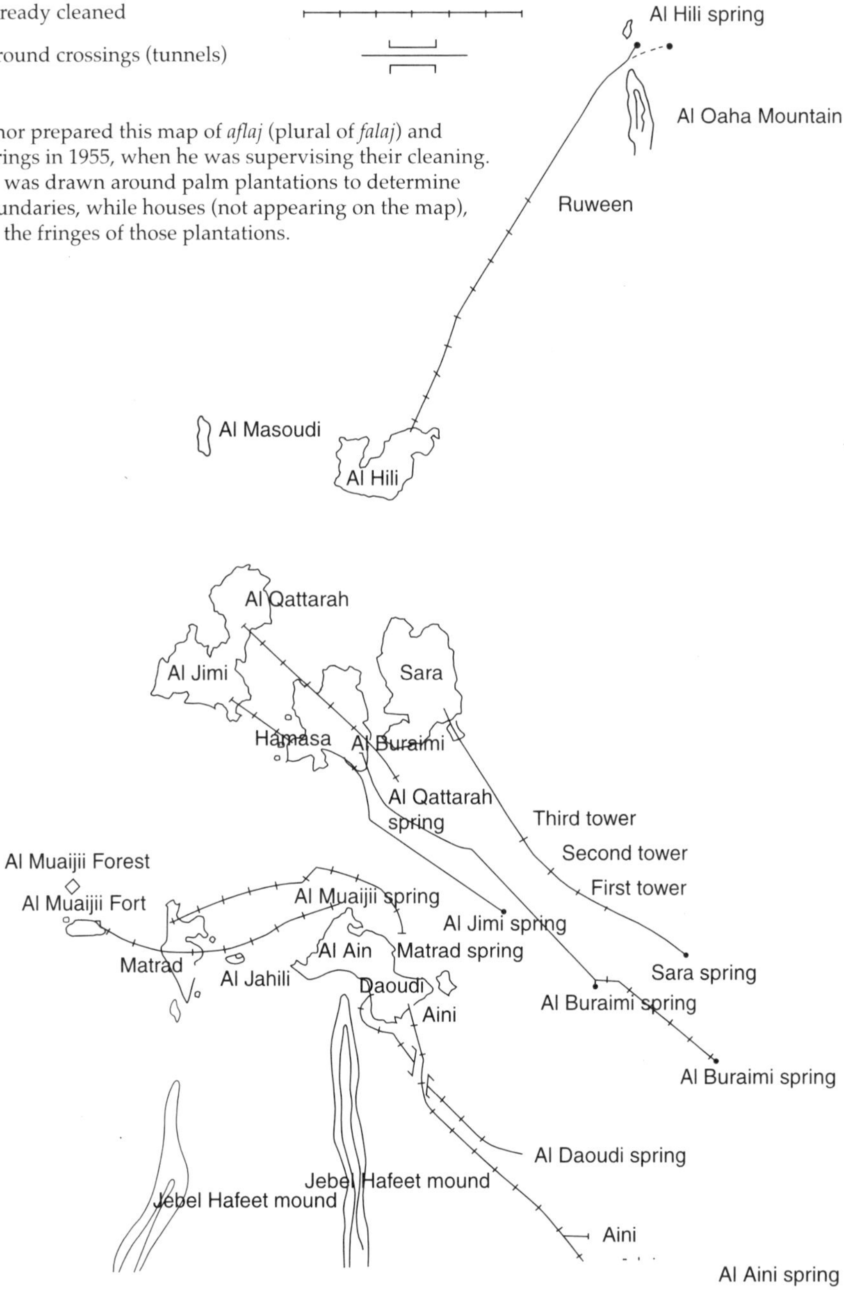

Chapter One

In the 1920s and 1930s I grew up in the easy, comfortable, perhaps rather self-satisfied, ambience of an English provincial city, Bristol. When I think of it now I seem to recall most easily all those intensely respectable occasions, christenings, weddings, the lace, the tulle and the heavily scented, over-starched and slightly, but only so slightly, over-dressed people.

In particular, the Jubilee year of 1936 stands out in my mind and, of the events of that year, the enormous military parade which covered the whole expanse of the wide parkland of Durdham Downs, a parade so huge that orders for its serried ranks had to be given by flag from the top of a scaffold. A few Bristol fighters, even in those days looking antique, flew over us with the fabric of their wings glinting and shimmering in the sun, while in front of us all someone rather important fell off his horse.

After Bristol came three years at Oxford, at Brasenose College; exciting in so many ways, but still to me it had the cloying atmosphere of the English provinces, albeit with Oxford's unique character pervading the mixture.

I suppose it was my fault that I found it just a little dull; I sought an escape in books, and in particular I devoured Liddell Hart, Gertrude Bell, 'The Seven Pillars of Wisdom' and others on Arabia. Much as I had grown to love Oxford, I began almost to ache for the Arab lands I read of, and I longed to go there and be in some special sense, in my imagination, free.

I read all I could find about Palestine and Jordan. In the process I inevitably began to form a view about the

Palestine problem. The books which I read tended to look at it more from the Arab side than from that of the Jews. But this was not invariably the case; historical textbooks tended to be dispassionate and tried to be objective. Churchill saw the problem through Zionist spectacles; and, after all like most Westerners of the day, the book I knew better than all others was the Bible. Like everyone else in the West, I started with a strongly in-built pro-Jewish prejudice. Like the majority in the West, I felt an obligation to compensate the Jews, and surely it was for us to do it.

I can record, therefore, that from reading widely and from what I learned from the contemporary press reports, the main conclusion I reached was that the Palestinians had suffered, were suffering and would suffer more. They were up against the Zionist ideology which the Western world accepted as being inevitable and right, and they seemed powerless to resist. I was then very critical of the Arabs in their failure to put their case, and in their repeated and apparently automatic reaction which was to boycott the many commissions of enquiry which the British set up, their standard way of trying to wash their hands of an insoluble problem.

I was often to come across, and began to accept, this same reaction in Arabia in later years. If an Arab feels that his rights are being unjustly trampled on, particularly in the matter of territorial occupancy or sovereignty, he will say simply: "Our rights are known." To his mind there is no point discussing it; it is undignified to have to lay claim to something which is known to be yours. You may have to fight, but it is pointless to discuss what is no more or less than fact.

I heard it put another way. If you have owned for many years an expensive rug and someone else laid claim to it and the authorities said it must go to arbitration in a court, you might perhaps at best, if you accepted arbitration, lose half of it. But if you refuse arbitration and the other party agrees to it, authority being what it is, you would lose it all. Such is the position of the weak among political giants, such was the position of the Palestinian who had his house and his lands, his way of life, his freedom, taken away from him by just such a process.

The war took me first to France, and then the scramble over the beaches of Dunkirk and an inglorious return to Britain (an incident which we perplexingly managed to make sound like a triumph). Then I went to Arabia, first to Palestine and Syria for the brief campaign there and then spent some time in Egypt in the western desert, before returning to the deserts of Syria and Transjordan. Afterwards it was back to Libya, followed by the Salerno landings, and then to Britain in time for 'D' Day in Normandy. I remained with the army (I was then in the headquarters of Armoured Division – the 'Desert Rats') up to the entry into Berlin.

I had met Glubb Pasha, Commander of the Arab Legion in Transjordan during the war. After it was over I applied for service there, although this meant signing on for another two years instead of enduring six months or so in Germany, followed by demobilisation.

It was a choice I have never regretted. In my earlier days in Syria I had been out with the bedouin, riding a camel and sleeping in the open or in their tents and now I would have the chance to see more of their fascinating way of life. Much of the next two years was spent in Palestine itself, but I had some opportunities to go into Transjordan and make further camel trips, and enjoy the freedom of nomadic life.

In the desert evening when I had been riding with one or two companions all day we would make our camp wherever we had reached at sundown. This meant hobbling the camels to let them be free to graze, collecting brushwood for our fire and spreading our rugs and blankets by it. Many were the times when, returning with a fresh load of brushwood, I would find our camels eating what we had already gathered of the driest sticks, seeming to prefer it to the lush green bushes which I, in my innocence, thought any sensible camel ought to enjoy. The fire lit, coffee beans would be ground, with the merry rhythmic ting-tang of our heavy brass pestle. A paste of flour and water would be thrown on the cinders for bread and this and dates would be our evening meal.

Some evenings we would come up to the low black tents of goats' hair, which the nomads call 'houses of hair', and we would be welcomed to join their inhabitants round the fire in the tent's mouth. There we sat in the glow of the fire on which the hawk-beaked coffee pots would be quietly sizzling, their coffee to be drunk from the tiny clattering cups in appreciative noisy sips. The long tent rope stretched out into the night to a wooden peg in the sand beyond our view, and outside the ring of the fire-light. Immediately above us was the tent's roof, and between the thick black threads of its weave the stars glinted, and out beyond it was the black sky and its festoon of stars.

Perhaps a dozen figures sat at ease round the fire, voices rising and falling. One of their number would hold forth in sonorous tones and others would join in the discussion; this was the scene for a night in the desert. One winter night in such a tent, when the talk had finally stilled and the glow of the fire grown a little duller, we each wound a blanket round us and settled to sleep by the fire. A little later the wind changed suddenly and started to blow into the tent's mouth. This was the occasion for our host to clap his hands and call to the women, who lived in the other part of the tent behind a wattle screen, to get up quickly to pull down the tent walls on one side and put them up again on the side from which this fresh wind blew. While this was being done the men lay still, luxuriating in their blankets, like the great proprietors they considered themselves to be.

Partly in the war years, while I was in the East, and more so after the war was over and I had returned from Europe, I experienced a little something, a taste of the Arab World, and saw the background of some of the scenes of which I had read. Like those who were there before me, I found the desert tribes and those of the wild hills and mountains fascinating, and above all, this was so when I was with them on my own. But even the presence of a single foreigner, albeit knowing the colloquial dialect and dressed for the part, must produce some disruption to nomadic life.

Yet on some evenings when there were many tribesmen round the fire, I would sit silent and slightly away, and I felt I had withdrawn just enough to observe the scene much as it might have been had I not been there; and strange and exciting it was to sit while a bearded patriarch intoned in rhythmic prose to his flock as his ancestor must have done a thousand years ago. Prose, I would rather describe it as poetry, and rhythmic and poetic were the responses of his followers.

In many such scenes, both by day and night, in hill village or in desert tent, I would see and hear around me nothing that would not have been appropriate to a similar gathering at any time in the last 1,000 years. Later I was to see in the Arabian Peninsula itself, in villages and in the desert, just such scenes. Then again, years later, I revisited some of these same places and saw the change which the arrival of a new world had made. It was a total change. The tiny pocket transistor may have caused as great a revolution as the arrival of tarmac, electricity, piped water or frozen food.

People sometimes say to me of a place once remote, now connected to the rest of the world by a direct jet airliner: "How this place must have changed since you first knew it." Weakly I agree, but in reality it has not changed; it is a different place. The old will not be known again; and even as I write, in Arabia at least, it is already too late to find the traditional life which was still being carried on much as it always had done until as recently as twenty years ago.

I spent nearly two years in the Arab Legion, and then by some quirk of the Army system I was suddenly posted to command a Service Corps company in 6th Airborne Division because I was a major. I was in Palestine and was a fully trained parachutist, this despite the fact that I only stayed on in the army because I had volunteered for service in the Arab Legion. Glubb protested, but to no avail. Such has always been the logic in the War Department.

Thus it came about that I spent the last six months of the Mandate up to May 1948 in Haifa on security duties. This drew me into closer contact with the Palestine problem than ever before. Hitherto I had been in country areas, again on security duties but mainly in Arab districts where we were on the friendliest possible terms with the Palestinians. Whenever we had been living very close to Jewish areas I also made it my duty to be as friendly as I could to them and many individual kibbutz secretaries responded by inviting me to their houses.

Here I will make a point which is missed, I think, by all apologists for Zionism in the West. It is claimed that the Israelis at least occupy Israel by right of conquest, and although this is rough justice, it is regarded apparently as acceptable. Even if it were true it would surely bestow on the Arab the right to re-conquer. But it was not true up to 1948 and it has been only marginally so since.

By 1948 most of the major Jewish towns, the main Jewish agricultural areas and the majority of the kibbutzim were already established as Jewish occupied areas. In 1948 and subsequently, Arab minority populations were driven out of some Jewish towns. Whole Arab populations were driven out of Arab towns (such as Jaffa, Lydda and so on), but the principal occupation of Arab lands by Jews had already taken place between 1917 and 1948.

It was not done by Jewish conquest. The Allies captured Palestine (and Syria and Iraq) from the Turks, the League of Nations gave Britain the mandate to rule over Palestine, tragically in view of the commitment to the Balfour Declaration. It was the British Government, pressed and bullied latterly by the Americans, who by an administrative process arranged for the occupation of the Arab lands by Jews. It is, I think, not right to blame the British people as a whole for this. Despite the fact that we run our country by what are sometimes laughingly called democratic processes, the British citizen, then as today, had in effect no more control over foreign policy decisions than his Russian opposite number.

A series of British governments from 1917 onwards were directly responsible for the wresting of houses and lands of Palestinian Arabs from their owners.

How was this done? Quite simply. The doors of that tiny country were opened to a steady and controlled flow of Jewish immigrants. The Palestinian inhabitants had no vote, no voice and they were never consulted. They were perhaps slow to realise the implications of what was happening to them. As they began to realise they protested, at first verbally, and then in the 1930s by armed revolt. Then by all the irony that history can squeeze from a situation they were outclassed in terrorist tactics by the fierce Irgun Zvei Leumi and other Jewish terror bands in their campaign of horror against the occupying power because the latter was not giving up the rights of the Arabs quickly enough for the liking of the usurpers. Could anything have been more ironical than the hanging of two sergeants by piano wire and the booby trapping of their dead bodies? The death of 95 British from a single explosion in the King David Hotel, and all the other countless brutalities of the time? There were we, the responsible sovereign power in the area, giving away the rights of the immigrants to a third race and being blown up by the third party to whom we surrendered for our trouble. The first people the Jews shot as their nation came into being were the people who made its creation possible.

Sitting as I was in the middle of this situation with first my Arab companions of the region and latterly my fellow Britons, its irony was never far from my thoughts. Some of my British companions could see the point partially, but the majority shrugged their shoulders and longed to be out of it.

I was in Haifa port for the last time on 14 May, 1948. I feared for the Palestinians. I could not see how with very little arms and organisation, they could hope to save themselves. The Jews were highly organised, dedicated and ruthlessly determined and, if not well armed, at least much better armed than the Arabs. All things considered, the Arabs did remarkably well, better than I had thought would be possible in their tragically difficult circumstances.

By the time the troop-ship had been at sea a few days, I really think most of my companions had forgotten the problem, but quite a few at parting had shown concern for the Arab inhabitants, and none of those that I heard talking at that moment seemed to think the Jews had any real right to be acting as they were. In this they differed from the mass of people in Britain who, when we got back, seemed able to remember only that in the Bible the Holy Land belonged by covenant to the Jews, and were surprised to learn (as the House of Lords had been when Edward Grey told them in the early 1920s) that the land of Palestine actually had inhabitants of its own.

I shall not go into details here as to all the methods which the Jews used to dispossess the Arabs. Before 1948 it was mainly encroachment by purchase. The Jewish leaders were among the most sophisticated, highly educated, able people. The Palestinians at that time were lacking education, and wholly untutored in politics and economics, yet a very intelligent people. In the early Mandate days, any Palestinian offered what he thought to be twice the value or more of his land would gladly accept. He was not to know that the real value was far higher. Thus the Jews first cut swathes through the Arab lands by purchase, paying mainly for two kinds of property. First was the best farming land in a country where good land is very scarce. Included in this was marshland to be reclaimed by modern methods. Second, and equally important, land round the frontiers was purchased by the Jews, as it were, to pin down the rug. From the beginning, this policy was resolutely, consistently and mercilessly followed. In the end the Arabs were left mainly with the barren hilltops, and, with the exception of their wonderful orange groves in the Jaffa, comparatively little of the best farm lands, which had been theirs for thousands of years. Later this policy was followed up even more methodically, and with the use of force in May 1948 and again on the West Bank from 1967 onwards. The subsequent building boom in Jerusalem was entirely political in motive to ensure that whatever happens, Jerusalem can never wholly be an Arab city again. The Arabs were being systematically pushed out, and the world shut its eyes and ears.

I am not suggesting that the British voters had any more right than His Majesty's Government (HMG) – had they been consulted – to make decisions affecting the future of the inhabitants of a foreign country; but constitutionally they were entitled to be consulted. Not only did HMG fail to consult them, it failed to spell out the implications of the decisions. The British Government had, for many years, regarded self-determination – the right of the inhabitants of a country to decide their own future – as a major principle of government policy. Here in the case of the Palestinians, it was something to ignore. Why should this exception have been made? It was a total reversal of everything which the British way of life and the British constitution stood for. The interests of the indigenous inhabitants were pushed aside in favour of those of a foreign race, the great majority of whom still lived outside Palestine at that time, as they had done for the last 1,900 years.

Chapter Two

On leaving the Army in October 1948 I joined the Iraq Petroleum Company (IPC) and was sent out to work for their holding company in Bahrain, known in those days as Petroleum Concessions Ltd (PCL). I was told in London before setting out that the main problem before us was to gain an entry into the interior of Oman; but it was not then made clear to me quite what part I was expected to play in achieving it. What I was able to contribute unfolded itself only gradually, but first I must explain the problem as we then saw it.

The Iraq Petroleum Company, of which PCL was a subsidiary, held all the land concessions, including the territorial waters, for all the countries on the Arabian side of the Gulf from Qatar inclusive eastwards, and round the corner southwards to include the whole of Muscat and Oman and its province of Dhufar. PCL was nearly half British in ownership and was British-managed on the same lines as its parent company, IPC. The headquarters in Bahrain was a convenient one for the area as Bahrain had direct air and cable connection to the UK, and made a good regional centre. Travel in the Gulf was still difficult since, in 1948, there was no civilian airline to serve the area, although we could sometimes use the Royal Air Force. However, the Company had its own small fleet of light aircraft based in Tripoli, Lebanon – the tiny de Havilland Dragon Rapides, and later Doves. One or two of these were often in the Gulf.

I was, in due course, to be based as company representative in Dubai where we had a small office, but the first task was to assist the Company's efforts at getting into the hinterland, south of the Trucial States, belonging to the Sultan of Muscat, Saiyid Said bin Taimor.

In each of the Trucial States we had full freedom of movement, but there was some risk from the security side. Fortunately, the people of the area confined their actual fighting to one another, and took considerable trouble to ensure that we foreigners, who had nothing to do with it, were left out. Arab ideas of hospitality even extend this far.

An example of this is that an IPC seismographic party was camped only a few miles from the scene of a battle when 50 were killed. That they continued to live and work, isolated and unarmed in the desert, even after they had heard this news, is a measure of the trust which the Company put in the local shaikhly governments and on the local bedouin in such trying and difficult times as these.

There was a security problem on the coast, therefore, but given the prevailing friendliness, the assistance of the shaikhs and the co-operative attitude of their tribes, even when they were at war with one another, we were prepared to live with this problem and take risks. In the outcome we were well justified. The problem in the interior of Oman was very much more complex and difficult, and moreover one of great historical interest. The key lies in the history of Oman from the 18th century onwards, and I will attempt a sketch of this.

The majority of the three quarters of a million or so inhabitants of Oman are of the Ibadhi persuasion. They call their leader the Imam, and he is elected by the elders of the tribes to lead the people in both the temporal and the religious field. A curious, perhaps unique, feature of the Ibadhis is that the nation may enter a period of *Kitman*, or abeyance, in which, for various reasons, no Imam is elected. During this period the nation continues to live as an Ibadhi unit, and may at any moment find it convenient or apposite to elect an Imam.

Oman, like many other countries in the East, has seen both changes in regime and changes of capital. Until the end of the 18th century, the capital was at different times at various places in the interior such as Rustaq and Nizwa. In the early part of that century, during a Persian occupation of part of the coast and when the capital was in the highlands of the interior, a major civil war took place in which the country divided into two factions, the Ghafiri and the Hinawiya. The origin of this split is obscure and may date back many centuries, but for our purpose the answer to this question need not matter. The country was undoubtedly divided into these two factions in the 18th century and to some degree still considers itself so divided. Although the two factions are not now at war, their existence needs to be borne in mind when thinking of tribal relationships. The dynasty which took over control of Oman as a result of the civil war, and which succeeded in finally ousting the Persians, is the present Al Bu Saidi one. The tribe is Ghafiri by faction.

At first the Saiyids, as the Sultans were called by the people of Oman, controlled the whole of Oman as Imams, but in the late 18th century the capital was moved from the interior to the coast at Muscat; and the ruling Saiyids ceased to be recognised as the spiritual Imams of the Ibadhis. The Ibadhi state thus entered a period of *Kitman*. In an age of poor communications this move progressively weakened governmental control over the interior, and this became less and less effective throughout the 19th century. By 1900, control by the Muscat government over parts of the interior was negligible.

In 1913, an Imam was once more elected in the interior who presented a challenge to the Ruler in Muscat. A revolt took place which caused bloody fighting for seven years. This was ended in a settlement in 1920 called the agreement of Sib, by which the tribes of the interior assumed that they had achieved home rule and the Saiyid at Muscat assumed that they had not. It was therefore an admirable agreement, from which both sides were able to draw what conclusions they wished, and like all such delightful arrangements, it deserved to endure. It did, in fact, continue to be effective until 1954.

Thus by 1920, in a part of the interior only, local government had come under control of a triumvirate consisting of the two head shaikhs of each of the great factions, the Hinawiya and Ghafiri, and the Imam who had been elected by the shaikhs and elders. On the coast and in Dhufar and part of the interior the Saiyid ruled directly. By now the Saiyid had become accustomed to being addressed by the outside world as Sultan of Oman, from a practice which appears to have been British in origin.

Documents held in the archives in Muscat show that certain state functions for the whole interior were exercised in Muscat alone by the Sultan's government. There, in the capital, all passports were issued, export and import duties were levied and commerce in arms was controlled. Certain law cases from the interior were sent to the Appeal Court in Muscat, and foreign policy, such as it was, would be handled in Muscat alone. To the outside world, Muscat was the seat of government, and every form of sovereignty relating to the country as a whole was exercised by the Sultan and not by the Imam.

There was no clearly defined boundary between the direct administration of the Sultan and the local government of the triumvirate. This absence of clearly defined limits applied both in the geographical and administrative sense. For example, the town of Ibri in the interior was a marginal town whose governor was paid and appointed for many years by the Sultan, yet it was within the area of influence of the lords of the interior. There was some coming and going of officials between the two areas and the two shaikhly secular members of the triumvirate would regularly visit Muscat and be entertained and given presents by the Sultan. The Imam himself, Muhammad bin Abdullah bin Khalili, who had been elected in 1920, did not leave the interior, nor did the Sultan leave the coast, save by sea to visit his province of Dhufar far away to the south-west. The Imam Muhammad was a saintly character, moderate in politics. It had been his election which had made the Sib agreement possible, and he was determined to keep the peace which had followed his accession to the rank.

There were areas of the interior where the Imam and his two colleagues had no authority, and where the Sultan exercised his power through tribal chiefs, but without any direct administration. From 1869 onwards the Sultans had made use of the fact that the Abu Dhabi shaikhs lived in Al Ain; and they had allowed them to help in the running of adjacent areas that were accepted as being parts of Oman. The rulers of Abu Dhabi had, as it were, a special position in the northern Dhahirah.

All this meant that, just as Muscat itself was cut off from the outside world, the interior of Oman was more remote. No people from outside could enter it; and apart from occasional visits by the American missionary doctor in Muscat to Nizwa, Christian visitors were almost entirely unknown. There were no soldiers, no police and no recognisable administration. It was an entirely tribal area. In the 19th century a handful of officials from the British Government in India managed to get some way into Oman. S.B. Miles and Percy Cox were two of these; and Bertram Thomas visited parts of the north and the extreme south in the 1920s. There were also the one or two visits of geologists, but otherwise it was an unknown land.

My company wanted to prospect southwards from what is now best known as Al Ain – but was formerly known by the name of one of the Omani villages in the oasis, Buraimi – principally into the lands grazed by the tribe called the Al Bu Shamis, and from there southwards and west again into the wide range of the Duru tribe. Our object was first to do geological work followed closely by geophysical; the first called for a light expedition of two or three geologists in vehicles and virtually no other equipment, the second for a more elaborate party numbering perhaps 15 Europeans with equipment carried in heavy vehicles.

Dick Bird was the IPC official who had been entrusted with the responsibility of getting the Company in; and he had spent a frustrating winter season in 1947, based on the Abu Dhabi sector of the Buraimi oasis, attempting to make progress southwards. I was to join him for another attempt in the winter of 1948/9 and for this purpose went out ahead with some of the preliminary preparations. After a brief stop in Bahrain I went on by RAF Dakota to the Sharjah landing strip. There I was met by Jackson, the company representative in Dubai.

Used as I was to the deserts of Iraq, Syria and North Africa, the Trucial Coast seemed altogether strange and new. Sharjah itself was a tiny place in those days, a huddle of small houses by the creek with, a short way inland, the single mud airstrip of the RAF – merely a piece of rolled salt flat, which is called in Arabic *sabkha*. The RAF Mess boasted one officer only who commanded some twenty or thirty men. There were no RAF aircraft stationed in the Gulf then, and few ever visited other than a weekly Dakota from Bahrain, itself based in Iraq.

Jackson I found a cheerful companion, lean, of medium height, scholarly and somewhat academic in approach, a fluent Arabic speaker and then busy learning Persian. We went in a Humber pick-up round the end of Dubai creek itself, a ride of 45 minutes, some at speed over the salt flats and some, more leisurely, over switchback dunes where the fat sand tyres bore us confidently and all was well provided we did not stop or go too slowly. It was October, still warm and sticky, but pleasant enough at night, and we came to a halt by a two-storey house overlooking the creek whose façade was broken by a series of white Moorish arches which fronted a long wide verandah. We were greeted by the guards who were in traditional Arab dress and a Persian cook in rather scruffy whites. A narrow stone stair took us up to the verandah which overlooked the dark waters of Dubai creek. The full moon was behind us, and I could see across the water the houses of Deira town on the other side and beyond them the glint of waves of the open sea. Small rooms led off the verandah, each with a hurricane lamp in it. The verandah and the rooms were well carpeted with Persian rugs, but there was little furniture save some camp beds, and in one room a rough table and a few wooden chairs of local origin. By the verandah wall were cushions; and after I had put away my things we sank down on the floor against the cushions and we were brought refreshments by the Persian cook.

There were no electric lights and Jackson explained that his battery charger was out of action. I later found that this was usually the case in this house.

He explained that the house was all the Company had in Dubai; the end room was his office; there were three bedrooms and a sitting-room and that was all it amounted to. There were then no other Europeans living in Dubai; the newly arrived manager of the British Bank lived with the RAF in Sharjah, and came over only for the day to open the office. He said that the Ruler of Dubai, Shaikh Saeed bin Maktoum, was very friendly and helpful, as indeed were all the shaikhs; there were five other rulers with whom we had concessions and I must call on them if time allowed, to get to know them before I was to go into the interior. In addition there were the shaikhs of Abu Dhabi whom I would meet later.

That summer, Jackson said, had been trying, very hot and humid. His small kilowatt charging plant gave him only a few lights when it worked, but he had no air-conditioning and no fan. However, life in the summer in those days went at a slightly slower pace than it does now in the Gulf. This was some compensation.

Leaning over the verandah railings we could see much of the town in the strong moonlight. Near by were two-storey houses like ours, fronting the creek and made from mud and coral with wooden beams. Beyond were hundreds of brown palm-reed huts called *barastis* or *'arish*. Most of Dubai was then built in this way. The creek in front of us was swiftly flowing with the incoming tide and perhaps 200 yards in width. Between us and the sea it serpentined first to our left and then back to the right to turn once again to a sand bar where it met the open sea. Small rowing boats, some carrying lanterns, plied quietly up and down like the sampans of the Far East, and these boats were the normal form of transport inside the town. The twin towns of Dubai and Deira lay on either side of the creek, and I was told that once feuding had caused a fight which was waged across the narrow water; but all was quiet now under the control of old Shaikh Saeed and his son, Rashid.

Dubai itself was a small fishing town and port with a major interest in the declining pearl industry, but with new activities beginning to take the place of pearls. When I first arrived the pearl boats had just come in for the winter and the owners were selling the summer's catch to Indian and Arab merchants. There was also much talk of lucrative smuggling of gold into India; but this trade at that time was in its infancy.

I soon got to know the names for the different kinds of boat: the perky little *jalboot*, the graceful *boom* with its long straight prow, and the *sambooq*, with its beautiful curved prow. Best of all was that rarity, still seen sometimes at that date in Dubai, the *baghala*, with high carved poop and stately carved bows, reminiscent of the days of Drake. One example I saw there had an elaborate carving on its stern based on the letters IHS, and doubtless its Muslim owners would have no idea of its significance. It was probably a design originating in Christian Goa.

I found the Ruler a delightful old man of some 70 years, sitting without any pomp whatever among his followers on a tiny carpet on a little verandah over the Customs House which was by the creek. With him was his son Rashid, shrewd, quizzical, friendly and alert. At first I found their Arabic somewhat hard to follow, Rashid's in particular since he spoke in a kind of shorthand and seldom seemed to explain quite what the subject was. One was expected to know.

His Majesty's Government had taken over the system which had been set up in the 19th century by the British Government in India before India, together with Pakistan, attained independence in 1947. A Political Resident was established in Bahrain, having just moved from Iran, and there were Political Agents in Bahrain, Kuwait, and Muscat. In 1948, a permanently resident British Political Officer was appointed for the first time in Sharjah to deal with the whole Trucial Coast. Previously the post had been run from Bahrain by the visits of officials from the Agency there. All these officials now came under the Foreign Office for the first time; and under our various treaties dating from 1820 onwards, Britain had responsibility for defence and foreign policy, and consequently exclusive diplomatic representation, in Kuwait, Bahrain, Qatar and the Trucial States. There was no such exclusive treaty with the Sultanate of Muscat and Oman and there, alone, all other countries had equal rights to have diplomatic representation; but in 1948 Britain was in fact the only country which maintained a diplomatic post in Muscat itself. Although this post in Muscat was then still called a Political Agency, in British-Indian fashion, it was in effect a Consulate-General.

In those days the British Government had no troops in the area other than a handful of RAF personnel to service visiting aircraft at the airstrips in Bahrain, Sharjah and at far-off Salalah in the Sultanate province of Dhufar. The navy maintained two or three frigates in the Gulf, and their presence was sufficient to maintain our political influence.

The object of Britain's special position had been to prevent piracy and slave trading, and to limit arms smuggling. His Majesty's Government also had responsibility for jurisdiction over what amounted to any non-Muslim and over almost all expatriates, including those from Commonwealth countries. This surrender of jurisdiction was at the express wish of rulers who dealt with crimes committed by their own people and by any Muslim in their own Islamic *sharia* courts. Similarly civil law cases involving personal status, if they involved Muslims, came before the *sharia* religious courts which, being run on religious principles, were not suited for dealing with cases involving non-Muslims. In those days, apart from Indians and Pakistanis – who were not then permanently resident in any large numbers – there were very few people who were subject to HMG's jurisdiction. In the state of Abu Dhabi, for example, there were none at all; and the same could usually be said of the smaller states to the north and east of Sharjah.

When it came to the problem of land wars between any two or three of the states, HMG had no direct responsibility by treaty, but would offer the government's good offices to try to negotiate a peace. A desultory war had gone on for years in the early 1940s between Dubai and Sharjah, for example. Ancient muzzle-loading cannons would 'exchange shots'. In this case it was literally true, since the bedouin warriors could sometimes recover the enemy's shots and fire them back at him.

While this war continued, Imperial Airways, the forerunner of BOAC, would still refuel their flying-boats on Dubai creek and send the passengers over to the fort in Sharjah for lunch. During this operation the war was suspended by mutual agreement between the belligerents, and passengers would pass through the 'lines' without, in most cases, realising anything unusual was afoot, since the air crews, who knew about it, had no wish to alarm them by explaining it. But by the time I had arrived this little war was over and no longer were there any flying-boats calling. Nevertheless there was always the prospect of such an affair starting again, and relations between Dubai and Abu Dhabi were still those of an uneasy truce. One outstanding question of stolen camels was the chief topic of conversation at the time, and this had been submitted to arbitration, the arbitrator being an elderly shaikh who very wisely listened a great deal and said absolutely nothing, in the hope, it was generally understood, that the camels would all be dead before he needed to pronounce.

I called on this old gentleman, and found him a master of desert diplomacy and almost professionally indecisive. He himself had almost no money at all, and was clearly in no position to make decisions on his own people's domestic affairs as there were few options to take; and this circumstance made him peculiarly adept as a cooler-off of the affairs of others. We could do with him, I thought, to deal with industrial strife at home.

It took me some time to adjust to the security situation, but when I did I found it altogether charming. None of the men of Dubai would ever go out of town unarmed since attacks on camel convoys, or even cars, by bedouin were always a possibility. We, on the other hand, were never armed and seldom took guards with us, as we were never attacked.

The co-operation of the local people made life very easy and comfortable. The one cause for disquiet to me was the absence of any state revenues in any of these territories to relieve the poverty of the people. The standard of living was low, but above subsistence level. People seemed happy as they had known nothing better; and, perhaps more importantly, there was a complete lack of juxtaposition of rich and poor. Medical care was not available in any modern form to those outside Dubai, and it was sketchy enough even there. Everyone, however, lived in the same sort of style and the poor were frequent guests at their rulers' tables, or rather at their carpets. Neither were the rulers themselves rich, and much of what they had, they would give away in hospitality and as presents to their people. Admittedly I was conscious that we ourselves in the oil company house lived a little better than most because we could afford to buy tins of meat, and tinned fruit and vegetables from the few shops which stocked such delicacies. But if we lived slightly better we did so unobtrusively.

In view of the forthcoming expedition to Oman that had been planned, I had a few days to become acclimatised before starting to check the necessary preparations. Jackson had in any case got most things ready: piles of tins of bully-beef and tinned vegetables, cans of petrol and four sturdy Chevrolet pick-ups with a team of drivers led by Firdullah bin Khairallah and Sabir bin Muhammad, Dick Bird's drivers of the season before.

Over the next week, Sabir took me to see some of the shaikhs and taught me something of his technique of sand driving in cars which had power only on the back wheels. To make up for lack of four-wheel drive we had wide, low-pressure tyres and carried tin sand-channels to put under the wheels when they were stuck; but try as I would, I could never equal the skill of either Firdullah or Sabir as sand-drivers.

We were to rely very much on these two excellent drivers. Both were amusing and informative companions, especially in any moment of adversity. Sabir had an oversize sense of humour, was lively, inventive and resourceful, and always cheerful. Firdullah seldom actually laughed except when a disaster occurred, and then he would go into fits, but, like Sabir, he was co-operative and resourceful. Both were self-taught desert drivers of great skill, and it amuses me today to see four-wheel drive Land Rovers stuck in places where Sabir and Firdullah would happily drive our heavily laden two-wheel drive Chevrolets or Fords without a thought to any difficulty.

All my real troubles in the desert have been when I was without either of these two, and especially when I was with a party organised by others. The moral I found was always to be in charge of transport, fuel and food yourself when going into the desert. Sabir's resourcefulness saved us, when at a later date I joined just such another desert party in our Land Rover. They were making such heavy weather of the trip that I finally decided to go home on my own, and we took our leave of them. It was winter and we were only 60 miles inland. We were in small steep cornice dune country, and I was driving, and coming off one of the high dunes I struck a bush and damaged the steering. The steering was easily fixed, but the serious matter was a cracked differential on the front axle. By then it was dark, and we cooked and ate our dinner and got into our blankets, and so spent the night. Next morning Sabir made a poultice out of dates and string, and tied this to the axle, filled up the differential with the spare oil we always carried, and we got home like that. On another occasion he fixed our second fan belt (the first had given up earlier), which shredded longitudinally, with the help of my leather bootlaces. These he plaited round it.

I had only just begun to taste the joys of life in Dubai when it was time to meet Dick Bird at the airstrip. I had met him briefly in London where he was based, and formed the impression that he was a man of vigour and ability, with considerable determination. This was what we needed for what looked like the insoluble problem before us. He had great experience of the Gulf area, having been in the Indian Political Service stationed both in Muscat and Bahrain. He was familiar with the local Arab dialect.

After his arrival we put the finishing touches to our preparations for the journey. We were to take with us a radio set which would link us on speech to Jackson in Dubai and, through Dubai, with the company office in Bahrain on key. Jackson had already sent a quantity of petrol by camel to Al Ain. This was the principal village in the Abu Dhabi sector in the group of oases of which the main Omani village was Buraimi. In those days in Dubai, petrol was still only available in the square, flimsy 'non-returnable' four-gallon tins of the war days, and each camel could take four of these in specially made wooden saddle boxes. Unfortunately, about one in four of these tins would prove to be a leaker, and would finish the journey partly or even wholly empty. Thus, although we had sent over 1,000 tins in this way to the store which Dick Bird had built in Al Ain, it was a matter for the gods as to how much had arrived.

Chapter Three

One bright November afternoon in 1948 we set off in three two-wheel drive Chevrolet pick-ups. The whole journey, as the crow flies, was only a matter of 120 miles or so, but to get through the sands we had to travel first almost to Abu Dhabi town, on its island off the coast, and then strike inland. In those days there was not even a graded track to Abu Dhabi and you followed the tyre marks of predecessors or launched out afresh onto virgin desert as the mood took you. It was essential to watch the texture of the *sabkhas,* the salt flats, to detect whether they were firm or soft. Rain, dew or a high tide could make them treacherous, and in the wet it was safer to follow earlier tracks through standing water, since where water stood the ground was firmer. We had tow-ropes, jacks, our sand channels and the know-how of our drivers to get us through.

On that particular day, it was a good and easy journey as far as the Abu Dhabi turn. There had been no rain and no recent high tides; the temperature was exactly right and all went well. We reached the Abu Dhabi-Al Ain track in two and a half hours. Then we turned inland and, heavily laden as we were, one of the cars got stuck crossing the first line of dunes. We stopped the other two on downward slopes, and all of us lent a hand. By dint of scooping away sand, lowering tyre pressures, pushing and using our sand channels, we got the truck going. By nightfall we reached a group of palm trees at the beginning of the massive pink sands and a well called Bidat Al Ajam (Well of the Persian). This was our objective and there we camped.

This process involved merely getting out our bedding, making tea and opening a few tins for dinner. Previous expeditions had found that tents were, for the most part, not essential since it so seldom rained. I found this reasonable enough except in the very coldest weather inland, when a tent is a comfort at night, and for the next few years much of my time was spent in the open. On the few occasions when we took tents, we usually regretted it because their extra weight meant that we could take that much less petrol or water. We set up the radio and got in touch with Jackson at nine o'clock as we had previously agreed. Speech was not very clear, but we were in contact.

Our plan was to wake early and, taking advantage of the dew-sodden, cool sands, get through the two lines of heavy sands which guard the approaches to Al Ain at sunrise. At about five o'clock, just before sunrise, the first flies had us properly awake, and after a cup of tea, we loaded up and got on our way.

We made good progress from Bidat Al Ajam over a mass of packed sand about five miles in extent. On either side rose hills of dunes with sharp crescent edges, their slip faces pointing south-east, and as we looked back at them, they glinted pink and yellow in the morning sun. The air was clear and cool; it was good to be alive and I was excited to see what lay ahead. The journey had been described to me and I knew that we had several big dunes to cross, but until we were amongst them I could not have imagined their majesty and solemnity.

The next range of dunes was easily negotiated where they fall away leaving a gap at Bu Samra well. Above the well is a huge dune. The experts say dunes cannot lie at an angle steeper than 32° on the slip face, but this one always looks like a small mountain and, whether you only look at it or try to climb it, it seems much steeper than that. We stopped at the well and exchanged greetings with the bedouin we found sitting there. Sabir made us all Arabic coffee while we began asking about the movements of the tribes in the area. Was Shaikh so-and-so at home? Where were his men? The bedouin were from the Awamir tribe, lean and tough. Their leader wore no headcloth as is the way of some of the bedouin of the high sands, but he had a thin head-rope of plaited leather tangled in his long black hair. Like the others, he wore a long coffee coloured shirt, or *thawb,* that reached down to his ankles and carried an ancient Mauser rifle, a camel stick and a piece of light cane about three feet long with a slightly curved handle. He spoke in a deep, thick voice in short phrases and the liquid accent of the sands with long pauses between sentences.

First it was: "No news. Praise be to God." And, then at length, he told us of the latest episode in the 12-year-old feud between his tribe and the Duru, the prospects of some settlement, the coming of their own shaikhs bin Rakkadh or Salim bin Hamm, and the possibility that Shaikh Zayed, brother of the Ruler of Abu Dhabi, might intervene.

The war had begun with a theft of Awamir camels by some Duru several years earlier, at which time two herdsmen of the Awamir had been killed. Since then, at long intervals, other incidents had taken place: camel thefts or very occasionally killings. To us it sounded as if the Awamir were up on the score and might agree to make peace, but we had yet to hear the other side. Although we had no immediate prospects of getting into Duru country, this was our ultimate objective; the most promising surface signs, geologically, of a possible oil-bearing formation, as we knew from our aerial reconnaissance, were in the middle of the desert which the Duru claimed as their own.

The Duru were the Sultan of Oman's people, but so remote were they from Muscat that the Sultan could only be in contact with them at certain times. The Awamir were a tribe which originated in the Dakaka of the Eastern Aden

Protectorate and roamed the territories of the Saudis, the Aden Protectorate, Abu Dhabi and the Sultanate alike. They would even be found, in some years, as far north as Kuwait and Iraq with their camel herds.

An important section of the tribe had been living for years in Abu Dhabi, using Al Ain as their base. They were regarded as Abu Dhabi subjects.

The most important news for us was that Shaikh Zayed, the brother of the Ruler of Abu Dhabi and his representative in Al Ain, was away on a hunting trip to the south but expected back any day. Since he was by far the leading personality in the area, he was the key source for information in the whole region as to the doings of the tribes. The sun was now higher, and we wanted to cross the next and last chain of dunes before the sands had really dried out.

The crossing point was the Haza Al Baush, a place that had become notorious for trapping cars in the soft sand. Dick Bird was a good sand-driver and he himself drove the first truck with myself in the front seat beside him. We crossed a bumpy bush-covered plain and could see in front of us the mass of the dune chain, and below one of its highest peaks was an obvious pass. As we approached, we could see that the tracks of previous cars which came in from either side converged at one point opposite the pass to be lost in the soft sand, and Dick drove flat out for this point. It felt as if we were airborne for half a minute, then the dunes were coming at us fast as we mounted a broad incline, rutted with car tracks, and once over the brow, we turned sharp right into a deep defile with a smooth mud-flat bottom. Across the mud-flat stretched one ridge of sand and this had to be taken at about 30 miles an hour to give enough speed to race across another short mud-flat for the hard climb over the last and biggest dune. On this occasion he timed it just right and we cleared the ridge, wheels in the air, landed on the flat, accelerated, changed quickly down and charged the steep red dune that seemed to tower in front of us. We could feel the soft sand gripping and sucking at our tyres as our speed fell off; another quick gear change and we just breasted the crest to have before us a totally new scene: no more high dunes but level sand with trees and scrub and, beyond, the dark, sombre crags and cliffs of the mountain, Jebel Hafit, which hangs over Al Ain village and the whole oasis of Buraimi.

However, it was no moment to admire the scenery. We were anxious to see what had become of the others, and we stopped the truck on the downward slope. We jumped out to walk back as Sabir's truck came roaring past to stop next to ours. He jumped out and shouted "I think Firdullah is stuck." Firdullah's truck had rather more load, and when we got to the crest we looked down at the mud-flat in the valley of sand and saw him stuck on the top of the ridge that bisected it, the car sitting astride the dune at an odd angle. When we got down to him we found him digging away at the back wheels and fitting the tin sand channels behind them. We helped him, while he gently reversed onto the channels and we pushed, the car was manoeuvered back over the ridge. Once he got on to the flat, Firdullah turned the car and drove as fast as he could right out of the dunes, and out of our sight. If he could get a clear run he would go right through; this was the only way. If he stuck anywhere between where we were standing and the little ridge, he would never get up enough speed to climb the big dune. A few minutes later, Firdullah's car could be heard and then we saw him as he came roaring over the first dunes and down to the mud-flat and took the ridge at about 40 miles an hour – a good bit too fast, I thought – but with the car swaying crazily and the engine and gears roaring and whining, he cleared the ridge like a show jumper, all four wheels in the air, to land below where we stood, on the salt flat, and then he aimed straight at the big dune. Even so, he only just made it, and with some relief we saw his tailboard disappear over the crest.

I was bubbling over with excitement. It was a *tour de force*. But I was told that this was nothing compared to the sands of the Liwa. That was sand. We walked through the soft hot sand back over the high dune to find the trucks all parked near to each other and Firdullah with the primus already lit for tea.

I found later, when in the Liwa, how much more difficult this was, but in the hot weather of the following June we had almost twenty-four hours, again in the Haza Al Baush, with two new and recalcitrant trucks whose track rods would not take the strain but bent under it. Firdullah and Sabir cheerfully took the track rods off, heated them up over a primus and straightened them. On that occasion Shaikh Zayed, who was camping in the neighbourhood, came over in his Chevrolet truck and we all had lunch together. It was the longest 'sticking' I remember, and we never took those particular trucks into the high dunes again.

Today the journey is done on a wide dual-carriageway tarmac road built above the sands. By optical illusion, the dunes have now diminished in size as seen from a passing car and are not so impressive as when you are among them, since they are dwarfed by the road. But let anyone leave the road and try the dunes at another point, and he will see the sands as we used to and experience their strange beauty.

We wound our way along an easy sandy track among the acacia trees into the oasis. This was a group of nine separate villages, three in Muscat territory and six in Abu Dhabi. Each village consisted of a cluster of low mud-brick houses set in large date groves, and in between the villages was open scrub. To the north was a small forest of acacia and other thorn trees; to the south were two gaunt ribs of Jebel Hafit and the main mass of the mountain which shuts in the oasis.

We made straight for the fort of Jahili. This was a mud-brick fortress with two large quadrangles set in high walls with corner towers and near the centre a robust but battered round turret, all of sun-dried clay brick. It was built by Shaikh Zayed's famous grandfather, Shaikh Zayed bin Khalifah, towards the end of last century, but the underground channel, called a *falaj*, which served it with water from a spring some three miles away, had 'died', in the local phrase, and the gardens had died with it, so that the fort had been abandoned and was partly in ruins. But it had a few sound rooms remaining, and these had been allocated to Dick by Shaikh Zayed to use as he liked, whenever he wanted.

We reached Fort Jahili and found it empty and forlorn. The rooms were bare, their floors of sand, and the windows unshuttered and without glass. This was to be our home for some months to come. We had brought no furniture other than rugs, but by the time we had laid them out, together with our bedding rolls, the place began to look more like home. Our rolled-up blankets with rugs over them formed useful cushions to lean on as we sat. In another building, we set up the radio with its poles outside, and in another we made a kitchen. It was real luxury. The one snag was the courtyard which was of loose sand, and every now and again a small whirlwind would cross it to blow the sand in clouds into our rooms. But this was a feature we had to learn to live with.

For bathing we were fortunate, since only half a mile away there was a bathing place in the *falaj*. Al Ain village was an excellent place for fresh water from the mountain spring.

We had been in the fort only a short time when we were visited by the bailiff of the shaikh of Buraimi village itself, on the Sultan's side of the oasis. His name was Saiyid Kamil and he worked for Shaikh Saqr bin Sultan Al Naimi, the paramount of the Naim and Al Bu Shamis tribes; that is to say, the leading shaikh on the Muscat side. The administration of the district from Buraimi to Dhank in the south was in Shaikh Saqr's hands, and in Dhank he had a governor. He was supposed also to be in control of the area to the north belonging to Shaikh Obaid bin Juma of the Bani Kaab, but that shaikh was not always so willing to admit Shaikh Saqr's paramountcy. Shaikh Saqr, we were told, was unpopular locally and had a reputation for toughness; he was, however, the Sultan's man and it was through him that we must deal with the bedouin on the Sultan's side.

The villages of the oasis area are typical of much of the interior of Oman. They lie at the northern end of the extensive Dhahirah plain. This plain is at about 1,000 feet above sea level and is blocked on the whole of its north-eastern edge by the range of the Oman mountains. Running through this range to the sea, there are three or four main valleys which give access to the Batinah coast, but at that time only on foot or by animal transport; they had not yet been opened up to motor traffic. The plain itself was mainly gravel, intersected by shallow water-courses or *wadi* beds across which the floods from the mountains would run after heavy rain. Much of the plain was covered with the low acacia trees and scrub, but in some places the sands of the desert invaded it from the west in thin tongues. The south-western edge of the plain is bordered by the desert which we call the Empty Quarter.

The plain could be crossed by car; it gave a very bumpy and uncomfortable ride, but it could be negotiated without any difficulty.

Due south of Buraimi, standing on the plain, was Jebel Hafit, a steep, partly eroded anticline rising to 3,000 feet and almost all of barren rock. Beneath it, under its eastern flank, nestled the village of Hafit with its green palms and mud-brick fortresses.

Like all villages in this area it depended for water on underground springs higher up the valley, with water brought by gravity to the surface by *falaj.* The water in these villages had only a very slight salt content. It was used mainly to grow date palms which flourish in this sunny climate. The palms were the main source of wealth to the villagers and provided the main crop. Dates were eaten locally or sold to the bedouin, and were also exported to the north, to the coast of the Arabian Gulf where water was insufficient to support palms in any number.

The trees were also used as a wind-break behind which other crops, alfalfa (lucerne) and some vegetables were grown. In 1948 the variety of crop was very limited but in recent years new ideas have been brought in, and the farmers were becoming more adventurous in their choice of seed as new kinds became available to them. Tomatoes and all the common vegetables now flourish in this area.

The nature of the crops gave the villages much of their character. Each one was really a plantation, principally of date palms, with mostly single-storey, mud-brick houses interspersed with the turrets of forts set along its edge. The village would present a dark green mass of palm fronds, with the light brown of the buildings along one edge and the grey gravel of the dried *wadi* bed beyond. Outside the village boundary there would be no permanent buildings; but the bedouin would often camp among the low dunes which reached almost to the villages from the west. Among these dunes were acacia trees and there were gravel patches on which bedouin might put up palm-frond huts and make small encampments. Some of the houses of the village consisted of palm fronds. There were also shelters among the gardens where it was pleasant to sit among the green trees and crops, under a palm-frond roof open at the sides to let in what breeze there was.

The largest villages had perhaps 1,000 inhabitants and in Al Ain village and Buraimi there were rudimentary markets or *souqs* where dates, dried fish, cloth and the simplest needs of a poor community could be bought. These *souqs* would be frequented by the bedouin, who would spend the day in the village, while their camels would kneel in a group by a water-place on the edge, only to depart at night for they disliked the life of settled places, and always made for the desert to sleep. The *souq*, like all the other buildings, was built of mud-brick with two rows of tiny alcoves – each a shop, separated by a narrow covered pathway. Each shop owner sat at the mouth of his dark alcove, with his wares piled behind him.

The immediate backcloth to the oasis itself was the towering whaleback mass of Jebel Hafit to the south, with its two arms coming out as if it were embracing the oasis. To the north and east lay the pale blue serrated edge of the main range of the Hajar Mountains, and to the west were the reddish sands of the first high dunes. The plain itself round the village had sufficient stumpy trees to give it a greenish carpet which from some angles appeared slightly raised above the grey of its gravel bed; for the trees were all shorn of lower branches and leaves by foraging camels, goats and other animals, and on their slender trunks the light green of the upper branches seemed to float above the general level of the plain.

In summer by midday the glare of a light blue, near-white sky, and the strength of the sun, gave only an impression of heat, dust and sand, which one could see as well as feel; but in the evenings and early mornings the plain, the villages and the mountains shone with a variety of colours in the clear air; the soil pink and yellow as well as bluey grey, the acacias light green, the villages dark green with brown edges, the local mountains ruddy in the dawn and the distant ones a pale blue. In winter, these colours would persist throughout the day and the sky would then be a darker blue, flecked with clouds.

In mid-summer the heat would be crushing and by early afternoon I sometimes found it almost unbearable. The air was bone dry but the heat itself had weight. By evening it would improve, especially away from any building and it was pleasant to find a slightly raised bit of land away from the trees on which to enjoy what little evening breeze there was.

Similar villages dotted the plain, and where each *wadi* made openings in the main mountain range, along its whole line towards the south-east, would be villages each guarding a water course, while at the same time being a vital point in the line of communication to the sea. These villages varied in size but all of them were of the same character as those in the Buraimi oasis. To the west towards Saudi Arabia stretched the sand, and not a single permanent building stood between us and Hufuf in Saudi Arabia, some 300 miles away.

The village houses were made of mud-brick walls about ten feet high with flat roofs supported on thick beams made of palm trunks. These beams had to be frequently repaired or replaced as they had little strength and became the home of insects, especially hornets. One house I lived in was noted for the arrival each evening of thousands of these insects which would stay quietly in their holes in the beams until dawn when, after a preliminary circuit round the room, they would fly out.

Terrifying at first, but one got used to it and I was never stung.

A particular characteristic of these villages was their forts. Each village had several, varying from single watch-towers, usually round and about 30 feet in height, with a crenellated top, to those in which the shaikhs lived, large buildings with a maze of one-storeyed rooms surrounded by curtain walls, with turrets at the corners and over the gate. Others again were taller three-storey blocks or towers with several rooms on each floor. All were of the same sun-dried brick, and for each fort which was still in use and in good condition, there would be many which had long since become ruins; and these ruined turrets graced the edges of every village. Buraimi itself had a large fort with a round tower at each of its four corners guarding the entrance of the village. Opposite, a mile away to the south, as if to challenge it, stood a massive tower of three stories standing by itself, clear of the date grove of Al Ain village.

To anyone who visits the oasis now, the scene is completely different. There are dual carriageway roads, gardens between the villages where before there were none, metalled streets and modern houses. The villages of course have lost their old character, the whole geography of the place looks different. Despite the modernity it is all far greener and more beautiful and the people now live in houses in comfort and all have access to medical care and schools. One may miss the romance of the old oasis, but the new one is far better and has acquired a beauty of its own.

Chapter Four

The main difficulty which the Company had run into in the 1947-8 season was that although our concession was signed with the Sultan, and our payments all went to him, and although the Sultan was happy for us to prospect in certain areas of the interior, and in this one in particular, the tribes also wanted a direct payment from the Company to them.

Despite the fact that they looked to the Sultan as their only overlord, there was no central administration which reached out effectively to their area, and they felt that the actual land was really theirs, even though it had to be admitted that the Sultan was their ruler. To understand their position, it is necessary to put aside all Western ideas of sovereignty. The bedouin take from a situation very much what they want. They have very positive ideas about their tribal rights, and these may differ markedly in character from place to place in Arabia.

In Duru country and among the Al Bu Shamis and some other bedouin tribes of the south and west of Oman, there is complete exclusivity of ownership of tribal grazing grounds. The Duru area is so large, so inhospitable and difficult to enter that before the days of the car (before 1954 in their region) they were impregnable in their fastness. No other tribe would dare enter their area for any reason, and whenever clashes took place with trespassers across their borders, fighting would be inevitable. Coming nearer to the hills and the sown land where settled people lived, this exclusivity was modified. Travellers who were acceptable could cross such semi-settled areas, and rights lay in ownership of ground for tilling or chopping of trees and especially the use of water for crops. Even here a traveller would be wise to take precautions, and the best safeguard, of which I made frequent use in later journeys, was to travel with a companion from some other tribe that was not at war with the tribe which inhabited the area one wished to cross. If you were killed while under his protection it would be as though a person of his tribe had been slain; and whether or not the protector survived, this would start an unending feud between two once-friendly tribes – an event of great consequence, which all bedouin naturally wished to avoid.

In about the year 1800, the Saudis had captured Buraimi, the Omani part of the oasis, and made their presence felt over much of the interior of Oman without directly ruling it in the modern sense. Their occupation of Buraimi was only intermittent, covering 13 separate periods in between which they had retreated; and in 1869 they were driven out finally by the then Sultan. In the mid-1920s, Saudi tax collectors came into the area on two or three occasions. This may have been a half-hearted attempt at a return to their previous position, but it was ineffective. Such was the fame of King Abdul Aziz Ibn Saud that when Bertram Thomas (then one of the Sultan's ministers) came into the region in the 1920s, he was told that the people of Buraimi at that moment accepted Ibn Saud as king.

People in an area not directly administered tended to be fickle about their allegiance and would, if one powerful personality were increasing in strength, attach themselves to him but, as it were, with fingers crossed. I am sure, however, that they did not accept the king as their ruler in the 1920s. It was simply a ruse to keep the foreigner, Thomas, out and as such it plainly worked. Later the Saudis quoted this as proof of their sovereignty, but I thought that this point was not a valid one to support their claim.

By the time I came to live in Al Ain, in 1948 and early 1949, there was no talk of the Saudis. The only powers recognised in Oman, were that of the Sultan and the triumvirate of shaikhs in central Oman, consisting of the Ibadhi, Imam and the leaders of the two factions, the Hinawi and the Ghafiri. But the Imam and his two shaikhly colleagues had no authority whatever in Buraimi or in the Dhahirah as a whole, which is not even Ibadhi country. There was one Saudi merchant living in Buraimi village, but he was always referred to as 'the Najdi' and was not held in high regard. As to the villages on the Al Ain side of the oasis they had belonged to the Abu Dhabi shaikhs for a very long time and never to the Saudis.

The area between Abu Dhabi and Saudi Arabia was frequented by both Abu Dhabi and Saudi bedouin in search of pasture, and for this purpose was used by groups of tribes migrating, sometimes because of a bad drought in any one area which drove them to seek water and grazing elsewhere. It was also very occasionally used by pilgrims on their way to Mecca, but these would be local bedouin tribesmen, as all other pilgrims would go by sea to the Saudi ports. I could find no evidence for a normal caravan trade route between Saudi Arabia and Oman. This desert crossing was so difficult that travellers preferred to go by sea. Only the real bedouin of the high sands would attempt it. Apart from a few – as it were – specialist tribes like the Awamir, the Al Rashid, and from Saudi Arabia occasional visitors from the Al Murra, no one crossed this waste of some 300 miles or more of rolling sands. Never in history has there been an established trade route across the desert between Saudi Arabia and Buraimi.

The position in the difficult area south of Buraimi, we hoped, was that the tribes would now accept Shaikh Saqr as their paramount and would, on his ordering it, allow us in. We were assured that the Sultan had recently reaffirmed all this in writing to Shaikh Saqr as the paramount shaikh of the tribes of the Naim, Al Bu Shamis and Bani Kaab; and he had directed him to deal with the company and arrange with the other shaikhs so that our geological work could begin.

Our intention was first to ensure that this plan was in good order and then go down to Muscat by truck with a small party of our company geologists and motor up to Buraimi, making a new, hitherto unused, route for vehicles up the Wadi Jizzi from the Omani coast at Suhar.

We felt free to call on Shaikh Zayed to advise us, and his friendly influence over the tribes immediately to the south of Buraimi was considerable; his support of the Sultan's position in the area through the Abu Dhabi shaikhs had historical precedent.

Although Shaikh Saqr lived only a mile and a half away in Buraimi fort, it took us some time to arrange to see him. His bailiff or general factotum, Saiyid Kamil, had already called on us within an hour of arrival, since Dick used him as his agent on the Sultanate side; and we had set about attempting to arrange an interview, but Shaikh Saqr was by no means easily committed to a meeting. We were also still awaiting the return of Shaikh Zayed from his hunting trip.

We busied ourselves with checking our store of petrol, of which about a third had been lost by leakage while being carried by the camels, tidying up the fort at Jahili, mending a dangerous-looking beam in the roof and doing a little exploring around the oasis. Dick seemed to know everyone, and after a break of seven or eight months was carrying on the bedouin gossip where he had dropped it at the end of the last season. He had a disarming and pleasant way, and after greeting the head of the house, would fold up his long legs to settle down and chat with an easy familiarity, remembering the interests and recent history of the person to whom he was talking, for this is exactly what the bedouin expected. They had excellent memories, and they expected you to remember all you had heard about them. They, likewise, have disconcertingly exact memories of all you have said in the past.

The villages were beautiful in early winter; the climate dry and warm by day and cool by night. Sometimes we would be invited to sit in a snug little room on the first floor of a brick house overlooking a garden. In the garden were date palms and, between the trees, vegetables and alfalfa. The rows of trees were intersected by irrigation channels, whose mud sluices would be broken and built up again systematically on a timetable to let the water run through by rotation every day or two in each part of the gardens. The water came from underground channels by gravity from underground springs that were, in some instances, as much as seven miles away under the foot of Jebel Hafit.

In the mornings the gardens would be very still, the only sounds a few birds, some parakeets and the creaking of the rope at a well worked by oxen. There were then no mechanical pumps and the noise of a car was a rarity. Among the palms, the gardens were a lush green with the darker green of Indian almond and other trees, and here and there the gash of colour of bougainvillea splashing down from a wall or a tree. Sometimes we would be invited to sit and talk in the gardens in an arbour, an outdoor *majlis,* or sitting place. Then, a large woven straw mat would be put in front of us and covered with bowls of dates, nuts, figs, pomegranates and pawpaws, while coffee and tea were served, the coffee in the tiny cups without handles and the tea in small glasses. Conversation rose and fell; neighbours dropped in for a talk. The oasis seemed so remote from modern life and so full of contentment. The fact that no one had much money really did not seem to worry people, and I envied them a way of life I could only share for a short time.

On one such visit we called on Shaikh Muhammad bin Khalifah, the senior member by descent of the Abu Dhabi ruling family. Here was a patriarch, interested in his people, his gardens, in hawking and visiting the countryside. He had gardens also near Suhar on the Batinah coast, and he was knowledgeable about animals, the digging of wells and water channels. Dressed like any of his followers in a white headcloth, black head-rope, white *thawb,* a thin *abba* (cloak) hanging from his shoulders with a gold embroidered edging, he wore at his belt a curved silver-handled dagger and on his feet the roughest locally made leather sandals. He talked in a soft voice, screwing up his eyes in the sunlight, always ready to see a joke in the passing scene. His people caught his mood and joined in. There was always laughter in his circle. Zayed, he said, would be with us tomorrow, or the next day perhaps.

Two days later we called on Shaikh Zayed at Al Muwaiqi fort. This was rather a forbidding square fortress with crenellated corner towers. To exclude the heat, the rooms inside were necessarily rather dark and had no furniture but the colourful rugs and cushions on the floor. Shaikh Zayed was then perhaps 30 years old. He was handsome with humorous and intelligent eyes, of fine presence and bearing, simply dressed, like his cousin Muhammad, and clearly a man of action and resolution. Although he was young and had only been formally in charge of the Abu Dhabi sector of the oasis and its surrounding deserts for some two years, he was experienced in the politics of the region and was already by far the most prominent personality in the area. He had a sure touch with the bedouin in both the Abu Dhabi and Muscat areas.

His brother Shaikh Shakhbut, the Ruler, lived mostly in Abu Dhabi but would visit his own garden at Al Muwaiqi from time to time. The Ruler had a considerable reputation. Although he had his critics, and although perhaps he did not have the touch which his brother Zayed could show in dealing with the tribes, he was a man who commanded considerable respect.

Shaikh Zayed showed a great friendship and co-operation towards us, and we had many pleasant evenings together while we were in the oasis. Shaikh Zayed said that Shaikh Saqr was being difficult over a number of matters, but this was only his habit. He listened to our plans for bringing up the geologists from Muscat and, although he thought it might not work, at least he considered it worth trying. He expected some opposition to our plans from the Bani Kaab and from Muhammad Salimin bin Rahmah, shaikh of the bedouin section of the Al Bu Shamis tribe. After a while we made our farewells, saying that we must now call on Shaikh Saqr who had agreed to see us. "I hope the old fox gives you coffee," said one of our friends as we parted.

The old fox did, but it was very cold coffee, and 'cold coffee' was the common term used to describe him. We motored over the light-coloured sand in front of Buraimi fort and up to its gloomy portal. Sabir had to knock many times before a small shutter opened and part of a face showed itself which proved to be that of Shaikh Saqr himself. With some noise and evident difficulty, he eventually unbarred the door and let us in. He seemed to be attended by only one servant, and he was reputed to spend the night with only one trusted retainer in the fortress. He was renowned for the money he reputedly held in the fort and seemed perpetually afraid equally of burglary from without and treason from within. Even Dick's easy way with the bedouin made no impression here. He was a small man, rather stout; he sat and waited for us to talk after he had, with apparent reluctance, shown us into a tiny and very dark room close to the fort's entrance, with a plain rush mat on the floor and nothing else to grace it.

Despite this introduction, the conversation went surprisingly well. The shaikh had heard from the Sultan that the geologists might come, and if his fellow shaikhs were agreeable, he said they might start working in the area between Buraimi and Dhank. He added that they must not go into Dhank itself, but he wanted some 'help'. This was the difficulty. The Sultan did not want us to pay for entry into the area; giving small *douceurs* without any particular terms attached might be overlooked, but payment for services rendered was out of the question. Shaikh Saqr really wanted his own oil concession and a large amount of money. But he also wanted work to start and he did not like to upset the Sultan.

It was agreed that the shaikh of the Kaab tribe and two shaikhs of the Al Bu Shamis, Rashid of Hamasah and Muhammad Salimin bin Rahmah, would meet us at Shaikh Saqr's fort in three days' time to agree finally to the arrival of the geologists.

Of course we did not meet in three days, nor in four, nor five. We asked Shaikh Zayed to help and he did his best. We made approaches through Saiyid Kamil, to no effect; we saw Shaikh Saqr twice more, and on one visit we did not even get cold coffee. We were given a variety of different stories as to why the meeting did not take place, but we were assured that the shaikhs concerned were not now very far off and we were to provide the transport to bring them from an appointed meeting place in the desert. We agreed to do so but arrangements fell through. At last, after two weeks of this, we heard that they had arrived and Saiyid Kamil came over to say that our cars were to go out to fetch them and they would come at five o'clock Arabic time – that is eleven o'clock Western time. At the time in Oman they still used the Arabic clock by which the day starts at sunset as if it were 0.00 hrs and is adjusted daily.

When we got to Shaikh Saqr's fort the scene was quite different from the previous occasion. There was a large number of camels and other animals outside. Our own two pick-ups which had brought the shaikhs were there with Firdullah and Sabir, the latter grinning happily. There was a group of bedouin on either side of the door squatting in the shade of the fortress wall and, wonder of wonders, the door itself was half open but held by a chain.

Sabir ducked into the fort under the chain to announce our arrival to the shaikhs, but it was some time before the chain was unhooked and the door opened. Shaikh Saqr was never one to show any form of enthusiasm at the arrival of a visitor. After greeting us in his usual sulky style, he took us to a rather larger room already crammed full of people. Here were all the other shaikhs and their followers. They stood and we shook hands with each and, finally, a tiny space was made for us to sit on the floor next to Shaikh Saqr. Then an endless and futile discussion began right away about the money we were to pay. Dick did his best to ride this out, emphasising that Shaikh Saqr was their declared spokesman, that he had agreed, and that the Sultan had agreed, to our operating without any specific payment to them.

The meeting went on until two o'clock, and, uniquely for Arabia, without coffee or any other refreshment; it finally broke up inconclusively by our leaving it.

The shaikhs stayed in the area but not as the guests of Shaikh Saqr. We called on them separately and they called on us. It all came down to money and they each wanted more than could be passed off as a modest *douceur.* We appealed to Zayed for help and he readily did his best. Although this matter was not the direct affair of Abu Dhabi, it had long been recognised by the Sultan that the Abu Dhabi shaikhs had a special position in the Dhahirah. At one time the Ruler of Abu Dhabi was actually paid by the Sultan to help him in the area, and there was a long history of co-operation over local tribal affairs between the Muscat authorities and the Abu Dhabi shaikhs. In such a place the exact boundaries of administration were in those days blurred, and the existence of frontiers between Oman and Abu Dhabi was only half-remembered.

In the course of the next ten days, small unofficial *douceurs* did change hands and sufficient agreement with the shaikhs seemed to be reached to make a visit by the geologists worthwhile. Dick and I went back to Dubai to link up with the geologists who were to come to Muscat with us and then return to Buraimi by the Batinah and the Wadi Jizzi. We left two of our people to look after our things at Jahili.

At Dubai we picked up three more vehicles which had been shipped in for this expedition and were joined by three geologists and a surveyor. We made our way over the desert and then down the coast to Muscat to pay our respects to the Sultan before beginning our journey back to Buraimi.

The journey in those days was of considerable interest as there were then very few vehicles which made this trip. There were no roads, and across the first 40 miles of low sand dunes the going was rough and bumpy. In that particular year, there had been a number of incidents in which the bedouin from the far south had shot up and robbed both car and camel convoys; for this reason traffic was particularly slack, and we met no other vehicle until well inside Muscat territory. According to some unwritten code the bedouin were not supposed to attack us as guests and foreigners but fortunately on this occasion we did not even encounter any hostile bedouin.

After crossing the sand dunes, the track became better defined and led up a long *wadi* into the mountains. The Hajar mountain range is mostly of bare wind-polished rock, beautiful at a distance but harsh and forbidding from close to. A very rough track, strewn with boulders, led us through a rocky pass at about 1,000 feet and on down the other side until, turning a corner in the narrow *wadi,* we glimpsed the sea. There the track flattened out on to a narrow plain with the mountains on the right and on the left rows of palms and gardens; beyond them lay a golden beach and the sea.

We camped that night on the Batinah coast in almost idyllic conditions. Because there is some malaria there, we carried mosquito nets; they also saved us from the attentions of the first morning flies. We tied the mosquito nets to a convenient tree, put up our camp beds, and that was enough.

The journey onwards next day was almost monotonously attractive, but the going was rough and very bumpy as the track wound its way among seemingly endless date gardens and tiny villages. We left some of our party at Suhar and in two trucks went on to meet the Sultan, in Muscat.

Muscat itself was then a fascinating little town. It is set in a crater which makes a horseshoe bay with dark crags at either end of the waterfront overlooking the sea. The circle of the waterfront was mostly taken up by the neat white palace, a government office and the British Consulate General nestling under the crag at the far end. On top of the crags were two old Portuguese forts, one used as the Treasury and the other as the prison. Both overlooked the little town which lay cupped in the rocks. The town was built of small white houses and was surrounded by an ancient wall, which in places ran right up the rocky slope behind the buildings. Only two streets within the wall were large enough to admit cars, but in those days there was virtually no motor traffic anyway. There were some curious and maddening rules and restrictions, most of which still applied until 1970: Europeans were not allowed out at night unless accompanied by an Omani carrying a lamp; special permission had to be obtained to drive a vehicle inside the wall; no smoking was allowed in the main streets; and musical instruments, including radios, were not allowed to be played anywhere in public, and only behind thick walls in private. These were some of the general restrictions, but far more onerous were those which were suffered by the Omani people themselves. The European community at that time averaged only about nine, including a bank manager and the British Consul General, with whom we were to stay.

We found the Sultan in excellent spirits. Urbane, courteous and very well-informed, he lived in a simple yet elegant and dignified style. The palace was a well-built two-storey white building on the edge of the harbour. On entering the tall studded doors through a little postern set in one of them, there was a wide flight of highly polished stone steps at the top of which the Sultan's secretary was waiting to greet the visitor and to conduct him to the Sultan's reception room. This was simply but tastefully furnished and had wide open windows which gave on to the shimmering blue and silver of the harbour. The room was cool, and spotlessly clean. The Sultan, who was dressed in a flowing robe and wearing an impressive and elaborate coloured turban, purple, white and red, rose to greet us. He spoke softly in almost perfect English.

We reached general agreement on the area which the geologists were to examine. He was most insistent that we should pay no rentals to the shaikhs; and our meeting passed very pleasantly, as the Sultan could be charming in an interview. He agreed to attach a government official named Yusuf to our party to help us with the tribes.

Early on the following day, we again took the long, bumpy and suffocating, dusty track up the coast past the hundreds of beautiful date gardens and by late evening joined the rest of the party near Suhar. The Sultan's trusted official was there to see us up the valley of the Jizzi. The Sultan himself had ordered the villagers to make a track up the valley which our cars were to negotiate.

We spent the night at Suhar and looked at the fine old Portuguese fort and great square tower which dominated the town. The gardens at Suhar were particularly beautiful, and the water was plentiful and sweet.

Early next day, we loaded our vehicles and set off up the *wadi,* Dick in front with the surveyor, myself at the rear, and our two geologists in the trucks in between. I had Sabir as my driver.

We soon left the plantations behind us and began crossing the grey rocky plain, not difficult driving but hard on our springs. As we came into the foothills, we were forced to drop down into the valley bottom; but there had been recent rain in the mountains and there were intermittent pools of water in the *wadi* bed. These we negotiated as best we could, sometimes going round them, sometimes through. We began to reach habitations, small villages perched on low bluffs near the *wadi* bed but high enough to be clear of flash floods which can suddenly sweep down these valleys without warning, carrying everything with them that lies in their path.

It was near the first village that trouble began with the vehicles. We could find no clear way round a particularly deep pool and had to use crowbars to clear a path round it through the boulders, with difficulty pushing and pulling the vehicles through the rocks on the pool's edge. When we came up to the village, we were immediately asked into one of the houses and entertained with coffee and mounds of dates served on basket mats. We asked after the track which was supposed to have been made as we could not see one. Our hosts took us across to see it. It was on the other side of the *wadi* bed, very rough indeed and not nearly wide enough; in fact virtually useless. The villagers told us, I am sure in all innocence, that they did not expect our vehicles to be so wide. They may have seen trucks on the Batinah coast, but they had certainly never tried to make a road before. We had to make up for the inadequacies of the track by the use of crowbars to clear the bigger rocks and the work was laborious; although the difficult stretch was only a matter of a few miles, it took us from morning until nearly sunset to cover it.

As we toiled up this difficult sector, the sun became hotter, the way dustier. The valley sides which had been gentle slopes became steeper, the dried *wadi* bed varying from 20 feet in width to 100 yards. In places it had three or four feet of water in it, but mostly it was dry. Sometimes the *wadi* bed took 'U' turns and we were able at a few of these places to climb over spurs to shorten our journey. The grey rocks were bare, polished and shining in the sun; but where the hard rock disappeared into the gravel and stones of the *wadi* bed, oleander sprouted luxuriantly. At places, looking up side valleys, we could see villages high in the rocks with a few palms or fig trees on tiny terraces hacked out of the cliff. At others, there were small plantations of palms and groups of huts right down in the valley only a few feet above what seemed to be the possible flood line, and at such places the villagers would come out and look at us in astonishment.

The tribesmen lower in the *wadi* offered us a gang of workers to help us to push the trucks through the difficult places. Yusuf, the Sultan's representative, had at last admitted he was a newcomer to the area, like ourselves, but he agreed to a dozen Shawami tribesmen joining us. They jumped on to our trucks and were to come with us as far as Hail and Rabi, two villages mid-way up the *wadi.*

At this point the front truck was just negotiating a particularly deep stretch of water, which we could see no way of avoiding, when we were greeted by a crackle of musketry, and one or two bullets came singing by us, ricocheting on the rocks around us. Needless to say, we all stopped and the front truck stuck, right in the water. Both Sabir and Firdullah characteristically laughed at this apparent misfortune. We switched off our engines and in the sudden silence after their roaring, the atmosphere seemed tense, brittle and electric. A few more shots came from a low bluff about 100 yards to our front and 50 yards above us. There were shouts from above and we shouted back explaining we were friends and had the Sultan's blessing. Then Yusuf took up the story and joined us in the shouting game.

We had all got down from the trucks which straggled down a steep and difficult boulder-strewn slope to the leading truck which looked half submerged now in the water. The slope was exposed to the tribesmen who were firing at us, and they were in good positions on the bluff above the water in front of us. They had us at their mercy; there was no getting back and no cover within 200 yards of us, or more, in any direction. Yusuf had a rifle and, I remembered with some concern, so did one or two of the excitable Shawamis; but they were by this time crouching behind the tail boards of the vehicles on which they had been riding, and those in the front truck had perforce to crouch in the water. Inevitably at such moments thoughts of other such incidents in Oman's history came to mind in which the victims either did or did not live to walk away. Which kind of incident would this be, I wondered.

Eventually two men appeared on the bluff and invited Yusuf to come forward. Yusuf did go forward a little, and we could hear the echoes of a shouted talk. He came back to us some minutes later and said that the villagers knew all about us and that as the Sultan had warned them of the trip, they would let us through with pleasure. But, why had we picked up those beastly Shawamis? Everyone knew, but not us and certainly not Yusuf, that Shawamis were not allowed on the territory of these two villages, and their plan to come as part of our party was just a trick to get them over forbidden ground. If we left them behind and took on some of their own villagers instead as helpers, we could go through.

In due course, but not without the Shawamis making a great noise, agreement was reached. We walked up to the village which was only just past the bluff, and we were offered coffee and dates: honour was satisfied. The disgruntled Shawamis went home on foot, having been paid off rather liberally to encourage them a little, and we took on a like number of the Bani Ghaith tribe who assured us that they were acceptable all the way up to Buraimi. So, it turned out, was the case. Our worst physical troubles with the 'going' coincided with the political hold-up, but the Bani Ghaith showed us a way round the wide water obstacle, and with their help we cleared a passable track.

Soon after leaving the village, we saw that we were now near the watershed and had come out of the area of habitation. From here onwards the valley was nearly barren, the rocks brown and grey. They rose on both sides steeply to the serrated mountain tops, the *wadi* bed itself being only 20 yards wide; and we mostly found our way along tracks made by animals some 20 feet up at the side of the gorge, not without some excitement and alarm as we put our trucks through places which their makers could not have had in mind for them.

From the watershed, about 1,200 feet above sea level, the going became gradually easier and nearly level until we came out at sunset between two arms of black crags on to the Dhahirah plain, and there in front of us was the familiar whale-back of Jebel Hafit. Turning northwards, we were soon among the trees and found our way across the bumpy gravel towards Buraimi.

It was dark and rather cold when we got into the village. We dropped Yusuf there, at his request, and paid off the Bani Ghaith. It was not until ten o'clock that we got back to Jahili fort. We had been at it since five o'clock in the morning, and were tired but happy to have got through. A brew of tea, our bedrolls laid down on the sand, and that was enough for the day.

Yusuf had fresh instructions from the Sultan, and we had a succession of meetings with tribal leaders on the following days. The geologists did manage a few trips a little into the Dhahirah, but Ibri and the south remained places we could not reach, and for that reason they began to have a strange fascination for me. What were they like, these places we could not visit?

Clearly, we were still making no progress and the geologists, although they could find a little work to do on the Abu Dhabi side, were wasting their time. Both Yusuf and Shaikh Saqr thought that it might help with the other tribes if Saiyid Ahmad bin Ibrahim, Minister of the Interior in Muscat, could come up and talk to them. We could hardly refuse to support this idea, and I set off with Sabir and two pick-ups, on our own, all the way down the wadi Jizzi again to see if I could persuade him to come from the capital.

Remembering the toil and trouble coming up, I expected that we would have trouble going down again, but Sabir assured me that if we took two empty trucks and two or three spare hands to help push us, we should be all right.

Apart from an alarming moment when the truck I was driving stuck near Hail, with one wheel on the edge of a 50-foot drop, all was well. We spent about an hour digging out rocks to widen the track at that point and we found that the rest of the track, though still rather difficult, was now usable. We had started early and reached Suhar in the early afternoon and began the trip down the coast to Muscat on the same day. The tribesmen on the trip down were all very friendly, but then we were careful to avoid any mixture of Shawamis and Bani Ghaith. Together they were a riot, but separately all smiles, coffee and dates.

The following day we reached Muscat and the Sultan agreed to Saiyid Ahmad's trip to Buraimi. Saiyid Ahmad was, even in those days, a venerable figure with a flowing white beard and, like the Sultan, he wore an elaborate turban. Charming and cheerful, he was an excellent companion. We travelled together in his aged Ford as far as Suhar, where I was lodged in a little villa belonging to the Sultan, in a lovely garden a mile or so to the north-west of the town, while Saiyid Ahmad stayed in the town at the Customs Post.

Early next morning, he sent me up by donkey from Suhar an excellent but, needless to say, rather cold breakfast of boiled milk, bread, dates and a kind of porridge; and he followed shortly afterwards. We set off in my two vehicles as Saiyid Ahmad's was not strong enough to face the wadi Jizzi, with myself driving in the lead and Sabir bringing up the rear.

Saiyid Ahmad had insisted on bringing several followers and quite a lot of gear so that we were overloaded, but I readily agreed, provided only that the followers walked over the very bad patches and pushed when necessary. I knew it would be hopeless to attempt to refuse this unwanted escort, since no man of importance can travel without followers in Oman if he is to retain the respect of the people.

With some misgivings we set off over the rough plain. Neither Saiyid Ahmad nor I were anxious to stop at each village; he because it meant giving a *largesse*; I because of the time it would need. The people were all glad to see him and wanted to give us lunch everywhere, but Saiyid Ahmad managed to prevent sheep being killed in his honour, and we got to Hail soon after noon.

There we had trouble with the vehicles. The steep pitches could not be negotiated with all the followers on the back, and the followers did not want to get off. However, after a particularly hair-raising slide, with wheels spinning, towards a nasty little drop to the *wadi* bed below, Saiyid Ahmad was thoroughly convinced that I was right, and at a snapped order from him all the men got down with alacrity and began to push. My trouble then was to persuade Saiyid Ahmad that it was all right for them to get on again. "No," he said. "They have legs, let them walk." However, we reached a compromise which allowed them to get on the running board of my pick-up, hanging to the sides, ready to jump down, and we made much better progress. Nevertheless, it was dark when we got into Buraimi and eventually said goodbye to Saiyid Ahmad at Shaikh Saqr's fort.

Saiyid Ahmad seemed to be doing rather better with Shaikh Saqr than we had, but such was the kaleidoscope of tribal politics that Shaikh Saqr in turn was getting on worse with Obaid of the Bani Kaab, and with both Shaikh Rashid and bin Rahmah of the settled and nomadic Al Bu Shamis respectively.

To appreciate the intricacies of this situation, not only is it again necessary to forget the conventions of Western political thinking, and any idea of uniqueness of loyalty, but it is essential to remember that each shaikh is living publicly in front of his people and if he appears to be weakening, he will lose any hold he has over them, and very soon his position altogether. In this part of Arabia a tribal shaikh has to be acceptable to remain in power; he is in a sense elected by his tribe and, if he appears to be failing to lead and benefit his people, they will begin to desert him. Only a very assured shaikh, who has built up a strong position over a period, can make decisions which concern the future of the tribe as a whole without going through at least the appearance of some process of consultation. Shaikh Zayed, alone of the shaikhs in the Dhahirah, was in a really strong position, but he was not directly involved as far as our entry to the south was concerned, except as a friend and adviser. In this he helped greatly.

Of the Sultanate shaikhs, Saqr was in the most peculiar position. Over-careful with money, he kept the proceeds of local taxes in his fort in boxes full of silver. He had a strong but small group of armed men both in Buraimi and in Dhank, 40 miles to the south. He owned and farmed more irrigated land than any other Sultanate shaikh in this area; he was feared for his toughness, but he had no popular following outside his immediate retainers. He maintained his position only with difficulty and, uniquely in this area, on the basis of his wealth and his group of armed retainers, rather than on popular acceptance.

Obaid of the Bani Kaab had a good presence and clearly had leadership; a pleasing personality, he was popular with his tribesmen. Rashid of the settled Al Bu Shamis had a reputation for being over-careful with money and was not popular; he resented the paramountcy of Shaikh Saqr over the Naim and Al Bu Shamis tribes (the two tribes were structurally one). Bin Rahmah was shaikh of the Al Bu Shamis bedouin group; he was clever and seemed to have considerable leadership.

From the secondhand accounts we received through Yusuf of the negotiations, it seemed Saiyid Ahmad was getting nowhere with anyone but Shaikh Saqr who appeared to be becoming more and more isolated from the other leaders.

To try to show us how good he was being, Shaikh Saqr suggested that the geologists should begin work on a small hill to the south of Buraimi. Early one morning we set off as arranged, calling at the fort for Shaikh Saqr who wanted to watch the geologists at work. As might be expected, he kept us waiting an inordinate time to show how important he was, and when he came to the door of the fort he hardly deigned to reply to my greeting. I showed him into the front of Dick's pick-up and off we went in silence. Even when we got to the rocks, Shaikh Saqr would hardly say a word. He, Dick and I sat by idly, alternately drinking coffee and tea, while the geologists pottered about and collected some samples which they put into small bags and labelled. After a couple of hours, Dick suggested we should pack up for the day. It was really only a trial morning and the shaikh was, not surprisingly, looking very bored by such a dull occasion. As the geologists packed up their gear, the sample bags were collected and put into one truck.

Immediately the shaikh noticed and said, "What are you doing with those?" Dick explained that they would be sorted out, examined and cut into fine pieces for microscopic examination, the most interesting ones being sent to London for further tests. The shaikh said that he thought that if they were worth sending to London, they must be worth a lot of money. He would keep these samples, and as for the future an 'arrangement' would have to be made.

You may think this sounds absurd, we certainly did, but in all fairness someone with no knowledge of the outside world, only recently introduced to car and radio, and more importantly cut off from his fellows and without friends or advisers, might be excused for such reasoning. Later,

Zayed laughed heartily at this; but what followed tickled us even more.

On the way back, pleased by his apparent victory over samples, Shaikh Saqr's tongue was a bit freer. He said that in the middle of all his arguments with bin Rahmah, the old bedouin shaikh had said "What is more, if they find oil I will have it carried out only on my donkeys and camels." "Silly man," said Shaikh Saqr in triumph. "I will insist that it goes on my own trucks, which I will buy just for this."

The next three days were taken up with talks between Saiyid Ahmad and the shaikh. But he had to report that he had reached no really satisfactory conclusion and, as the best season climatically for geological work would come to an end within a month, we decided to delay our project until the following year, and we recommended in this sense to our London office.

I drove Saiyid Ahmad back to Suhar and had a much easier trip. On our journey up, he had given instructions for parts of the track to be improved and this had been done. Also we now knew its difficult points and we managed to get him to Suhar and ourselves back in Jahili all in one day. By now the track looked almost as well established as the other routes which we had been using, and it demonstrated that in Oman the passage of a few trucks is enough to establish a well-worn main route at once.

We spent the rest of the spring between Jahili and Dubai. The last weeks were hot and trying, and in the early afternoon we used to sit in the comparatively cool irrigation channels to make the afternoon heat endurable.

I remember that period of spring in Buraimi and Al Ain for the pleasant companionship of Shaikh Zayed, and sometimes one or other of his three brothers, of evening meals sitting on a rug in the sands, of lunch in the date garden beside the clear water of the irrigation channels, and the atmosphere of quiet repose and remoteness which the oasis still had in those days.

Although I was still a newcomer to Oman, I already felt rather despondent about the future – would we be permitted to search for oil in Oman? Here was a people friendly, lively, delightful; yet, what future had they otherwise? The chances of oil in the area south of Buraimi were, we hoped, very good indeed. The Sultan did not have enough money to administer the area from his far-away capital. The history of the bedouin tribes in Jordan, Iraq and Saudi Arabia proved again and again that the bedouin will continue their raiding and tribal feuds until central authority can make itself established in the towns and, by using modern methods of communication, can reach out from the towns into the desert. Until the invention of the motor car, the modern rifle and machine gun, bedouin were undisputed masters in their deserts. Settled people can hire bedouin to fight each other, can raise guards from among them or pay them to let trade cross their land; but before the car was available to them the settled tribes found it difficult, if not impossible, to control the bedouin who could raid any line of communication which crossed their deserts or was within easy reach of them.

I was quite certain that all that was needed in the area south of Buraimi was a small locally raised force in trucks, perhaps no more than a squadron in strength. This would allow a survey party, followed by drilling rigs, to get in, find the oil if as we hoped it was there, and bring prosperity to the people. Without some show of strength, the tribes would never allow exploration to take place in the desert, and the hills were of little interest to us from the point of view of oil. The key lay solely with the Al Bu Shamis and the Duru tribes. But as things looked, progress and development could never come to them as long as the bedouin themselves prevented the essential preparatory stages, albeit unwittingly.

The Saudis had never administered the area, and had never occupied the Abu Dhabi sector of the oasis, and, at those times before 1869 when they had established themselves in Buraimi, they had used it only as a centre for raiding and for conversion to the Wahibah code of Islam.

To me, renewed Saudi interest now seemed unlikely. The desert journey from Dammam to Buraimi must be over 300 miles; and, unless one used the coast route almost to Abu Dhabi town itself, the hundreds of miles of sand dunes presented a terrible obstacle to mechanical transport. Moreover, it was an area which only the hardiest bedouin, lightly equipped and specialists in the region at that, would face, with camels trained to do many days' march between water holes. I discounted such a danger but Zayed was more cautious. Only two years before Saudi tax gatherers, collecting *zakat,* the religious tithe, had entered the Abu Dhabi plantations among the high dunes of the Liwa. This, Zayed said, would not have been done without a reason. He regarded it as a preparatory step.

In June we finally packed up in Jahili, said goodbye to Zayed and our other friends and returned to Dubai, where I was to take over from Jackson, for the time being at least, but I was to keep an eye open and be ready for further expeditions inland while Dick went home to London. From this time my hopes centred on the Duru country and the sphinx it harboured, the anticline called Jebel Fahud, which might be full of oil.

Chapter Five

I was based in Dubai for nearly three years between 1948 and 1951; during much of this time Ronald Codrai was with me as my colleague and we lived in Jackson's former house. We did a considerable number of trips inland, and up and down the coast, mostly in the cooler weather, but sometimes in the heat of the summer when sensible people expect to stay at home.

The Trucial Coast is mostly flat and sandy, and much of the strip along the seashore is at, or even just below, sea level. The areas that are lower than the level of high tide are protected by a barrier of sand dunes, except at Dubai itself and in neighbouring Khan and Sharjah where tidal creeks have formed. In the case of Dubai this stretch of water runs twelve miles inland, and is the *raison d'être* for the town.

Dubai in those days must have had a population of something under 20,000. The indigenous population was Arab, mainly from the tribe of the Bani Yas, which had first settled on Abu Dhabi island in the second half of the 18th century and had spread to Dubai. Bedouin tribes have a tendency to split up and rejoin in different formations over long periods of time; these changes are usually due to the rise and fall of big personalities and success or failure in war and raiding.

Which personality caused the coming together of several tribes to form the Bani Yas is lost in the mists of local history, but by the 18th century the process was well-established. In Abu Dhabi other tribes had also adhered to the main Bani Yas group in that they acknowledged the shaikh as their paramount, and yet had not merged themselves with the tribe, keeping a separate identity. In the last part of the 18th century and the early years of the 19th, the Bani Yas in Abu Dhabi and Dubai were under one shaikh, and it was not until 1835 that Dubai finally split from Abu Dhabi; from the same tribe originally, the two states tended to be at rivalry with each other, and a series of conflicts ensued, mostly over grazing rights, camel thefts, individual killings and similar causes.

For the first half of the 19th century, the Saudis made themselves felt in the area by their occupation of the villages of Buraimi and Hamasah in the Buraimi oasis, inland, on several different occasions.

By the beginning of the 19th century the Qawasim, based in the towns of Ras Al Khaimah and Sharjah, had seriously disrupted trade in the Gulf: many was the merchant ship they had captured. It took the British government of India the first 20 years of the 19th century to bring maritime peace to the area. This involved occasional landings of troops and, in particular, the landing of a considerable force at Ras Al Khaimah itself. A treaty was signed in 1820 with the shaikhs of the whole coast, and others followed it; and as is plain from the texts of these early treaties, it was the object of the British to prevent fighting at sea and the carriage of slaves by sea. The British sought only to suppress slavery and to keep the peace at sea and in this they succeeded magnificently.

The British sailors engaged in operations were using tiny wooden ships, under the hardest possible conditions. In the case of the operations on the east coast of Africa, they were in open boats; heat-stroke and scurvy took their toll; and the operations to stop this trade must have cost the lives of hundreds of British sailors in the 19th century and exacted a toll of hardship and privation from those who managed to survive.

As I have mentioned earlier, for a short time after the Second World War Imperial Airways continued to alight on Dubai creek, but by 1948 these had stopped and no scheduled air service operated to any part of the coast. The normal way then to reach Dubai was from Bahrain, or Karachi by British India (BI) steamer, and with no air-conditioning in those days, this was a most uncomfortable way of travelling.

The arrival of the BI steamer was an occasion in Dubai. The 'goer up' or the 'goer down' as the ship was called, would anchor off Dubai about a mile or more out to sea, and small boats would scurry out to bring her passengers ashore.

The narrow ladders up the side of the ship would be packed with crowds trying to go up and down at the same time, mingled with 'coolies' lugging packages on and off. I made several trips by British India and one night at Bandar Abbas I was entertained for many hours by the fact that the gangway ladder happened to be exactly opposite my porthole: many passengers were disembarked there, but also several tonnes of ghee (cooking fat) in square four-gallon drums were manhandled individually by the 'coolies' down the same ladder, both with and against the stream of passengers. The din, the shaking, the smells which assailed me all night were quite astonishing. On such trips, when at sea, I normally slept on deck, where it was hot enough, but not like the cabins which were stifling, and on one occasion my cabin shared a bulkhead with the engine, a bulkhead which was too hot to touch. But in port one could not sleep on deck, since all open spaces were crowded with people, luggage, and cargo, the boat deck uncluttered but out of bounds to all passengers be they steerage or first class. On that particular night in Bandar Abbas, exasperated, I went up on deck and found a ship's officer and asked him why the ghee could not be unloaded in bulk by crane. "I don't know," he said quite frankly. "They always seem to do it this way here."

Our house in Dubai was directly on the creek's edge, with only the roadway and one small jetty between us and the water. It stood at the point where the creek curved in a great S-bend out to sea. The water was about a quarter of a mile across at that point. It is now about half that width, since it has been made narrow in order to deepen it and create a strong current to move the silting sand. At the bar there was only about two feet of water at low tide and about eight at full tide, so that only country craft and the small lighters for unloading cargo ships could come in.

The majority of these country craft were *jalboots* (from the English 'jolly-boat'), short, stumpy, wooden sailing ships with a vertical plank for a prow, a single mast and a lateen sail. More and more of these little boats were being fitted with small diesel engines. There was one which we used to charter from time to time for carrying company stores up and down the coast and for our own journeys. She was called *Shaheen,* the Arabic word for peregrine falcon, and had a crew of five. When on board, we lived on deck, and I used to sleep on an air mattress since I found the lurching of a camp-bed intolerable; in anything of a sea it was a case of lying on the bare deck anyway.

In addition to these small boats, there were the much bigger *booms* which would sail from Kuwait to Dubai and southwards as far as Zanzibar. These were often two-masted and the habit of fitting an engine was at that time just beginning; even those so fitted would use their sails as well if the wind was favourable. They were long, beautiful ships with their billowing lateen sails and purposeful raked prows. Dubai creek was an endless joy to watch. Apart from little *jalboots* fussing up and down

Schoolboy, Clifton Preparatory School, Bristol.

During the Second World War.

In diplomatic uniform, Bahrain.

Family portrait on the occasion of the Queen's birthday party, Qatar.

Fishermen releasing a truck from the rising tide. (*R. Codrai*)

As British Consul in Jerusalem 1961-1964. Greeting Governor of Jerusalem Anwar Nuseibe on the occasion of the Queen's birthday party.

Negotiating the settlement of withdrawal – then as Political Agent of Qatar, seated with Sir William Luce and Shaikh Khalifah bin Hamad Al Thani, then Ruler of Qatar.

A ferryboat on the creek at Ras Al Khaimah. (*R. Codrai*)

Accompanying Ahmed bin Khalifa Al Suwaidi, adviser to His Highness the President of the United Arab Emirates, and Sir Wilfred Thesiger during the latter's visit to Abu Dhabi in 1990.

With Shaikh Nahyan bin Mubarak Al Nahyan and former British Prime Minister Margaret Thatcher, who opened an exhibition of Sir Wilfred Thesiger's photographs in Abu Dhabi, 1992.

Members of the large Duru tribe in the Dhahira. (*R. Codrai*)

Visiting old Jahili Fort in Al Ain, 1994, where the author lived in 1948-1949.

with the pug-pug of their little engines, there were the larger country craft plying the creek at high tide, majestic under sail. On each occasion they would have to pull in the sail and furl it on the spar, pushing it under and past the mast which, with lateen rig, is raked steeply forwards, and set it in order to go right about on the other tack to catch the wind and fill the sail as the helm went hard over for the bend. Among them scurried little *abras*, two-oared ferry boats, literally 'crossers'. There were hundreds of them in those days, and none of them had motors. They would ply as taxis across the creek or up and down it, since all the houses were close to the creekside.

The town was divided into three districts. We lived in Dubai itself on the south side, to the north of us was Deira, then a growing community but no bigger than Dubai, and to the north-west was Shindagha, a purely residential district on the same bank as Dubai, but sometimes cut off like an island when a high tide and strong wind coincided. There some of the shaikhs lived, but in very modest 'palaces' indeed.

On Deira side there was an increasing number of cars, perhaps two dozen by 1948; and on the Dubai side, the shaikh had two or three. We had five mainly for our inland expeditions, and apart from occasional visitors from Deira, there were no others on our side of the creek. The track outside our house dived almost at once into the cavern of the *souq*, the market, which was not then wide enough for cars to enter. The traffic in front of our house was limited to donkeys and foot passengers, but noisy and busy it was. The town noises were punctuated all day by an old beggar, sitting a little way down our street, whose strange cry was rather distressing until you became used to it. He seemed to collect quite a lot of money, much of it in the tiniest coins of all, worth about a farthing, and we contributed regularly as he, as it were, belonged to us.

At our door sat Ghanim bin Ali, a genial man but nearly blind, much mocked at by his friends because he had nine daughters and no sons. He was our chief guard; we had two others, not that they had any guarding to do, but they seemed to be necessary appurtenances to a house in those days. They helped to keep away small boys if they became too bothersome and noisy. More important, they kept us in touch with local events and advised us on social etiquette and acted as messengers, in the days before the telephone had reached Dubai.

Dubai *souq* was about 200 yards long, covered-over and dark, with the shops on either side of a central lane. Each shop was a small rectangle, the back being in darkness. At its entrance sat the owner, cross-legged on the ground, with the more attractive and recently bought wares around him. If you wished to buy, he would offer you a small stool or the corner of the rug on which he sat, and then he plied you with coffee, or if he was an Iranian merchant, with sweet tea. The *souq* had a subdued hubbub about it, for this was before the days of transistor radios. The strolling crowds, almost all in long Arab *thawbs,* or robes, made a murmur of voices punctuated every now and then by a small boy on a bicycle much too large for him, warning of his headlong approach with a squeaky horn.

In Dubai *souq* the shops were of different kinds. In one, meat would be cooking while next to it another would stock a pile of dented tins of soup, baked beans or sardines. The next shop might be an Indian tailor or a cloth shop, but many sold a little of everything so that at first sight these dungeon-like cavities seemed unlikely to have what you wanted but often, after the shopkeeper had rummaged about in the dark recesses, he would pull out the article you were looking for. The drawback to this was that the farther back in the shop the article was found, the older it would be, as fresh goods always took pride of place at the front.

If you could not find what you wanted on the Dubai side, or if you were after cloth or a battery for your radio, you would walk through the half light to the end of the *souq*, where suddenly you were faced by a dazzling and noisy opening between the houses, and you were at the water's edge. Here, bumping against the rough stone steps, would be twenty or thirty little *abra* boats, jostling for custom. As soon as anyone appeared from the darkness of the *souq*, anyone who looked a likely customer, the *abra* men would all shout together, each one certain that his eloquent persuasion would induce you to pick his boat.

Once aboard, the excitement died; the *abra* man would push the boat out and his competitors would give him a friendly shove from either side. Then, in a standing, stooping position he would push, not pull, at the oars which were each tied by a loop of rope to a wooden pin stuck through the gunwale. In this way, the boat would go quite fast over the choppy little waves of the turquoise blue creek, whose sudden brightness was cheerful after the gloom of the *souq*. The journey took you a little further up the creek, as the other *abra* station in Deira was not opposite the one in Dubai.

A little beyond on the right could be seen the long building of the Ruler's old palace. Of two storeys, with a plaster-decorated front, and with verandahs the whole length on each floor, it looked imposing simply because it was the biggest building, and it had an almost quaintly Victorian look about it; but it also looked unused and decayed. Next to it was the Customs House where the Ruler and his son, Shaikh Rashid, held court on the verandah. In front of the office was a wharf and on it a small iron crane with a hand crank, and there were always some small barges moored alongside. It was not until I had been in Dubai for some time that I discovered that the lower floor of the old palace itself was absolutely full of merchandise. In particular the first sacks of cement were here, the cement which was shortly to transform Dubai and turn it in a few years into the very different place which it is now.

Meanwhile, the *abra* man had rowed the little boat almost to the other side of the creek, at the same time keeping up a running conversation to describe to his fare the events of the day and his philosophy of life. The first thing to be seen as one bumped through the crowd of boats at the Deira *abra* station was the British Bank of the Middle East's very special lavatory. I always thought the boat would hit it, but it never did. The bank itself was right on the creek's edge to the left of the landing point. It was a modest single-storey building with windows on to the creek and its chief ornament was its lavatory which was really no more than a platform sticking out over the water, with the essential slit in its middle, tastefully boxed in and screened from view with palm branches. Whoever was inside had a rather broken view of the outside world, but the outside world could not see in. I think it was the most prominent lavatory I have ever encountered and it was certainly a landmark. "Go past the BBME loo and turn to the left," one could say by way of direction.

If one were Deira-bound it would be an automatic drill to drop in and pass the time of day with Mark Stott, the bank manager, and at that time our only European colleague in Dubai. His bank was in Deira, but he then lived at the RAF mess in Sharjah. Not only was his lavatory odd, but his office had an unusual feature. At his back, set in the window, was a fan run by a tiny paraffin engine which went clank, clank, clank, and turned a small blade round, it seemed to me, very slowly. I always maintained that the paraffin engine made more trouble with its heat and smell, than any comfort it could provide, as it brought in the remarkably unfresh air from the creek in tiny quantities. However, Mark robustly held that it made life bearable and he would not be without it for anything. He was a hefty, solid and jolly man, much more like a cavalry officer than a banker; it was a pleasure to exchange gossip with him and sip a glass of rather warm lime juice, for he had no fridge, before leaving to visit the Deira *souq*.

Later Mark moved into Deira where he built a house a little way out of town. It is almost in the centre of the new Deira town and still stands – something of a museum piece. He had seen service in the Indian Army and when the house was completed he held a house-warming party for all the British community on a hot day in August when he chose to provide us with a curry lunch. The new house, which was somewhat pokey, boasted an electric generator and was meant to be air-conditioned. It seemed to me rather hotter inside than outside, but it would have been churlish to comment on such an occasion. But when we all, some eight of us, moved into the dining room for the famous curry, it became hotter still, for through the dining-room windows, which were shut for the sake of the air-conditioning, streamed the midday sun.

Even Mark was sweating and I suggested that perhaps we should have his paraffin fan to warm us up. He said that the air-conditioning had only been turned on for the first time that morning, and perhaps it had not quite settled down. It would doubtless be better soon. As we plied ourselves with the hottest curry I can ever remember, I looked up, perhaps hoping for help from above, and saw over our heads a large ceiling fan, motionless. "For goodness sake, turn the fan on, Mark," I said and my neighbours supported my plea vigorously.

"What! And ruin the curry?" cried our host. And so the fan stayed motionless throughout what remains in my memory as the hottest lunch I have ever eaten.

After lunch someone had the good sense to suggest we should look at the garden, although we all knew there was nothing in it yet. It was cooler outside and there was a little breeze. When we got to the back of the house by the dining room someone gave a shout of surprise. "Just feel this," he said. Out of the exhaust of the very Heath Robinson central air-conditioning unit came cool air. The fans had been put in the wrong way round. It was as simple as that, and we had been air-conditioning the garden, and breathing in the exhaust.

However, this was all a year or two later. From Mark's hospitable office we would go to a tiny square and thence into a choice of black holes. One was for cloth, one was for household goods, another for carpentry and so on. These *souqs* were long, narrow and dark tunnels, arranged in the traditional Eastern style, unlike the *souqs* on the Dubai side; each *souq* to its trade, miniatures of the arcaded *souqs* of Aleppo or Isfahan. The cloth *souq* was cool and comparatively quiet, and was heavy with the smell of camphor and of the new bales of cloth. Other *souqs* were redolent of spice, of cooked meat, or of tobacco. The alleys were narrow and small, but they had great character, and the shopkeepers, naturally glad to see a customer, made one very welcome; and whatever one bought or not, it was impossible to stop without taking coffee or tea. Those who liked to gossip could do so there all day.

The Eastern style of putting all like shops together in one street I always find puzzling. You could look at any two shops side by side or opposite one another, and it was a problem to tell one from the other: they each seemed to have identical wares. I suppose the difference must ultimately lie in the price or, more importantly, in the fact that Ahmad was your mother's first cousin, whereas Muhammad next door was only her second cousin twice removed. Of course no price was marked and you bargained, that was really the fun of it.

Another road led out of the Bank Square and even in 1948, so far had progress then reached Dubai, the occasional car would force its way down it, since it was just wide enough. On either side there were low stone or mud-brick buildings, mostly shops, workshops and storehouses. The road was roofed over, and a car would come honking down it disturbing the walker, and those sitting outside the shops would have to grab their stools and retreat indoors until the car had passed. The crowds that wandered in this street, like the others, would mainly be Arabs in white *thawbs* or robes, and those who were the Ruler's men would carry their rifles and wear curved daggers at their belts. There were also Indians, Pakistanis and Iranians, but the Arabs were the distinctive figures, and in those days everyone wore their traditional national dress. The Arabs from Oman wore coloured *thawbs,* and bright Kashmiri scarves wound round their heads like an untidy but colourful turban. They walked gracefully with short steps, heads held back and slim bodies graceful and lithe. The women also walked this way but this was from the habit of carrying loads on their heads; the hillmen, too, were accustomed to carrying loads on their heads, but quite why all the Omanis have this characteristically graceful walk I could never make out.

Then there were the bedouin from nearby tribes like the Manasir. They showed their pride, and the young bloods would strut through the town as if they owned it. At that time, they were not allowed to walk in town armed, but they were always armed when they went out into the desert. Even without their rifles they had a roguish, attractively overconfident air because the bedouin all looked down on the townsmen. The shaikhs of all the towns on the coast, mainly bedouin by descent, still very much affected bedouin ways, and they could, therefore, keep on easy terms with the desert folk, although they were half-way to being townsmen. This was more particularly marked in Abu Dhabi than in Dubai, but along the whole coast the bedouin were the aristocrats and the blue blood of a shaikhly family was from the wholly nomadic tribes of the interior.

It was in this street that I called one day on a merchant friend who has since become remarkably rich. After the usual coffee and tea, I started to ask idly about his business and what he traded in. "I trade in everything that comes to hand," he smiled. "Come and look at this." He took me out of the shop, round a corner and up a back alleyway. He came to a door and shouted. Up sprung a boy, it seemed from nowhere."Please open it up," he ordered. A small postern was opened which was set within two big double doors, and I was shown inside. When I got used to the dim light, I could see we were in a long low mud-brick warehouse completely full of bicycles. "But," I said in amazement, "there are no roads here and very few people ride bicycles." "My friend," replied the merchant smiling, "of course I shall not sell them here, one or two perhaps. I shall smuggle them into Pakistan, that is how I have got a similar number of Singer sewing machines off my hands in this same way."

We went out again and he took me further down the road until we came out on the bank of the creek. "You see that boat? That one and all the others moored above it are smugglers' boats; they have bigger engines than the others, but they look just the same." "But why do all the smugglers moor their boats together?" I asked. "I don't know," he replied, but it seemed to me that as in that neat and inscrutable manner in which the *souqs* are laid out – all cloth sold in one street, all tin cans in another – so the legitimate traders moor in one place, and the illegals are snugly tied together in another. If you could explain the first practice, perhaps you would find the answer to the second.

Some of the stone or coral and plaster houses on both sides of the creek had the picturesque and stately wind-towers called *badgirs,* of Persian origin, which were found then on both sides of the Gulf. They look rather like our own village church towers and are attractively decorated with ornamentation in plaster. These are efficient as a means of cooling the rooms below, as the four sides are really scoops designed to push the wind downward into the house.

Our house, unfortunately, had no such tower, but the wide verandah which ran its length faced the prevailing north-west wind and there were three passages right through the house to enable the wind to blow across the verandah at these points. Although we were without air-conditioning, or even fans for much of the time I lived there, we usually had a draught of air blowing through the house. The worst times were those frequent nights in the summer when humidity was maximum and the air was too still even to stir the thick mist which rose out of the creek. Maximum shade temperature was 49°C, but normally the day temperature was around 41°C in the summer. The trouble came from the high humidity and from the high night temperatures which in late summer were sometimes not so far below those of the day.

In the autumn of 1949 we had the inspiring sight of the pearl boats returning from the *ghaus,* the diving season. Ten major and many smaller boats came into Dubai that year, although this was many fewer than would have been seen in the 1930s and before. We could see the ships lying off the bar waiting to come in on the high tide of the early afternoon, and in the afternoon we put out in an *abra* to watch them come in. The first two were the largest.

They set their sails and headed for the bar. As they crossed it, the wind dropped and we could see that instead of relying on sail, they had their long sweeps out, ten to each side in the largest boats, and with three men pushing on each sweep, they crossed the bar and entered the creek at quite a speed. All Dubai was on the banks, or like us, out in small boats to greet them, for they had been away at sea for months. The two leading boats were almost abreast as they rounded the bend and they raced with tremendous vigour, great sheets of water splashing up at every stroke, to the anchorage further in. High in the stern of each was stationed a young lad with a screaming falsetto to urge on the rowers, and the rowers themselves shouted in unison, a harsh menacing cry in rhythm with the thump of the oars. As the boats swept in, one after another, it seemed more like the start of a battle than the end of a long voyage.

Specialist pearl merchants had come from India and Pakistan to examine the catch and make purchases. Shortly after the arrival of the boats, I watched these merchants at work examining and bargaining. One particular merchant would hold court on a verandah overlooking the creek, the merchants and boat owners bringing their pearls to him in large red or yellow cloths which they would spread out on the carpet before him. The old merchant, dressed in the flowing clothes of India, with a white turban-like cloth on his head, would let the pearls trickle through his fingers in a full stream. He looked, and seemed, centuries away from us.

This was the last year that a major fleet went pearling from Dubai, and their numbers have dwindled ever since to almost nothing, partly because of competition from the cultured pearl industry of Japan, partly because this arduous work is unpopular, and now because there are other sources of income available. It is hard to imagine how they lived, each crew, as much as one hundred men, cooped up in a tiny boat, the divers diving all day, never getting ashore for perhaps four months at a time and relying on other boats which brought them food and water. When you are diving you must have an empty stomach so the divers could not eat at all and took only sips of coffee in working hours, that is in daylight, and this through the height of the Gulf summer.

Wilfred Thesiger was a welcome guest, either at the beginning or at the end of some of his magnificent journeys across the Empty Quarter. He mentions in his book 'Arabian Sands' how on one of these occasions he was still accompanied by two of his bedouin who stayed with us in our house, and we introduced them to European food and our ways. I have been many times a guest of the bedouin and as many times entertained them to meals at my house or at a camp in the desert, but this was the only occasion I had real bedouin living with us as house guests in something like a European *ménage*. As Wilfred recalls, they delighted to waken me before first light with cries of "Up to pray! Prayer is better than sleep."

On one of these visits Wilfred and I went down by launch, a *jalboot*, to Abu Dhabi. It was a convenient way to go in those days when Abu Dhabi was still an island, but it meant that when you arrived you had no car, and there were virtually no cars in Abu Dhabi at that time. It was a pleasant, calm trip and took about 14 hours in the *Shaheen.*

On arrival at Abu Dhabi, we anchored off the foreshore and went ashore in the tiny canoe-like dugout through the surf. We walked through the soft sand half a mile or so to the big fort or palace which then seemed to dominate the tiny town (now the town in turn totally dominates it). Shaikh Shakhbut, the Ruler, was at his most charming and courteous and was amused by Wilfred's explanation of my name as meaning 'bin Hender' ('son of Hender' in

Arabic), and it is as 'bin Hender' that I am known to some of the family to this day. Shaikh Shakhbut would hold forth on any subject and had the shrewdest questions to ask, whether about flying saucers, the population of Bristol, or the rainfall in Scotland.

We were put in the only substantial house on the seashore, two storeys of mud brick known as Bait Al Shamali, 'the northern house' or the 'guest house', but most of our meals were taken at the palace, to which we were invited by a messenger on foot. One lunch was at the guest house itself and the Ruler and two of his three brothers came to join us for it, the fourth brother, Shaikh Zayed, being still at Al Ain. Here Wilfred and I parted; he to go inland by camel to Al Ain and from there to start one of his journeys, and I to return to Dubai. This was just the first of many interesting and enjoyable visits for me to Abu Dhabi.

Abu Dhabi was in marked contrast to Dubai in those days. Since the death of the great Zayed bin Khalifah in the early years of this century, trading from Abu Dhabi had gone downhill. Moreover, the fall in the pearl trade had hit Abu Dhabi particularly badly. Last century and in the opening decades of this, Abu Dhabi was one of the leading centres for the pearl trade, but by the time I first arrived few ships of any size set forth for the pearl season, and the pearling fleet consisted mainly of small boats which could not venture so far, nor for so long, as in the old days. There was a row of three or four stone-and-plaster-built houses along the front which were then already in ruins. The *souq* was tiny, and the majority of houses in which the inhabitants lived were of the palm-branch, *barasti* type. The foreshore of the island was three to four miles in length, and the town occupied only a tiny fraction of this. There was a thin scattered line of date palms just inland of the coast, and there was the cluster of huts which formed the town; then near the palm trees, the large fort.

The island was in the shape of a narrowing tongue of bare sand and salt flat surrounded on both sides by wide lagoons and was totally devoid of any vegetation except the thin clumps of desert grasses on a few of the dunes and the dark mangroves in some of the neighbouring lagoons. At its apex, this tongue came near to the mainland, leaving a quarter of a mile or more of shallow sea water which could be forded with difficulty by cars and camels at one place at extreme low tide. Once on the mainland, one's troubles were not over because there were ten miles of salt flat or *sabkha,* as it is called, which a high tide, a strong wind or rainfall, or worse still, any combination of these, would cover to the depth of a foot or more thus making the going impossible to car and camel alike. Evidence of this lay in the camels' bones which covered it, camels which had fallen in the mud and had broken a limb and had had to be slaughtered ritually and cut up for meat on the spot – the only salvage operation that was possible to recoup a little of their value.

I said goodbye to Shaikh Shakhbut and to Thesiger, and ploughed my way back to Dubai in the launch with regret because, despite the simplicity of the place, its very remoteness and the charm of its people were very attractive to me. Even as it is now, anything but remote, its hinterland still has a certain magic, if you can get away from the motorway.

In Dubai I was brought back into the 20th century with a bump. The RAF had brought part of a squadron of twin-engined Beaufighters to train over the desert, and as the village names on their maps were incorrectly shown, I was persuaded to go with them on one of their flights to identify the various places. It was by then already warm. They apologised for being unable to give me a proper seat and I was perched behind the pilot on the wing spar, where I had a good view; but the sun beat hard on me through the perspex. We had an exhilarating ride, mostly as far as I could judge at a height of 20 feet in close formation with four aircraft together. We visited more places in those few hours than I could normally hope to do in a year.

We first went north to Rams and Khor Al Shaam and looked at that remarkable feature the Musandam Peninsula from uncomfortably close quarters. The blue of the sea and the grey, red and brown of the rocks made a striking contrast below us. In places, 3,000-foot peaks are perched on the edge of the deep water and their bases are actually overhung. In one place the whole peninsula is a ridge of such rock at the head of an inlet, and the peninsula there is less than a mile wide. On the other side is the Indian Ocean, at that point called the Gulf of Oman. We flew low over this narrow neck and then turned back. From there we flew low over each of the coastal towns and villages to turn inland and roam over the desert to Buraimi, climbing steadily with the rising ground to some 1,000 feet above sea level, and then up to 3,000 feet and more among the crags of Jebel Hafit. Back we came to the coast along the edge of the rocky foothills of the Oman mountains where the desert in many places seems to lash itself like an angry sea against the hard rocks, and where deep dunes pile themselves up against the cliffs. I could see why we found this area difficult to cross on the ground. Here and there was the sudden splash of greenery, a group of palms and acacias, an acre or two of crops and a little pool, the sudden contrasts which make this country so attractive.

Afterwards we had lunch at the mess with the crews, and Ronald Codrai, himself a wartime RAF pilot, felt we should give them all dinner and invited them all over to Dubai there and then. On the way back in the car I protested: "You know, we cannot possibly sit as many as

16 people at a table, and we haven't even enough plates or knives and forks." "Never mind," said Ronald. "I will think of something." He conferred with the expert, our nearly blind old Ghanim.

The charging plant was working that day and Ronald fixed up lamps in the courtyard at the back of the house which was some 20 yards square, and which boasted two little almond trees. Our guests were due at half-past seven by which time it would be dark. We had plenty of beer and whisky and sent out for more glasses, which when they came were gaily painted with flower designs. Ronald contracted a cook in town to bring up everything needed for a monster kebab. But the *piece de résistance* was the party of dancing girls and sword dancers. There were some 20 girls, some of them distinctly mature, but a few were lithe and attractive, and about ten men – jugglers, sword dancers and a conjurer, a 'gully gully' man. All of them were Baluchis from Pakistan, and they were the standard entertainment in Dubai at that time for weddings.

Ronald had them concealed under the back verandah with all the lights out. The guests all arrived together in a couple of RAF trucks and when they had all been given a drink and we were leaning sedately over the front verandah admiring the peaceful moonlit creek, Ronald disappeared to give the signal. The lights went on, the drums and cymbals banged and out came the colourful dancers in dresses of green and gold, the girls wearing, at the beginning at any rate, the face masks which are the local habit. Our guests dashed to the back verandah and stood fascinated for the next two hours, while skewers of kebab and fresh glasses were pushed at them from behind. No-one noticed the shortage of plates.

Our friends the shaikhs heard about it and were most amused. "But how did you get them out of the house, those girls?" they asked.

Chapter Six

A friend once told me that he thought that in the 1950s the Court of the Ruler of Dubai was the nearest thing in the world today to that of the Plantagenets. I felt this a piercing observation, since although its traditions and culture were far from those of the early English monarchs, much of its flavour and character, especially the nature and activities of its courtiers, were very similar.

Court might be held in the mornings at the Customs House overlooking the glittering lagoon, with hundreds of little ships carrying rich cargoes to Dubai and bearing her valuable re-exports away again to Iran, Pakistan, and India. Court might be held in the late afternoon at Zabeel, in the simple spacious palace surrounded with palm trees and set among low white dunes: or it might be held in a desert hunting camp or in the summer palace on the Jumairah beach.

Wherever it was held it would be dominated by one personality, simple in dress, indistinguishable in outward appearance from any of his subjects, this was Shaikh Rashid bin Saeed who as I have mentioned earlier, was the aged Ruler's son, but was in all but name the Ruler.

The patrician nose, the alert shrewd eyes, the quiet humour and a dignity which eschews pomposity, these were the facets of a warm, complex and fascinating personality.

He was dressed in a white cotton headcloth, with a plain black head-rope to keep it in place, a white full-length *thawb* or shirt, and over the shoulders a plain black robe, with the thinnest gold piping down the front edges, and on his feet were pattering sandals, locally made in the Dubai *souq*.

With him would be the courtiers in exactly the same dress. Some would be merchants, some his retainers, some visitors, some palace officials. The shaikh's presence held their respect and calmed them, and there was much quiet, dignified movement among them; speech not addressed to the shaikh was in lower tones, for although respect for the shaikh's presence must be shown, business must be done and this was what the shaikh wanted; and he enthusiastically assisted any of his subjects if they only concentrated on making money. Even in those days, many of the courtiers were becoming comfortably rich, but like their leader seldom had any liquid money, it was always out on loan. If the courtiers and their shaikhs had one thing in common, apart from the style of their clothes and their outward appearance, it was the possession of large overdrafts.

In those days, in order to see the shaikh, one would simply go round to the Customs House in the morning, mount the steep, narrow and uneven staircase, and at its top walk out on to the wide, level, dazzlingly bright concrete verandah which was open to the sky and looked out over the lagoon. On the inland side of this open space was the crowded room, furnished only with carpets and cushions. It had white bare walls, unglazed windows with their wooden shutters fastened open, and was Shaikh Rashid's morning *majlis*. Within sat forty or fifty figures dressed in black and white as I have described, shoulder to shoulder in a line with their backs to the wall; they sat looking through the open door and windows towards the lagoon. From the *majlis* would come an animated buzz of talk and this would hardly be broken as he rose to stalk out with quick steps to greet one of his friends. This tall, slightly stooping, impressive figure would come towards them with a hand outstretched and a welcoming smile, to take the visitor perhaps (if he wanted to speak privately) to another smaller room further along the verandah overlooking the creek, furnished only with a red Persian carpet and a few easy chairs.

A little later in my acquaintance with the shaikh the telephone had, sadly I thought, arrived. Then one might think it polite to warn him of one's arrival and intention to call. It would simply be a question of finding out from one of his followers the number of the telephone which would be next to him. He would answer it immediately himself. "Welcome, welcome, I shall be pleased."

But in those days we were not yet blessed with the telephone, and one would simply call unannounced, and as soon as one was in his small room looking on to the water, the talk would start while we were sipping coffee from the little cups and looking out on the radiance of the passing scene, the bustling little boats, the glistening blue and silver of the water.

There would be the immediate opening questions to begin with. One's health, the health of the people in the country one had just left, and sometimes if one had arrived by air,"How long was your journey?", and always "Was your journey a good one?".

All this would be addressed to the visitor with charm, and with plenty of evidence that the shaikh really wished him and his friends well; but it was equally clear that these opening phrases, which with other shaikhs might occupy half an hour or the greater part of several visits, were also only politeness which both parties wanted to get through as quickly as possible. I think it must have been Shaikh Rashid who set the now current fashion for the brisk business-like meetings which may be more characteristic of the Gulf today.

After a few moments of this he would shout, for the second time, "*Qahwa*" – coffee – but this did not mean he expected his visitor to go yet, as it might with other hosts. The little rattling cups would be brought and sucked quickly dry, each to be filled twice in quick succession.

Then the shaikh would ask a brief perhaps half-formed question, sometimes, disconcertingly, on the subject which the visitor himself wished to discuss and about which he had reason to assume the shaikh would know nothing. Such assumptions were invariably unwarranted in his case.

No sooner had the main problem been explained than the shaikh would have a cryptic, usually humorous, comment which gave his view in a nutshell and showed how well-briefed he was. This might leave very little further to be said on that topic. Then there would be an exchange on current events, the shaikh producing a stream of shrewd comments, sometimes with devastatingly accurate and amusing interpretations of what people really must have meant when they said what they had said.

None of this would be easy to follow because the shaikh spoke quickly in often half-finished sentences, as if he were already tired of a subject and assumed one would know what he meant before he had fully unburdened himself. No subject on its own would, after all, have the right to demand much more than a sentence when there were always so many other fascinating subjects jostling in the queue for his attention. I once thought to myself as I watched his eager face silhouetted against the dazzling, dancing lagoon that it was like talking to an impressionist painting: his conversation was a series of deft, apparently unrelated touches which gave you a sparkling and complete picture.

Yet with all his eagerness to get on with the next subject, he would cheerfully repeat a phrase in different words if the visitor admitted he had not quite followed, and once when I must have looked blank at a quick question from the shaikh, his man, who was at that moment handing me the coffee, said rather peremptorily and testily: "Well, can you come to dinner this evening?"

One needed to keep one's wits about oneself when talking to Shaikh Rashid, but it was rewarding if one could manage it.

A Plantagenet court? While all this is going on, people come into the room, to linger a moment, whisper something in the shaikh's ear and in return receive what were often, to me, incomprehensible instructions. Apart from that cryptic invitation to dinner, I like to think there was little that the shaikh said to me which I could not understand. But I could seldom follow the exchanges between the shaikh and his court: and this was not only because part of the questions might sometimes be in a half-whisper; it was because of the special language of immediate mutual understanding in which he communicated with his followers.

Courtiers would come and go. Business concerning millions was done with a nod or a wink. The signs and shibboleths of the sale room are tame and slow compared with the way in which affairs of finance and state were dealt with at Shaikh Rashid's *majlis*. People who could not keep up dropped out: it was the case of the survival of the swiftest, the sprightly and the shrewd.

I have seen Shaikh Rashid in solemn conclave with others on some subject of importance to him, something of necessity near to his heart, otherwise he would not have allowed the meeting to happen. One of his slower colleagues, and some of them tended to be slower, would hold forth in sonorous tones. After about four minutes of this Shaikh Rashid's eyes would look up to heaven as if for succour, and they would appear to glaze slightly, his face would take on a grey dull texture and his cheeks look haggard. He would run his hands over his face as if to say "God deliver us."

He would, however, remain silent until all had had their say, and finally, with a look of relief, add something himself – brief, cryptic and entirely to the point – or if the occasion was, he felt, too awful, instruct one of his courtiers, with a look, to do this on his behalf. This final comment would be one to which there was no answer, and with a swift mumbled "Goodbye" he would be out of the room before any of the others knew what was happening.

Thus was business done in Dubai: and business was done.

The court was, in consequence, lively, brilliant and friendly. Its leader held the affections and inspired the enthusiasm of his people, and anyone who worked with him became devoted. Things got done in double-quick time and those who were not quite up to it would disappear, gently, discreetly.

And the result? Oil boom conditions and an expanding town 15 years before any oil was discovered. "Goodness, what will he be like," asked someone "if he does find oil?"

Chapter Seven

It was my duty to give a large sum to Shaikh Shakhbut periodically, and always in cash, as part of the payment due from the Company for the right to explore for oil.

One year we had a slight argument over the question of a receipt. The Company suddenly insisted that I should obtain this in writing, having in previous years waived this modern formality. No representations of mine could convince our London office that such an insistence on modern formalities would be taken amiss by the Ruler.

I therefore had to ask for a signature. "This means they do not trust you, and I do not like that at all," he said at once. However, after some light-hearted banter on both sides, I had his signature.

On the next occasion I went at the appropriate date to his castle – a day's journey. I found that he was out. "Where?" "Hunting of course – this is the season." I asked for a guide and off we went into the desert, carrying petrol, food and water for several days. We followed the shaikh's tracks and came to the place where he had spent a night. My guide, a tracker, knew exactly where in the camp site had been the place of each tent. The shaikh had several cars and had made several excursions from this one camp, but the tracker knew at once which was the main exodus route used when camp had been struck and the tents loaded. We set off to repeat the same performance twice more, and it was not until the sun was setting behind the silhouetted crescent dunes that we saw a light and came up to his latest camp.

I was made very welcome, and after coffee and the usual exchange of greetings and pleasantries, shown to a tent which had been allocated to me. We sat again around the coffee fire, and soon dinner. Several houbara bustards – killed two days before – on piles of well-cooked rice were in front of us. It was a delightful meal and the shaikh was at his shrewd and witty best – as indeed he invariably was when out in the desert; castle life depressed him, desert life seemed to release his spirits. I mentioned my suitcases full of bank notes. "Let that wait," he said. "You must stay another night and tomorrow we should have some sport, Allah willing."

By about ten o'clock that night I took my leave of the shaikh and retired to my tent. The night was cool and I was glad of my roll of blankets laid out on the sand. I lay listening to the rise and fall of conversation, and to the lulling effect of this sound drifted off to sleep. Before dawn there was the call to prayer, and I heard the shaikh and his followers saying the morning prayer in the half light. Then came the merry clink of the brass pestle for grinding coffee and I could smell the coffee fire and thought it right to join them. The shaikh had a happy look in his eye at the prospect of a day's hunting and greeted me warmly. A weak-looking sun had just risen in a cloudy east; it was still winter. We were among beautiful crescent dunes which fell away to the north to the lower rolling sands which lay between us and the sea. This was not the high-dune country of the Empty Quarter, but nevertheless these dunes, some 100-150 feet high, of creamy sand, had the same magic attraction. Their subtle curves, which are accentuated by the shadow cast either by a rising or a setting sun, have a great beauty. Between them in the hollows were the tufts of bush and grasses which one day's rain will create, to survive, on night dew alone right through a summer.

The shaikh had with him some 25 followers and four of the pick-up type trucks. Ten of the followers carried on their arm the *mangal* (glove or leather sleeve), and the lure (a bunch of feathers on a chain) for a falcon. These birds, sitting each on a crooked forearm, seemed alert and ready for a day's sport. Each had a leather hood over its head which its falconer would occasionally remove as if to whet the bird's appetite.

Falconers and followers sat in a ring on the sand, the shaikh in their midst, while the little cups of coffee were handed round. Each cup has only a small amount of coffee, bitter with the cardamom that is in it. As I had found in Syria, it is polite and customary to have the cup refilled twice, and then to shake it between forefinger and thumb to indicate enough. At first, nothing was said. The coffee cups were sucked at meditatively, then the shaikh called his chief tracker and hunter. "Which way today, oh Salim?"

"May Allah lengthen your life, the west: Bida Mughayim offers sport. There was good rain there two months ago, about so much." Here he indicated on his arm a distance of nine inches, showing that the rain had penetrated the sand to that depth. This is the bedouin way of measuring the quantity which had fallen in any one storm. "The green foliage will be good there, and, Allah willing, we may see some game."

"Allah willing," said the shaikh and stood up. He motioned me to get into one of the pick-ups with him and the driver (he himself did not drive), and into the back piled several falconers and his chief tracker. Some of the others climbed into a second vehicle and off we set over the dunes, threading our way between their crests towards the west.

The tracker would, from time to time, bang on the roof of the truck and shout fresh instructions. Suddenly he called "Halt!" He jumped down to examine the tracks of a bustard. Not satisfied that they were less than an hour old, and, therefore, worth following, he jumped back on to the pick-up and off we went again. Some minutes later he banged once more. This time he did not even need to get down, and we too could see fresh tracks. "Half an hour only," he cried. "Follow those."

Then, a dodgy business, the car was made to follow the bird's tracks. These led mainly to the hollows of the dunes but sometimes over the crests. To keep the tracks in sight, the driver, Ali, would take abnormal risks and follow a line which made even an agile and tough Chevrolet protest. Occasionally the shaikh would shout, half laughing, "Oh Ali, have a care!" Salim, from behind, would, on the contrary, shout in protest if the driver went too far from the tracks in order to pick an easier path for his car. It was exhilarating and exciting, but I had nothing to hang on to and was alternately bounced on to the driver and the shaikh. The whole thing was taken in the highest possible spirits, laughing and shouting; at such moments, the shaikh was no more than one of the boys, the driver taking note only of what Salim said, often ignoring the shaikh's instructions. This went on for some 20 minutes. I was getting bruised, but I had lost my original fear that we should all be overturned.

Suddenly, another bang on the roof and we stopped. All the men were quiet; we jumped down and, at a sign from the shaikh, one of the birds had its hood removed. The falconer stood up in the back of the truck and held it as high as he could. There in the distance I could see two bustards in a hollow grubbing amongst the grasses. These were the birds whose tracks we had been following. The falcon was released, stooped and with a lovely curving, infinitely graceful flight, went right to its prey and, in a great fluttering of wings, seized one of the bustards and dug its beak into the breast again and again. Meanwhile another falcon was released to attack the second bustard which had half flown, half scampered to some larger bushes nearby as if in hope of finding cover. The shaikh and his followers, now all on foot, ran to the scene, and the falconers started to entice their falcons back to the lures with pieces of goat's meat which they had ready as the reward. Trained falcons will hold and wound a bustard without killing provided they can be enticed off the prey in time. It was essential to cut the bustard's throat and draw blood while it was still alive in order to make it lawful to eat its flesh.

The trucks had come up behind us and while the followers were fussing over the successful falcons and stroking their breasts, coffee was served from a small thermos flask, followed by tea.

The bustard was duly dispatched with a knife and put in the back of the truck. The remaining eight or so falcons on their falconers' arms looked excited under their hoods, their heads going this way and that as if to say, "Is it my turn next?" After a short break, we climbed aboard again, and the whole process was repeated.

The third kill of the morning was the most exciting. A single bustard was attacked close to some tall tamarisk bushes, and, as the falcon stooped and flew in to the kill, the bustard backed up against a bush and opened its beak in defence. This upset the falcon and, just as a dog which has unexpectedly got to grips with a cat which holds its ground will suddenly pretend to lose all interest and wander off, so it changed course and flew right away. Immediately a second falcon was unhooded and stooped on its prey which was not courageous enough to withstand a second assault. The shaikh told me he had seen two bustards together beat off several falcons but eventually they had succumbed.

I had in earlier years been hawking on camels. That had been even more exciting, much more sporting and difficult.

It is undoubtedly a good and exciting sport. It needs skill, especially in the training of the falcons which must be carefully schooled. They are mostly purchased now from the northern Arab States and Iran, and may fetch enormous prices. But falcons are occasionally still caught in Eastern Arabia. The falconry season in Eastern Arabia is from November to March, when the prey – Macqueen's bustard – migrates into the area from Russia.

I have seen a falcon catcher at work, near Dubai. He makes a deep hole in the sand, covered with branches, and in this he hides. String, some hundred yards long, is run out though steel loops set in the sand in the shape of a rather open 'L'. At the corner a net is set across the angle, lying flat on the sand in such a way that, when the string is pulled, it swings upwards and over to come down on the sand within the L-shape. At this point there is a loop in the sand and another string. One end of this string goes to the catcher in his hole, and at the other is a pigeon secured by a leg. The catcher, when he sees a falcon, lets the pigeon go a little way and it flies trailing the string. The falcon takes a good look and if the catcher is well concealed, will stoop at the pigeon, which the catcher pulls back to the hoop. As the falcon seizes the pigeon and digs his beak into it, the catcher pulls it home to the ring and releases the net, which springs up and over the falcon and pigeon together. The catcher then comes up out of the hole and walks across to sort it all out.

Once caught (or, more often nowadays, bought) the falcon is hooded. For four or five days its eyelids are actually sewn together with a single fine thread, and the bird is starved to tame it until, from hunger, its breast bones stick out sharply to the touch. Then the eyes are released, but it remains hooded and retained by a loop of cord round the leg. All this time it is on its handler's leather sleeve and near the bait, which is a bundle of feathers. At night it is put on a wooden block – a small circular platform, three or so inches in diameter – on the end of a wooden stake which stands in the sand. The falconer must remain with the falcon day and night. He gives it a name, and calls to it in a high falsetto, which the falcon learns to recognise and hear at a distance.

Each evening the falcon is handed to another falconer, and its own falconer goes about 100 yards or so away with the bait and about half a pound of raw meat. He calls to the falcon in a falsetto, waves the bait, while his comrade unhoods it and the bird stoops low and gracefully over the sand to the falconer, to take the meat and submit to recapture. These early essays are exciting and important, since even a valuable bird may be lost by careless handling. On some afternoons the training will consist of letting the falcon stoop at a tethered pigeon, and then getting it to leave the prey by enticing it away with meat. This is to teach it not to kill at once, and to expect a tit-bit if it holds the prey without killing it.

The trained falcon which proves successful in the hunt will be kept over the summer and autumn for several successive years. An indifferent performer may be released at the end of the hunting season. Sometimes a hawk that has been released will be recaptured the following year by its previous owner.

On this particular occasion after the brave, but vain defence put up by the bustard, we were kept waiting while several followers in one of the pick-ups chased and finally recaptured the unsuccessful falcon which, frightened by the resistance put up by the prey, seemed to lose its wits and would not return to its falconer. It was finally recaptured and we returned to camp for lunch, which was again bustard, eaten from a bowl on the sand amongst us all.

We spent the afternoon inspecting newly dug water wells in the neighbourhood and visiting camps of the bedouin. Only a part of a shaikh's hunting expedition is for amusement. The more important aspect is the chance it gives to visit his people. Different bedouin visit the *majlis* at his camp fire each evening and tell him their woes and ask for help in various ways. In the desert, the subject sits next to the shaikh or in front of him and addresses him by his first name only, seldom using his title. His talk will be a mixture of information and aphorisms and, with many a "May Allah lengthen your life", will usually end with some form of request for help. The popularity and strength of a shaikh must depend on his accessibility and the wisdom of his manner of treating his subjects. If, as until recently, he has little money himself, he needs very considerable intelligence, leadership and good sense to hold his people together and make the best use of his meagre resources. If he suddenly hits oil, as has happened recently in the Arabian Gulf, his problems are suddenly altered but not made more easy. They will become even more acute; but in the early stages at least of the development of the new society, the *majlis* will be the main institution on which the shaikh must rely.

It is fascinating to watch a capable ruler dealing with his people in this way, off the cuff and in public. He has to have a ready answer to each question or request, and at times he has to make what are really life and death decisions. The shaikh of a nomad tribe has to decide on the spot what is to be done in cases of murder, or war, or feuding. The settled shaikh has his *qadhis* (judges) to help him, but the true nomad does not have professional help, unless he has tied himself in some form of alliance or allegiance to the nearest settled chieftain or uses him as a referee as is sometimes the custom.

As usual, the party all gathered for coffee after evening prayers which were said by the shaikh and his followers standing in a line on the sand. At prayer time, as in so many other ways, Muslims are egalitarian, and among the desert folk this is especially marked.

Dinner followed not long after, a few large trays laid on the sand inside the tent, as it was now cold. We clustered round it and ate mainly in silence as it is polite to do. After most of us had eaten I tried the old bedouin joke, "Where is the wind blowing from?" My friends looked at the pile of rice to see which side had been eaten away the quickest; just as the wind hollows out the sands, so do the eaters hollow out the rice. "From the west," they all murmured in agreement and pointed laughing westward to fat Sultan who, as usual, had dug the deepest.

After dinner, coffee and tea followed one another as often as we felt inclined. Some of the bedouin would then tell stories. The shaikh would be asked questions on tribal politics or on any subject that occurred to his companions. If so prompted, he would then hold forth at length giving a considered view on the question raised using simple flowing language, sometimes quoting the Quran and sometimes the bedouin heroic poems. When this is done there will be a chorus of voices finishing the verse and adding others. Then one of our number would recite a new poem he had composed and memorised. The whole goes with a beautiful rhythm, and in describing this scene one gropes in vain for epithets; these occasions have a flavour that is unique. The more serious moments were always interspersed with joking and laughter.

At nine o'clock there was an interruption from the news on the ancient and battered radio run from the car battery. The shaikh would listen every day to Cairo, Kuwait and London. This gave me a chance to stretch my legs a little. As a guest I usually found myself beside the shaikh on these occasions, with cushions for my elbow and my feet tucked away in the sand. The tent was lit by two hurricane lamps and some 20 to 25 could sit at a time inside it. Others were round the camp fire outside attending to the perpetual coffee-making. From time to time visitors would drop in and talk so that the circle in the tent would change repeatedly. As a guest one was free to get up and walk about, to sit and listen or, if one felt inclined, to speak. I usually did not talk, unless to answer a question, as it is fascinating to watch how life goes on when no-one from outside is there to influence behaviour.

In due course, the conversation would become less general. I would have a private chat with my neighbour and there would be some long silences. Silence amongst such a group may be lengthy, and it is perfectly acceptable in bedouin society. Eventually, when I thought a suitable moment had come to take my leave and to wish my hosts a good night, or rather, in the Arab phrase, "A happy arising in the morning", I would retire to my tent.

Even in winter, when tents are a comfort if you are not to suffer from the piercing cold of the desert at night, there is a wonderful freedom about the desert camp. One particular joy to me is that there is no noise that is unattractive. There are the low murmur of voices, the crackle of a thorn fire, the clinking of the coffee mortar, a cry to a companion to fetch something. Above us all, the stars, clear and bright, and the surrounding spaces are so still, so wide. I slept well on such still nights.

The next day after breakfast with the shaikh – eggs fried on rice and put on a tray with cheese, olives and the thin sheets of Arab bread – I again mentioned my suitcase full of money. The shaikh laughed: "Where is the receipt? Let me sign it."

I gave it to him and he handed it back signed. I rose to fetch the money but the shaikh motioned to me to sit and called again for coffee.

"I don't want your money here, when I am hunting. If you see my brother in town, give it to him." He mentioned the name of his younger brother.

After some further talk I took my leave and set off back to town leaving the shaikh to enjoy another few days in his beloved open spaces. I, of course, had both the money and the receipt. A nice way, I thought, to show his regard for people who insist on receipts.

In town I did meet the brother in the street a day later. He came to have coffee with me and, as he left the house, I gave him the suitcase of money. He took the case and threw it into the back of his car like any other piece of luggage and drove off.

Chapter Eight

Like so many visitors to the East, I find that Arab hospitality, Arab manners and their traditional attitude to gifts attractive, and the West may have much to learn from them.

One day, after taking lunch at the home of a very old shaikh who lived in a village consisting of a huddle of white houses and palms nestling in a deep valley in the mountain-side, I made my usual speech of thanks. "You have honoured me. You have lightened us by your presence." So far, so good. Then I said "Thank you."

"No," said the old man, shaking his finger at me sternly. "Thank your Lord."

On reflection, I knew that the rebuke had been justified. Allah is responsible for all things, and the giver of lunch is only a vehicle. "Thank you Lord!"

Another day, I was interpreting for a business friend who suddenly asked the Arab shaikh on whom we were calling: "What is the time?" Instead of translating I said in English "Twelve o'clock." "Don't be silly, I know well enough what it is, but I want you to ask him." It later transpired that on a previous visit he had given the shaikh a particularly splendid gold watch. I suppose, in his very Western way of thinking, he thought the watch would be produced and a chord of friendship struck, a memory revived.

How wrong he was. Our host clapped his hands and in came a follower who was asked the time. He looked at his Ingersoll and said, "Six o'clock". So it was, Arabic time.

I told my friend that I thought this might have taught him a lesson. Are gifts worth giving if you seek to attach an obligation to them?

Once my oil company presented a car to the shaikh of a small tribal group in whose territory they were prospecting. I had protested at the choice, a make of car that shall remain nameless, good enough for the town but a poor performer in the desert. The shaikh concerned had no car and I knew he would want one for his desert trips; there being not one yard of tarmac for hundreds of miles, all journeys were over sand or salt flat. However, the car had already been ordered and shipped, and in due course it arrived and I went round to make the presentation. After a good lunch and coffee, I said: "Oh shaikh, the Company has asked me to bring you the motor car I mentioned before, and today I have brought it."

We went down and out on to the sand. I showed the shaikh the car and he said he was delighted and thanked God. I set off and did not see him again until one evening there was a knock at the door of my house: he had called for coffee and a chat.

When he came to take his leave I saw him downstairs and into his car. I was surprised to see an aged and battered Chevrolet pick-up, and I said in my innocence: "What of the ...", mentioning the make of car the Company had given him.

"Oh, that! I sold it and bought two of these."

I considered this attitude rather admirable; but when I regaled my oil company with the tale, it evoked no response.

The Arabs are justifiably famous for their ready and generous hospitality, and those very few who do not follow their traditions are laughed at and despised by their fellows. But it is not only the generosity of their hospitality that so impresses me: it is the attitude behind it, the lack of obligation either way.

In one of the little fishing villages on the Arabian coast there was a shaikh who had granted our company concession for exploration. He had a small area of desert over which our technicians had done the normal geological and geophysical surveys; but no good prospects had been found. However, the Company had not given up hope altogether.

Tall, thin, stately and with an impressive beard, the shaikh was an active out-of-doors man and spent much time in the deserts inland from his village. When at home he was usually to be found in the market talking to his merchants. He lived in a crumbling fort or palace perhaps half a mile from the main market of his capital; and if I warned him in advance that I had some important visitor to see him, he would sometimes be waiting in the port to meet us. But he used the old-fashioned traditional way of telling the time: sunset each day being twelve o'clock, hence at the equinox, sunrise likewise was at twelve o'clock and midday would therefore be at six o'clock. Before and after each equinox, the time of day would be more difficult to estimate; and a rough guide I used was to look at my watch upside down, noting the hour hand only. In that latitude this does not give a bad estimate, and the nearer it is to the equinox, the more accurate it will be. However, even if one worked out the hours exactly, others might not; and this meant that with this shaikh, as with all who used the same system, appointments were not easy to keep.

Sometimes when I had taken some important person to the fort, and found the shaikh to be out, a messenger on a donkey would be sent to warn him. He arrived on a camel from the market, where he held court daily, perhaps half an hour late. On such occasions, the shaikh would apologise and say laughing, "You see I have no telephone, so that I did not know you had arrived."

I decided to call his bluff and give him a telephone, with the lines strung from the palace to the market. The next visitor whom I took to see him remarked on seeing the telephone in the *majlis*, and the shaikh obligingly turned the handle on the instrument to call the other end to demonstrate the new amenity. There was no reply. Not to be outdone, the shaikh clapped his hands and called for one of his sons, saying: "Oh Ali, run down to the market and answer the telephone." Everyone laughed, especially the shaikh who was as usual in cheerful spirits. Some ten minutes later the telephone rang and the shaikh had to talk to his son; and he afterwards explained to us that the merchant in whose shop the other instrument had been fixed was evidently out, calling on friends, and the boy whom he had left in charge had been too awed to touch it.

Arabic time may be a little difficult because it changes every day of the year; and in our northern latitudes we can find this really awkward (except perhaps as another excuse on the British Railway); but I found unexpected advantages in the Arabic calendar. One of them was, oddly enough, to show me the way.

When driving along the coast it was the habit to follow well-worn routes across the salt flats, upon which the car wheels would create a surface almost as smooth as asphalt. Most of these flats are affected by the tide, and where there are shallow lagoons running into a low-lying coast, a fresh wind can have remarkable effect on the height of the tide. It required an experienced driver to negotiate what on occasions spanned ten miles of water up to a foot deep during high tide, and the penalty for failure to keep to the submerged track was to stick in the mud. If the wheels went through the hard crusts, the truck would sink to its axles, at once with the tyres spinning helplessly in the muddy water. We sometimes used winches from other trucks to retrieve a vehicle that had sunk to its axles, or jack it up on steel sand channels and push-start it.

The first time I drove across one of these very large flats it was the summer and there had been little wind. I was driving and came to one of the many places where the track split and offered three or four choices. I said to my driver, "Which do I take?" He astonished me by asking in reply: "What day of the Arabic month is it?" In those days I was accustomed to thinking in both the Arabic and European calendar, and I therefore knew the answer and told him. "Then take the right hand road," said the driver.

It was a few moments before I could work out his reasoning. Then I realised that all the tracks led to the same place and that the right-hand one was for use at spring tide, the left at neap tide, and the others in-between according to the wind and the day of the Arabic month.

General use of the lunar calendar is helpful for sailors, as they can manage without the need for tide tables, and those who live by the sea become accustomed to judging the height of the tides by the day of the month. But it can cause difficulty over weather. As in most parts of the world, the seasonal variations in climate, although they differ somewhat each year, are sufficiently regular for a solar calendar to be of some guide as far as the weather is concerned. The fishermen therefore use a calendar of roughly 365 days, which they divide into tens and hundreds. Each seasonal period is called by its nearest whole number of tens and when each hundred days is reached they start again with another series of tens, to the next hundred. The wind that blows in the first ten days might be called by the Arabic name for the number. A wind that comes between the fiftieth and sixtieth might be called therefore the *khamseen* (fifty). In the Gulf the term *khamseen* is not used, as it is in Egypt, for a particular wind, but a sailor will say that he expects a gale or a calm in the next *khamseen*, for example. I have often wondered if the real explanation for the Egyptian term *khamseen* for the hot desert wind does not come from such an origin. Explanations for *khamseen* which I have heard, such as there are 50 such winds in a year, have always seemed to me lame. Winds are also called by stars, and on the Trucial Coast, although star names are given to ordinary winds from particular directions, date names are used for special storms that occur at particular times.

The expertise of the old people of the coast on weather is, as one would expect, remarkable; but sometimes they become impatient if an expected storm does not come at its appropriate date and then they will take risks. On one such occasion when the Ruler of Dubai, Shaikh Saeed bin Maktoum who was at that time at least 75 years old, set off in a small boat for Iran, at a time when a generally expected storm had not come. They were two-thirds of the way over when the fierce gale hit them. The boat's captain soon gave them up for lost and resorted to prayer, but the old shaikh himself took the tiller, gave orders to the crew, weathered the storm and brought them safely into port when the wind had slackened. The same old shaikh was equally adept at finding his way over the deserts on a camel or in a car.

I myself grew more experienced at adapting to the changable climatic elements, and for this reason, made many trips by boat – two to Muscat from Dubai and countless ones to Abu Dhabi, as the mud flats were difficult for our cars to cross during high tides and when it rained. In addition to the mud flat, there was the further obstacle of a ford through the sea to reach Abu Dhabi island. In those days, to get from the end of the mud flat on to the island where the capital stands, one had to follow a route through the water made originally for camel caravans. Stones had been laid on the sea bed to give a footing, with stakes to act as guides, and to indicate the depth. One had to await dead low tide and then manoeuvre a car some 500 yards through the water. It took an experienced driver to make the passage. Many was the time when I had driven the two hours or more then necessitated by the journey in those days over the open desert from Dubai, to find that a north wind had sprung up and the tide was firmly in. On other occasions one would get across and then be unable to return for several days. For this reason I would frequently go by sea, hiring a 40-foot launch for the purpose. When the weather was rough we could cover half the journey behind the islands and through the complex system of creeks. Even in fine weather I would sometimes take this route, especially if I had a visitor with me, in order to see the marine life in the shallows. Particularly exciting were the enormous stingray, manta and others with a 'wing span' of 15 feet or more. Experts told me not to be afraid of them if one meets them swimming as they are timid. "So" I used to say, "am I."

Another opportunity to experience the varied marine life along the coast arose when I accompanied a hydrological survey over the islands and seas of Abu Dhabi. We landed on 75 islands in three weeks, and most of these landings involved long walks, wading waist-deep through shallow water for sometimes up to half a mile. We carried harpoons, but the noise of our splashing certainly seemed to frighten away stingray, shark, barracuda and sea snakes, which all abound in these waters; and we never had a single scare or even a narrow escape, so far as we knew, all that time. From the main ship, a converted landing craft, we did see some wonderful sights; and once we passed close to a monster hammerhead shark laying motionless under the surface.

As we passed it flicked its tail and left; and my guess was that it measured over 15 feet in length.

On the survey we had with us a first class pilot, Thani bin Murshid. He had done many years' pearling and knew the Abu Dhabi waters intimately. Once we realised how astonishingly accurate his knowledge was, he was able to save us hours of time each day. I would stand on the bridge of the *Jamila*, our landing craft, with him and our captain. The charts which we had showed very little, if any, of the underwater topography. Our ship drew one fathom and Thani was able to say almost exactly what the depth was ahead of us, and which way the ship must turn to find a channel of just a little more than six feet of water. This saved us hours of sounding with a hand line and lead as the boat inched forward. We had an echo-sounder which of course showed us the depth immediately below us and with this we checked Thani's running estimates as we went along. He was remarkably accurate and never once led us into a channel which we could not navigate. Under his guidance we could go ahead at good pace in the narrow channels.

We used to tell of his pearling exploits, and once, when one of the British members of our crew challenged his claim to be able to dive to 15 fathoms, he straight away took off his shirt and headcloth and dived over the side returning after a minute and half with a lump of mud in his hand to show he had been to the bottom. We were in 14 fathoms at the time, and he explained that he was out of practice, and that he could go into very much deeper water if he was in trim – down to 20 fathoms.

Like the bedouin of the desert and especially the expert trackers, who can recognise footsteps of individual people or camels in soft sand, invariably Thani knew everything that went on around him at sea. We would see a tiny sail far off on the horizon and Thani would say: "That is so and so bin so and so. Must have bad news at home or the boat is leaking, he should not be making for port today." Then later we would come up to them and find a tiny boat with three men in it, and it would all be as Thani had said, they were making a journey for some unusual reason. We experienced this not once but many times: he would always know what each boat was and where it would be going from the sight of its sail in the distance.

Thani interrogated all the crews we met and we used to give the fishing boats water and sometimes food. Thani knew the names of all the reefs and banks on the chart, and we were thus able to replace some of the English names which naval surveyors had recorded with the right Arabic ones. For example 'Bill Island' became 'Halat Yabir'.

Thani was not only excellent as a pilot, we found him very interesting company and I much enjoyed our work together. We have often met since, and although times have changed and Abu Dhabi is becoming a modern state we both, not unnaturally, look back with pleasure to those days. It will not be long before such expertise about the sea bed as Thani's will be unobtainable.

During the survey we came upon a large pearling fleet at anchor and watched the divers and their crew at work. They seemed to have no fear of sharks, but would, when necessary, wear cotton shirts against jellyfish. I never heard of losses to pearl divers through the attacks of barracuda, although two fishermen were killed by these fish off the coast, while setting nets in the shallows, when I was in Dubai. Although the Gulf teems with predatory fish, the loss of human life to them is remarkably small – in contrast to the Indian Ocean, the Red Sea, and the Pacific. What the reason is I have never been able to discover. I wonder whether the sea is so well-stocked that sharks are plentifully supplied, and will not bother with strange things like a man's leg. The real and inescapable danger to the diver was damage to his health from the pressure underwater.

We may perhaps regret the passing of a romantic tradition with the virtual end of the pearl diving, but we should be glad for the sake of those who were engaged in it that it is finished.

Chapter Nine

For me, those happy years on the Trucial Coast, spent in Dubai, Abu Dhabi and the hinterland, formed an interlude between our attempt to enter central and southern Oman in 1948-9 and the more elaborate expedition which was to set forth in early 1954.

During this period, several things happened which altered the position as far as company work in the area was concerned. The first was the formation by HMG in Sharjah in 1950 of a levy force, known to begin with as the Trucial Oman Levies, later to be renamed the Trucial Oman Scouts. They started modestly with one British officer, from the Jordanian army, a small number of Arab officers and fifty non-commissioned officers and men, but within a few years they grew to the strength of a small battalion. Lightly armed and mounted in Bedfords and Land Rovers, they soon commanded all the deserts of the coastal area, inland to the borders of Oman and to the oases of Buraimi and Al Ain.

Their very creation produced an immediate improvement in the security of the area, particularly in the desert bordering Oman, and as they grew stronger and operated small armed patrols to the north and east, they were able to exert a pacifying influence on the tribes. This patrolling put an end both to bedouin raiding on the part of such tribes as the Al Rashid and the Al Afar, and to any resort to fighting in order to settle the quarrels of the tribes over rights to water, grazing and travel. What is more, they were able to achieve all this without any shooting. They worked skilfully and with patience, handling all the disputes between tribes and villages under the direction of the British Political Agent at Sharjah.

Disputes continued over wells and grazing as they had done before the formation of the Levies, but instead of a dispute working up to a fight the Levies would step in at the critical moment to gain a cooling-off period during which the shaikhs or the Political Agent, with the aid of the tribal leaders, could ensure a fair and open discussion of the problem; and this would usually, after much toil, lead to an acceptable solution; but many border questions remained unsolved. It was found essential in such cases to prevent the first killing of a tribesman which would start a vendetta often lasting many years.

To advance from being an area in which one might almost expect trouble to being an area where one could go out into the desert assuming that there would be none, took a matter of perhaps three years. Abu Dhabi was, however, a special case since in that emirate, after the ending of a Dubai-Abu Dhabi war in 1948, no insecurity at all was experienced. This was because of the effective control exercised by the Abu Dhabi shaikhs: the Ruler, Shaikh Shakhbut, on the coast and his brother, Shaikh Zayed, in the interior at Al Muwaiqi and in the Buraimi oasis.

The beginning of an era of security in the hinterland of the Trucial Coast greatly facilitated oil company exploration, a considerable amount of which was done in the 1950s and 60s, culminating in the finding of oil in Abu Dhabi on land and later, both in Abu Dhabi and Dubai, under the sea bed.

The second important event was, in contrast, a disruptive one. This was the occupation of the village of Hamasah in the summer of 1952 by a small Saudi force who came in civilian clothes under the Amir Turki bin Ataishan, apparently at the invitation of the shaikh of the Al Bu Shamis tribe in Hamasah, Rashid bin Hamad.

I have explained how, between 1800 and 1869 the Saudi emirs had put a force into Buraimi itself on several different occasions. From this vantage point they had made themselves felt in this interior of Oman by means of raiding parties, reaching on occasion as far as the Sharqiyah in the south-east of Oman.

From 1869 to the late 1920s the Saudis had little or no influence in the area. On a few occasions and at infrequent intervals in the late 1920s, mid-1930s and late 1940s, small tax collecting parties, mounted on camels, would make their way into southern Abu Dhabi, and on one occasion reached Buraimi itself, although it is not recorded that they took any tax there and perhaps one is permitted to wonder why they did not. The tax which they sought to collect from bedouin whom they met in the desert was the holy tax, the *zakat* or alms, a tithe to be paid by the faithful for the benefit of the poor. Payment of the tax is religious due, and experts dispute as to whether it implies sovereignty on the part of the collectors. In those days the bedouin had no conception of frontiers, and if any party of officials on camels met bedouin in the desert the latter would submit to them as a matter of common sense. If the bedouin had no money the collectors would first have to give *largesse* from the king in order to give them something from which to pay.

From 1935 to 1938, the Saudis had discussed with the British Government the claims which the Saudi king had made to the territories of both Abu Dhabi and the Sultanate, and agreement was almost reached on what became known as the Riyadh Line. However, final agreement on the details could not be reached and negotiations had lapsed by the time the Second World War broke out.

In 1949, ARAMCO, the American company which held the Saudi oil concessions, started sending out survey parties which made forays into Abu Dhabi territory, reaching even Khor Al Ghanadha near the Dubai frontier, where I bumped into them and talked to one of their party leaders who pretended he was lost. Perhaps he was. Later the political officer, Pat Stobart, met them when they were in company with a Saudi emir in rather tense circumstances on Abu Dhabi territory further to the west. The British Government, on behalf of Abu Dhabi, complained about these intrusions through diplomatic channels. In the same year, the Saudis had put forward a claim to Abu Dhabi and Sultanate territory which far outreached their claims of the 1930s. Among other things, they laid claim to the whole of the Buraimi area, and consequently this affair, involving as it did a Saudi claim to much of Abu Dhabi's whole territory, has been known ever since as the Buraimi Dispute.

In 1951, by the London Agreement, both sides (Britain, for Abu Dhabi, and Saudi Arabia) contracted not to put forces into the disputed area. In January and February 1952, discussions took place in Dammam between the Saudi Government on the one hand and HMG on the other. HMG's representatives were assisted by the shaikhs of Abu Dhabi and Qatar (whose territory was also involved). No conclusion was reached.

In 1952, Rashid bin Hamad, shaikh of the settled Al Bu Shamis in Hamasah, went on the pilgrimage to Mecca and apparently, as we later discovered, agreed to a Saudi force coming to occupy his village. Saqr bin Sultan, shaikh of Buraimi village and paramount of the Naim, was also approached by the Saudis, but he would not agree to the Saudis entering Buraimi itself; thus the village which gave the dispute its name was not, ironically, itself directly involved in the subsequent Saudi occupation.

On his return from Saudi Arabia by air, the aircraft in which Shaikh Rashid flew as a passenger was forced to land at Abu Dhabi instead of Sharjah, its intended destination, and Rashid wisely took to a camel. The aircraft had lost its way and become short of fuel. Had the forced landing not turned out so well, the Buraimi problem might never have happened. The aircraft, an Anson, used some of the petrol I kept for company cars in Abu Dhabi; fortunately Ansons go quite well on motor fuel.

In the summer of 1952, in clear breach of the London Agreement, a small Saudi expedition went in motor vehicles from Dammam to Hamasah, crossing hundreds of miles of undisputed Abu Dhabi territory, to which the Saudis had laid no claim, in order to achieve its objective. Once established in Hamasah in 1952, the Saudis set up lines of communication with their homeland through the port of Abu Dhabi, just as they had done when in occupation of Buraimi in the 19th century.

The Sultan and the Imam of central Oman together gathered considerable irregular forces numbering thousands of men on the Batinah and in the Dhahirah. These would have proved overwhelming, but, wishing to avoid bloodshed, the British Government intervened to prevent fighting. First, there followed a Standstill Agreement in October 1952, and later in 1954 an Arbitration Agreement.

At the time my company was preparing a second major attempt at effective exploration in the search for oil in the interior of Oman, the Saudis maintained a small police force of a commander and 15 men encamped in the oasis area. Likewise, the Levies had a force of the same size under the terms of the arbitration agreement, but the Saudis and the Levies alike were supposed to be exerting no political influence outside the small camps which they occupied.

For me, an interesting feature of the Saudi claims was a fascinating little view of the back-room boys at work. As an oil company official, I went over to Dhahran in 1951 to meet George Rentz of the ARAMCO research department. A scholar of the Arabic language, he had acquired a wonderful library and a very great knowledge of Saudi Arabia. When I called there, I found him busy attempting to stretch this knowledge into Abu Dhabi. I had just previously come across the Arabic version of a book of his called 'The Eastern Reaches of Al Hasa', which I had borrowed from a friendly Saudi. I had made copious notes on it and had guessed, and later determined, that it had been put together by the process of interrogating many bedouin at great pains in Dhahran. The results, as must be inevitable from such a process, were, to say the least, inaccurate. In the case, for example, of the Liwa oasis which contained then some forty settlements, the huts of which were more or less permanent, but mainly only seasonally occupied, the book listed some three times that number. In my view, the book was largely inaccurate.

The Manasir tribe, which is primarily an Abu Dhabi one, has a section, the Al bu Mundhir, sub-sections of which sojourn for periods in Saudi Arabia. One part of this tribe which, I was able to establish, contained only a few adult men, not much more than a family, was credited in the book with some 20 separate settlements. Subsequent investigation showed that what had happened in this and other cases was that the individual bedouin interrogated each claimed quite wrongly ownership of a whole settlement, and in naming them each had used the name of a particular little group of trees within the settlement. Any one settlement could have a dozen such names, and so they came to be listed as separate settlements.

I was George Rentz's guest and most unfairly, I am afraid, while sipping his whisky (liquor was not yet illegal in Saudi Arabia) in his room in Dhahran after dinner, I looked into his (locked) glass fronted bookcase and found 'Eastern Reaches of Al Hasa'. I did not say that I had just studied it for some weeks. "Could I take this for a bedside book, please George?" I asked. "Sorry old boy, although that looks like a bound volume it has never actually been published, and I'm afraid it is confidential", he replied.

However to cheer me up he went over to a table and picked up some papers. "Let me give you this, and please feel free to comment – write your comments in pencil. It is my draft for the new edition of the 'Encyclopaedia of Islam'; it is the article on Abu Dhabi." Then with a disarming smile, "You have been there I believe: I haven't."

The result was amusing enough. I took the draft off to bed with me. Apart from recommending the exclusions of some personal comments on individuals which seemed to me unfortunate, I neatly put in ink (not pencil), the following: "Several of the villages of Buraimi belong to Al bu Falah." (See 'Encyclopaedia of Islam', Volume 1, page 166). I was astonished when perhaps a year later I saw that this had been included in the article. Al bu Falah is the name of the ruling family of Abu Dhabi. Although it is not the name which they themselves now customarily use, it is the correct name of the sub-section from which all the ruling family descended.

Thus over the signature of George Rentz, Dhahran, Saudi Arabia, comes the surprising assertion, very firmly expressed in perpetuity in this learned work, that several of the villages of Buraimi belong to Abu Dhabi's ruling family. This information comes from a man who spent quite a large span of his life trying to prove just the opposite. I thought for one wild moment when I first saw it that George Rentz had been misled by my use of this particular name for the ruling family of Abu Dhabi. But George Rentz is a great scholar and an expert on Arabia and could not, I feel, have made such an elementary mistake.

I twitted him about this article when he came to lunch with me in 1970 but I did not get much more than a faint and rather embarrassed smile.

To return to the problem of our proposed expedition, it was more the attitude of the Al bu Shamis and their desire for special treatment which they had shown in 1948 than the actual arrival of the Saudis in Hamasah that suggested to us the approach to central Oman should be from the south.

If you look back at the history of the country the idea of getting into the interior of Oman from the south from the Hugf area is an exciting one. That most forbidding and barren shore was explored by Bertram Thomas in the 1920s during his camel trek round the coast of Oman, otherwise I have no record of its being visited save by the comparatively few bedouin who frequent it.

It is exciting because in the second half of the 19th century, and in the 20th century particularly since the Agreement of Sib in 1920, the tribes of the centre of Oman have always kept themselves largely cut off from the coast by the command of the passes, and notably the Samail Gap, which the tribes are able to maintain. To land in the south would be to open up Oman from inland, a thing which had hitherto been impossible.

In Oman there was no standing army save the tiny force in Bait al Falaj near Muttrah, commanded by a major; and this was scarcely more than a local garrison with no modern equipment and virtually no transport.

The interior was a region into which few foreigners had ever penetrated, and the rare journeys of those few who had done so were well documented in history. Most of the villages and many of the towns had never been visited by anyone from outside the country, much less by

Westerners. For these reasons the interior had already taken up in my mind the image of a strange never-to-be-reached country; I had heard and read so much about it, I really never expected to see it.

The first problem was to get to Jebel Fahud itself which as we could see from the air was a perfect anticlinal structure and was the likeliest oil prospect; the second was to establish lines of communication and secure the area sufficiently to allow the establishment of drilling camps; the third would be to make agreement with the Imam and the hill tribes for the transit of the oil by pipeline. Once oil was found we hoped to solve the political problems which the mountain area presented. Its people would clearly benefit, and the only alternative outlet for the oil would be to pipe it across to the Masirah area; but this presented serious practical problems in relation to a sea terminal on that difficult coast.

Having seen the Batinah coast and explored some of the valleys inland of Muscat, parts of the Dhahirah plain and the Wadi Jizzi, I was beginning to know something of the Omanis and I came to like them very much. They are sturdy and intelligent and like most hill people, individualists. Their material surroundings were notable for what they lacked. The beautiful, but rugged and harsh scenery, the water and fertile soil of the valley bottoms were their only apparent physical assets. It was fascinating to think that such a lively people who had so little in the way of food or clothing or comforts might suddenly, through our efforts, enjoy the fruits of oil. Most of them had never seen a car or heard a radio; most had never known tinned food; fresh food was severely limited in variety and quantity and they seldom were able to serve meat to their families. The simplest of our possessions were luxuries undreamt of to them; of modern medicine and modern science, they had no knowledge.

The urge to find the oil for which we were looking was strengthened for me and for many of us very much more on account of the benefit it would bring to the Omanis than for what it would bring to us. This was a natural emotion, and I say this without any wish to be thought either patronising or self-righteous. It was exciting to be given the political responsibility in the field for such a venture.

But if it was exciting when I thought of what there might be in front of us, it was rather depressing when I thought of the difficulties which then seemed to me insurmountable; and it was ironic that the very people who would be the ones to benefit seemed to present the main obstacle.

The Sultan had not yet raised the force which he regarded as essential. I was not yet in contact with the Duru; the attitude of the Imam was uncertain; the Saudis were to our north; no Western-type expedition had ever penetrated right into the interior. These were only some of our difficulties.

The vital factor was to be the attitude of the Duru tribe towards our exploration of their lands. They were only partially within the sphere of influence of the Imam but, although they were not under the Imam's direct control, they were vulnerable to the other tribes of the interior since their date trees, which were all they had of any real value, were in the towns and villages on the edge of the settled area, especially in Ibri and Tanaam. Their ownership of these trees was the vital point and the key to all that followed; it was a simple obvious point, but almost all the people involved managed to overlook it. In some cases I was glad they did so. Fortunately the Imam was old, not very active, and had no standing force of any kind and no administrative machine. We would have to win over the Duru; and if the shaikhs of Ibri, the key town, could be got to help us, the Imam might be unable to affect the issue, unfavourably to the Sultan, even if he wanted to do so.

I made many visits in 1953 to Muscat and far-off Salalah by light aircraft to see the Sultan and his officials. During this time, the Sultan was building up his mobile force and gathering information. The force was to be called the Muscat Field Force (the MFF).

Many were the nights I spent at Salalah, the capital of Dhufar, either in the tiny RAF camp or in the Sultan's guest room before or after an interview with him. He was spending almost all his time in that province. Dhufar is an attractive region. Strangely, the south-west monsoon, which blows from the beginning of June right through the summer, just catches the mountains of this corner of Arabia and precipitates a gentle rain for three months or more, and during this time the sun is hardly ever to be seen through the low cloud base.

The result is that, unlike the remainder of the region, the southern slopes of the foothills and the plain of Salalah are lush green with long grasses and thick bush. On the coast, in place of the date palm of the Gulf, they grow the coconut palm with its tall, slender, shiny trunk, a pleasant contrast to eyes that are used to the rougher, thicker date palm and its often dusty leaves.

The Sultan's palace, right on the beach, was stoutly built of stone, with the roaring waves of the Indian Ocean seeming to pluck incessantly at its solid foundation, as if trying to drag it into the water.

The palace interior, like that of the palace in Muscat, was immaculate, the staircase of slippery stone dangerously well polished.

Kindly in his attitude towards a visitor, the Sultan was a pleasure to meet, and I should have enjoyed these long talks by the window overlooking the roaring waves of the Indian

Ocean much more if I had had more reason to believe that we should ever achieve what we were aiming at.

The Sultan spoke almost perfect English in a soft voice and had a great calm about him. He told me he was already forming a force of 400 men. This, he said, was a mystic figure in Omani battles. The leader who had 400 men would win; he would almost be allowed to win and probably without any need for fighting.

Omani battles are fought according to conventions which I believe we have never tried to understand, and the Sultan may have been right when he said a force that numbered 400 would win. This was because in a country where the inhabited areas were split from each other by impassable mountains, where the only form of communication was on foot or animal, where distances were great, and where there is no central administration and no standing force, it was both extremely difficult to gather an army and, once having gathered it, to maintain it as a cohesive force. The position was somewhat analogous to that of the Middle Ages in Britain, but in this case applied to a country that was divided by high mountains. The Sultan believed that if he could send in a force of this size and maintain it in the field by modern methods, especially if the Sultan's position became stronger financially and thus militarily, he must win.

Circumstances were such that if I could not persuade him personally of my views, I had to accept the Sultan's decision and live with the consequences. But I saw the problems ahead of us rather differently from him. Provided we could gain the support of the Duru and keep it, using a landing point in the south we could work at Fahud and at other sites in their area and find out whether or not oil was there. Once oil was found, then would be the time to worry about getting it out. There would then be money for the Sultan to extend his centralised administration over the whole of Oman, to raise a gendarmerie and create some structure of modern government. The area might (I supposed) have to be very gradually detribalised, and in the process the tribal chiefs kept in funds and their loyalty held.

I saw the need to land on the southern coast of the area at Duqm (a site chosen by our marine department), to gain the support of all the desert tribes and to advance inland to Ibri. It was essential to make sure of that town, to be certain that the Duru would not lose their vital palm trees to the control of the Imam, were the latter to attack Ibri. Ibri must not, therefore, remain as it were a marginal town vulnerable to the tribes which were closest to the Imam.

For the preliminary landing we would need merely a small force since the area was inhabited only by a few nomads. For the advance across the desert, likewise, a very small force of camp guards would suffice, but only providing the Duru were agreeable to our presence. For the final advance into Ibri we might need a larger force to ensure a bloodless entry to the town although we knew its shaikh to be loyal to the Sultan. The Shaikh of Ibri was also on the best of terms with the Duru as the shaikhly families of the two tribes had intermarried.

The Sultan was having difficulty in raising and training a force quickly, as he had virtually no sound basis on which to enlarge his small existing force as it lacked all the necessary training facilities from which to work. However, he was determined that when we landed in the south at the beach we had chosen, the whole force would be ready to land with us.

I explained that in my view it would be a mistake to concentrate so large a force on the beach in the early stages. We had little hope of finding water, there was no firewood, no shade and no material to make it, nothing on that barren shore. We would have to bring everything with us. The maintenance of 400 men on the beach posed an unnecessarily big problem.

I argued that we would land with only a small force and then build up our base; and, in due course, when we had sufficient transport, petrol, water and stores ashore, advance into the centre of the Duru territory on the Wadi Amairi where there were good prospects of finding plentiful water. Then we could land more of the force if necessary and pass it through towards Ibri, using both Duqm and the Wadi Amairi area as our base camps, and thus avoid holding too many men at Duqm at any one time. I pleaded above all that we should have direct contact with the Duru and the Shaikh of Ibri as soon as possible. The Sultan agreed with me entirely on this last point, but time went by without any contact being made.

The Sultan's military advisers agreed with my thinking in regard to the troops, but the Sultan wanted it otherwise; he insisted in the first instance on landing all four hundred men as quickly as we could, within a week or so, before doing anything else.

Naturally, I reported my misgivings to my company and looking back on it, I see that if I had been sensible I could have persuaded my company by using stronger arguments and even greater emphasis, that my plan was right and the Sultan's was wrong. The operation would then have been stopped. As things turned out I suppose it was better that I did not succeed in persuading my masters; but I will not attempt to conceal the fact that from an early date I had no faith in the plans as they now evolved.

Despite all this, the Sultan's enthusiasm was infectious and, after all, we supposed he knew his country (I was constantly being told this by company officials in London). I must confess the Sultan and the Company carried me along with them on a road in which I myself had little trust.

Much of 1953 I spent in travelling between Bahrain, Qatar, Dubai, Muscat and Salalah. I was involved in a study of the tribes and also in keeping track of the Sultan's military preparations, which by this time, after a false start, the Sultan had put in the capable hands of Colonel Percy Coriat, a British officer of great experience who had formerly served in the Sudan and had newly entered the Sultan's service.

While I was paying my visits to Muscat and Salalah, the Company was preparing ships, transport and stores for this quite elaborate and, by no means easy, operation. We had two naval-type vehicle landing craft and other smaller vessels including *Jamila* for the landing, and a fleet of six-wheeler Nubian load-carrying trucks, together with Dodges and Land Rovers as personnel carriers for the desert journeys. Our equipment included, in addition to tentage, a water-desalination plant, a generator and other quite heavy gear, as well as a mountain of tinned food.

All these preparations went on during the summer of 1953. I continued to press for contact with the Duru. Eventually, I was told that contact had been established, but I was unable to gain access to them myself, as I had wanted. This alleged contact appeared to have been made in the usual complex, uncertain and remote way I had begun to realise is customary in the tribal contacts in Oman.

I was to go down by truck to meet the little oil company fleet, or that part of it which would sail from Muscat. There the soldiers would be embarked and all of us taken to the beaches at Duqm.

It was a distinctly interesting situation in the interior that we sought to penetrate.

Chapter Ten

One bright February morning in 1954, I set off from Dubai with Sabir driving and Firdullah in the second truck hoping to reach Muscat easily in two days, stopping for the night on the beach near Suhar. From there onwards to save the endless bumping of the coastal track we risked the beach, since the tide was low, and still just ebbing, as we set off in the morning.

We made fine progress for the first 50 miles, until suddenly and without warning we reached one of the little estuaries which intersect the coast. Sabir did his best swerving inland towards some very substantial palm trees, which I thought we must hit. But the soft sand gripped us, and in it we sank before the bumper hit the first tree. Fortunately Firdullah was a good way behind and managed to stop on firm sand. But it took us a hot and sweaty hour before we got the first truck out. Then we had to turn back and find a way through the gardens to the coastal track, which here ran a mile or so inland. Once on it we endured its bumps, and the inevitable slowing down, almost to a halt, to cross each water course.

As you approach Muscat the coastal plain of the Batinah becomes narrower, and the mountains close in towards the sea. The last big village with extensive gardens is Sib, the scene of the famous agreement. After it is Hayl and the line of the coastal palm plantations begins to be crowded out between the blue of the sea and the rugged greys and browns of the bare rock of the foothills. And the sea is such a deep blue, different in quality from the water of the Gulf for this is a part of the Indian Ocean itself.

In front of us we could see where the rocks of the foothills finally reach the coastline to form Muscat's famous bay; and as we came closer it seemed impossible that there would be a way through for our trucks.

At the last moment a little valley among the rocks opens inland and a short way up it is the Customs Post. There a careful check was made of our passports and driving licences, since, although we had spent the night before near Suhar, and had been travelling a day and a half over Omani territory, this post was in those days the first you came to on the road from Dubai to Muscat.

The valley track leads on past the village of Ruwi, shut in by the mountains, peaceful and green, with its well-watered garden of palms and fields of lucerne.

Leaving Ruwi we turned north towards the sea again and across the narrow plain in the deep valley of Bait Al Falaj, its soft gravel bed marked out unconvincingly as an airstrip and in those days only usable for light aircraft (but only one of these had landed there since 1945). Towards the seaward end was the small white house and diminutive barracks which housed a major and a company of infantry. This little unit and the tiny police force in Mutrah and Muscat had been the only uniformed forces in the whole country, until the Muscat Field Force (MFF) was formed.

A few minutes later we were winding down a bumpy track into the outskirts of Mutrah, Oman's biggest port and commercial centre, a considerable and densely-packed town and possibly a larger one than Dubai at that time. Many of its buildings were of rough dark stone; but the sombre colours of the houses were relieved by the gay colours worn by the women of the Baluch who lived in the quarter at the entrance to the town. They dress in bright red full skirts, red and white upper garments and bonnets.

The road took us round the edge of the town but we could see into its crowded, partly covered, streets which went down the water's edge. These were always thronging with a cosmopolitan crowd; Pakistanis, Indians, Omanis, Iranians: it was almost like an exhibition of national costumes.

As against these attractions, there were off-putting features to the place. In particular anyone coming from the clean air of the Batinah coast would be assailed by the horrid stench of drying fish; for in the very middle of Mutrah stood, in those days, the fish factory, where many tonnes of small fish, mostly sardine, were laid out to dry in the sun. Some of the resulting dried fish might be eaten locally, but the bulk was destined for export as fertiliser.

I had on earlier occasions spent some time in Mutrah and found it a fascinating place in many ways, more colourful than the towns of the Gulf itself. The *souqs* were well supplied with locally made wares and particularly attractive were the bright colours of the woven Nizwa belts.

At one time we were thinking of renting a house there for the Company and I was shown one or two examples of buildings by our cheerful Indian agent, all of which he regarded as eminently suitable. One imposing building of three storeys, right in the middle of town, seemed at first sight attractive; but mounting a twisty, very narrow and shaky wooden staircase to the first floor, I was shown into the best room. I was a little surprised to find it inhabited by a large and elderly cow.

"Oh, she will be taken away Mr Henderson, never you mind her; and all the walls will be repainted."

Nor was I encouraged when opening a window at the back I discovered we looked straight out over the drying fish.

"Better to keep the windows always shut."

We did not take the house.

So with Mutrah behind us we sped along the track, first taking an interesting tour for half a mile round a narrow corniche, with the sea lapping onto the track, then we turned inland and up a steep little pass which took us over the tip of Muscat's volcanic crater.

There we stopped. Muscat was immediately in front of us and a little way below, a sight I have always found alluring, beautiful, but at the same time rather eerie and unnerving.

Muscat is I think unique, and once one is familiar with it, this view from the little pass has that strange quality of all really unique views, perhaps for example rather like that of our own Big Ben from across the Thames in London or that of St Marks Square in Venice. When you return and see it again it seems to strike one somehow more real than reality.

It is only rather a small group of houses that form the town standing at the inner curve of the bay; the silent dark crags embrace the harbour, its sparkling blue, ringed with white sun lapping at the foot of the cliffs. It all looked perfect, delicate, perhaps rather diminutive; and it is certainly a tiny place for a capital. But the scene was silent, apparently motionless – even the tiny waves hardly seemed to move and in that distance could not be heard; and it was the silence and stillness that make it eerie. What other capital appears to have no inhabitants?

The most hard-bitten, unromantic traveller would I think stop his truck, and get down to wonder at this enchanting little view; but in appearance it is the view of a deserted town.

We drove on down to the gateway in the town wall, where after a bit of a discussion with an Omani guard our special pass, which the authorities had given us on a previous trip, gained permission for us to take the cars into the old part of town.

We wound our way through the narrow streets which only had room for one car at a time, to get to the Political Agency, hoping to find a boat there to take me out to our ships anchored in the harbour.

At this point, I had to say goodbye for a time, with much regret, to Sabir and Firdullah who were to go back to Dubai with the two trucks we had come down in. Land Rovers were already loaded on our ships (for the surveyor, the geologists and me), and we had to economise on staff as much as we could. This meant taking drivers only for the bigger trucks and driving the Land Rovers ourselves. We had to watch the logistics problem very carefully on this operation.

By late afternoon I was on board the company vessel, the *Jamila,* a former wartime infantry landing ship. This was the same vessel I had sailed in earlier in the Gulf on survey work. Now she was loaded with stores and would also carry some of our personnel.

Near us lay another company vessel, the *Jasoura,* a vehicle landing craft which carried our vehicles.

We were to rendezvous at Duqm later in the week with the other similar ship chartered by the Company and likewise loaded with stores and vehicles. The beach had been chosen by air photography, but we would have to go ashore first in a small landing craft so that the ship's officers could check the beach profile before committing the vehicle landing craft to the landing. For myself the operation was all a bit reminiscent of Salerno and Normandy, but this time our aims were peaceful ones.

Our general manager, George Heseldin, who was responsible for all our company's exploration, was on board, together with those company officials who were in charge of the administration and logistics of this operation. Heseldin and the others wanted to see the landing, on which the Company had spent such a great deal of money, before returning by *Jamila* to Muscat and thence back to his headquarters in Tripoli, Lebanon. Also on board were Nick Fallon, our surveyor; Morton and McGinty, expedition geologists; Brown, a senior geologist; and three officers of the MFF, Colonel Percy Coriat, Mike O'Kelly and Frank Haugh.

We dined that night on *Jamila's* deck. It was a lovely evening with not much wind and it was just the right temperature for sitting out of doors. The gaunt crags rose up on either side of us and the town, with only a few faint lights, lay in between them. In the moonlight we could see the patches of grey on the crags which showed where, over the years, the crews of visiting ships had painted their ship's name in white paint. There were hundreds of them, many dating back a long time; many were of the British frigates which had called there. Every ship seemed to have been in competition with her predecessors to get her name in a more prominent, more difficult position.

On *Jasoura's* decks near us a hundred or so newly recruited soldiers of the MFF were sitting, eating their evening meal. *Jasoura* was later to do further trips back to Muscat with another ship to pick up the remainder of what I called the 'Mystical 400'.

Over dinner we discussed again points of detail in regard to the operation, and as we sat after dinner I felt I had to say once more how poor I thought the prospects were for getting as far as Fahud and setting up a continuous operation there with full-scale drilling and all that this would entail by way of equipment and men stationed out in the desert. If we could not work in the Fahud area what was the point of all this expedition? We could of course do geological work in the Wahibah and Janaba areas, and if we thought it worthwhile to bring in the equipment we could follow up with geophysical work. I saw no likelihood of trouble on the coast if one expected the logistical task of feeding, watering and sheltering four hundred unnecessary soldiers there.

However there were no exposed structures in the south. Fahud was the classic anticline all good geologists dream about and there were other possibilities in the same region inland, but all were in Duru country.

The general manager said, of course, the object was the Fahud area, but he himself was confident we should be there quite soon, I was being too pessimistic.

I reiterated that I thought that the Sultan must be persuaded to get in touch effectively and quickly with the Duru. He claimed that he had done so, but I had not met them and we had no Duru with us. I also feared that the arrival of the expedition on the coast would in itself arouse the antagonism of the Imam. I doubted if he would do more than complain, as he could do nothing to oppose such a landing physically; but the danger of his then using our arrival to influence the Duru against the Sultan (if he could reach them first) was one we could not disregard. If that happened, our chances of getting inland would virtually disappear, and Oman might break up into a series of small and unrecognised states. Political instability of this kind would prevent any company searching for oil, perhaps for many years to come.

Percy Coriat largely agreed with my argument. He was, he said, very worried about his force. The men had been recruited in far too great a hurry without the necessary training facilities and he had no properly equipped base; he had no cadre of Arab officers and NCOs to draw on. He had two British officers, on contract to the Muscat government, who had retired from the British Army. He had a group of Adenis who had

His Highness Shaikh Zayed bin Sultan Al Nahyan in 1952. Shaikh Zayed became Ruler of Abu Dhabi in 1966, and President of the United Arab Emirates in 1971. (*R. Codrai*)

Pearl merchants and their wares. (*R. Codrai*)

A pearling boat sets out for the season. (*R. Codrai*)

Camels crossing the ford to Abu Dhabi before the causeway was built. (*R. Codrai*)

A desert expedition. The author is standing in the truck. (*R. Codrai*)

Sabir bin Muhammad. (*PDTC*)

We had no four-wheel drive in 1949. (*R. Codrai*)

Water taxis in Dubai. (*R. Codrai*)

Guards were on alert as soon as vehicles stopped or broke down. (*R. Codrai*)

'Spudding in' at Ras Al Sadr, February 1950. Ronald Codrai (left) talking to Shaikh Shakhbut, while Patrick Stobart, British Political Officer, and the author look on. (*R. Codrai*)

His Highness Shaikh Shakhbut bin Sultan, Ruler of Abu Dhabi 1928-1966. (*R. Codrai*)

Building the causeway to Abu Dhabi, 1950. (*R. Codrai*)

Company vehicles near the border of Oman. (*R. Codrai*)

His Highness Shaikh Rashid bin Humaid, Ruler of Ajman 1928-1981 (left centre), at the Company house in Dubai in 1949. Among those with him, left to right, are Shaikh Ali bin Rashid, Ronald Codrai, the Ruler's secretary, the author, and Muhammad Abdul Rahman who was on the staff of the Company. (*R. Codrai*)

Khan Sahib Hussain. (*R. Codrai*)

seen some service in the Aden Levies, and he planned to use these as his non-commissioned officers, but they were out-of-work soldiers of fortune without much training and it was already evident that they did not get on well with the Omani troops. Even without any enemy to bother him, Percy thought he would have difficulty with his own force. Some of the men had only been in uniform a few weeks and they had virtually no basic training.

Moreover, he did not yet have an effective organisation to back him logistically. He was short of equipment and he had very little qualified administrative staff. It was, he thought, ludicrous to field a force of this kind in this manner. To begin with, the Company would have to give vehicles to him in order to carry the force inland. This was accepted by the Company for as long as he was awaiting his own transport, which was on order; and until it came he would have to rely entirely on us logistically whether at Duqm or inland. This in itself he found most unsatisfactory. So of course did we.

The general manager said that it was too late to go back, we had to do the best we could with things as we found them. I pointed out that I had raised many of these matters earlier, but it was only now that we had assembled the expedition, such as it was on the military side, that some of our weaknesses were quite so apparent.

The general manager ended the discussion by saying that it was too late to hold up this operation; we had to do the best we could with things as we found them. The Sultan did not want to achieve our common aim by means of physical force and certainly had no intention of fighting, otherwise we should not have gone along with him. He agreed that with the bedouin some show of strength might be needed, but just the presence of troops was all that would be required.

After the general manager had left us, Percy and I went on talking. Percy said he had been so preoccupied with the difficulty of raising this force in a few short months, that he had not had the opportunity to study the political position. He was, after all, a newcomer to the area. It looked to him as if, on top of what had seemed almost insuperable difficulties on the military side, he now had to face problems of even greater complexity politically. However, he remained cheerful, pulled my leg about being a Cassandra and said we must look on the bright side; after all, a miracle might happen.

I was of course very pleased with this reaction. I had chances to talk with Percy on my previous visits to Muscat since his arrival but, as he said, he had then been so preoccupied with the problem of raising a force out of apparently nothing and with very little time to do it in, that we had not discussed in enough detail the political background which was all new to him. This was the first opportunity we had had to talk about the political problems fully and to brief him. The political position had never been really clear, and it was not until the very last moment that I had finally realised that the Sultan still had been unable or unwilling to do anything about the Duru on the lines I repeatedly asked.

Percy was an impressive figure, tall, lean, and tough, with a black patch concealing the loss of an eye as a result of a war wound. He had a handsome, prominent nose and a thin weathered face. He looked the part of a colonel who had had years of hard service in tropical countries behind him. Much of this service had been in the Arabic-speaking parts of the Sudan and he was familiar with the language and quickly adapted himself to the local dialect.

That night I went to bed on *Jamila's* deck, my mind full of anxiety. However, I hoped to see the Sultan on the beaches at Duqm, which he planned to visit by sea from Salalah some time, after we had landed. I could at least discuss it all with him then, putting forward my recommendations yet again. It had been nearly two months since I had last seen him.

On the following day, we put into the port of Sur to pick up Shaikh Salim bin Nasir, the paramount shaikh of the Janabah tribe, a section of which frequented the Duqm area in the autumn, winter and spring. Salim had his instructions from the Sultan but he did not know exactly when we would come to pick him up, and there was no way in which we could have told him, as there was no speedy communication out of Muscat to other towns. We already had with us two government representatives who were supposed to help us with tribesmen whom we met ashore, but I soon found that they knew very little about the tribes and nothing whatever of the geography of southern Oman. They would not, I thought, be any use, and I counted on Salim to help us, at least in regard to any of his own people whom we came across.

I did not expect to find the Janabah in very large numbers ashore at Duqm. They would, I was told, be friendly and I did not expect any difficulty with bedouin at the landing point, but there could be difficulties when we struck inland to the north into Wahibah country since the latter are not on good terms with the Janabah, and we had no representative from the Wahibah with our party. The Muscat government had either failed to produce one or, perhaps rightly, felt that to have one alongside Salim might have been awkward for us. The tribes were not actually at war, just 'unfriendly' I was told and, in these circumstances, we felt we should have had a representative from both. I had done much the same elsewhere when I had been with tribes and got away with it.

We should also expect to meet another tribe, the Harasis, but they were a small weak tribe who were on terms with the Janabah and I did not expect any trouble with the few whom we were likely to meet.

We sailed well before dawn and, early the following morning, we put in at the port of Sur. I had one of the Janabah with me and he and I were to go ashore to pick up Shaikh Salim bin Nasir and one or two followers. "Mind it is only one or two," were my instructions from Heseldin, and "We sail at four." "More like fifteen or sixteen and sailing tomorrow," commented Percy Coriat sardonically.

However Percy promised to come ashore with me to help, and in the event the general manager and his party came ashore also, to look at the *souqs* and to take photographs.

Percy said he was particularly interested to see Sur, since it was the place where the British-Indian Army landed in 1821, after which they attacked the tribes in the hills inland and a whole brigade of British-Indian troops under British officers were cut to pieces. "Not," he said firmly, "that I think anything like that will happen to us."

It took us some time to walk to Salim's house and we got there only to find he was out. We eventually ran him to earth in another house and managed to persuade him to go back to his own, after having coffee. At his own house, of course, he disappeared from our view. Percy was amused by all this and prophesied that we should be kept waiting the rest of the day. "Never mind about your general manager!" he said. "That's all very well but he is not your general manager," I replied.

Whilst we were waiting for Salim, we took a short walk along the waterfront. Sur is not a very beautiful town. The main part of it, where the Janabah live, is on the peninsula which guards the entrance to the extensive but rather shallow creek. This part of the town is almost flat and, since there is a very poor water supply in the town itself, it has no gardens or trees and the low, flat-roofed houses have a singularly colourless, unattractive air.

But it is a considerable port for country-craft and for the large sailing ships (called *booms),* partly powered, that went as far as Zanzibar in one direction and Kuwait in the other. There were a number of wooden ships, berthed and pulled up on the beach of the creek. Some were under repair and boats were being built at the water's edge.

I walked a little way up a small hill hoping to catch sight of Bilad Al Sur, the inland part of the town, which is well watered and has extensive gardens, but I was unable to see it and we did not have time to walk further; I had no adequate map to see how far away the gardens were. All the water for the port of Sur is brought on the backs of animals from Bilad Al Sur, I suppose two miles or more away. Bilad Al Sur is reputed to be an attractive place and one I should like to have visited.

On the far side of the creek is Ayqa where the Bani Bu Ali live, but we had no reason to go near them since they do not visit any of the country our expedition was planning to explore. This is a section of the famous Bani Bu Ali tribe, the bulk of which live inland of Sur, who overcame the British-Indian brigade of which Percy told me. In turn, they were defeated a year later with great loss, and paradoxically have always been reckoned to be very well-disposed towards the British in consequence, but we did not have a chance to test this.

Salim did his best to make us stay for a late lunch; it was already after three o'clock in the afternoon. He wanted to bring about 20 tribesmen with him and a great deal of kit, but he was persuaded eventually to cut it down to six and a good deal of kit, despite the fact that I had explained that we had in the ships sufficient tentage, bedding, food and cooking utensils to make them all very comfortable. We finally got all this gear down to the beach and put it on board the waiting motor launch. When we reached *Jamila* it was already five o'clock, but Percy thought we had done very well to bring only so few so quickly.

Salim proved very pleasant although a bit pernickety and fussy. But I felt I could rely on him when dealing with his own people. He was sure he could also get us through the Duru area, but I was absolutely certain that he could not. The general manager asked him just this question and, with me interpreting, he heard Salim's confidentially affirmative reply. "There you are; your fears are groundless," I was told.

The general manager wanted to visit the curious nearby harbour of Khor Al Jaramah that evening but it was now too late in the day to negotiate the entrance. *Jamila* stood off the coast and waited until first light when we turned towards this most unusual waterway.

At Ras Al Hadd, which is the cape at the elbow, as it were, of Arabia, there are three creeks, one at Sur, another about 12 miles to the east, called Khor Al Jaramah, and, just beyond it, Khor Al Hajar, right on the tip of Arabia.

Early next morning we sailed towards the shore.

The entry to Khor Al Jaramah was difficult, but fortunately the tide was slack as *Jamila* sailed into the narrow twisting entrance with the rocks close to us on either side. Once inside the channel, it opened up suddenly to an extensive creek over two miles long and more than a mile wide with deep water inshore to the north.

We spent about an hour exploring it; there was no sign of human habitation and it seemed to us that it was a very fine harbour going to waste. It might be useful later. According to Salim, the reason for its disuse is that there is no fresh water within reach of it. If there had been, the port of Sur would surely have been built there instead, since it is a far finer harbour than Sur's own shallow creek.

We sailed out again and passed by the entrance to Khor Al Hajar but we did not go into that creek since the entry to that large but shallow inlet was not deep enough for a vessel as big as *Jamila.*

Just to the north of this creek, between it and the sea there is an unusual airfield. I had once landed on it in a company Dove on the way to Salalah. We simply wanted to see what it was like and put ashore to look at it. It had been built during the war for anti-submarine coastal patrolling aircraft. It still had in 1954 two beautiful asphalt runways, but no buildings. When the Dove had landed we walked about for a bit and could see no one, and flew away once more. Two wonderful deserted harbours, and an airport, not even up for sale.

Jamila sailed on. We still had plenty of time in hand and two days later we made our rendezvous with the other ships off Duqm. It was seven o'clock in the morning and coming on deck I saw that the two vehicle-landing craft were anchored in a line just off the shore. It was just like 'D Day' in Normandy in miniature.

We lowered into the water our very small assault landing craft, which we carried on the after deck. It was arranged that a small party of soldiers with Percy Coriat, Salim bin Nasir, Heseldin and myself would go ashore first in this small boat. As we were making these preparations, we were astonished to see five sailing boats being launched from the beach. A number of people climbed into them, put the sails up and came straight out towards us.

Before we could get our motorboat ready with its little party, the five sailing boats sailed right through our fleet without apparently giving us a look. I naturally asked Salim what it was all about and he replied perfectly calmly, "Oh they are going fishing. They do that every morning this time of year."

Never before in recorded history had such a landing been made on this wild and barren coast and yet this was the remarkably cool reaction of the only inhabitants.

In front of us, to the left, was a low cliff jutting out to sea, ending in a pointed rock; inland the ground rose to perhaps 100 feet, but it looked higher. The escarpment then ran back inland leaving a sandy bay behind which were low dunes dotted with stumpy trees.

We could make out a few people on the foreshore and one or two small sailing boats and dug-out canoes drawn up on the sand, but we could see no huts or tents. Smoke was rising in the area of the stumpy trees and this must be where the Janabah fisher-folk lived.

We climbed aboard our little assault landing craft and were soon chugging through a fairly calm sea to the shore. We drove hard up on to the beach, after the manner of landing craft, and being well used to this I was hanging on as tightly as I could, ready for the sudden stop. Heseldin and Percy Coriat were standing on the half-decked stern and quite what happened I did not see, but Heseldin fell overboard with a splash and Percy just saved himself at the last moment. Heseldin claimed Percy pushed him but the latter denied this. However, no damage was done and we all got ashore dry except for Heseldin who had seen nothing at all amusing in this little incident.

Percy was soon marching about with his long ash stick which he always carried, flicking the dust into the air to see how the wind took it and looking for a suitable place to put his tents away from the worst dust. The motorboat went back with a message to the others that all was well ashore, for the main landing operation to start and, perhaps even more important, for a change of clothes for Heseldin. Meanwhile, in another small boat, the ship's officers were taking soundings and examining the approaches to the beach.

Salim and I walked through the soft sand to where the bedouin were. We spent some time talking to them and I was astonished by how calmly they had accepted our arrival. They saw nothing remarkable in it.

Later in the morning our three ships weighed anchor and steamed in abreast; each made a successful landing about 100 yards apart and got their doors down on to the dry sands of the beach. It was a perfect landing place. Out came the men and the first of the vehicles. Unloading proceeded until the tide began to turn and the ships pulled off to return to complete unloading on the high tide the next day.

As soon as my Land Rover was ashore, I went for a tour in it with Salim and some of his men. We went first to Nafun, a tiny encampment where it was hoped to base the MFF, since there was brackish water which the bedouin stoically drink; this would at least serve us all for washing, even if we were not tough enough to drink it. There we found a small encampment of Janabah. They greeted Salim warmly, but again expressed little surprise at our arrival.

This section of the Janabah was a strange group based on distant Sur where they owned palm trees and houses. The tribesmen spent some of their time, especially in autumn and winter, on the coast in the Nafun area fishing. They also grazed camels there. Some travelled there by camel, some by small boat, usually remaining until just before the monsoon and the dust storms, which made living in that area almost impossible for most of the summer, as we were to discover for ourselves later. Others of the Janabah lived permanently in Sur town and others again in central Oman. All together they were a very large tribe.

At Nafun the escarpment comes almost to the sea and there is a small plain covered with thorn and other small trees between it and the water. The sand is light-coloured and very fine, in many places just dust, the trees gaunt and scraggy and the whole of this coast has a depressing, almost lunar landscape. The Janabah lived in harsh conditions; they simply placed their few belongings under trees in wooden chests and they also used more fragile boxes, placed vertically against the diminutive trees, looking rather like small wardrobes, for storage of some of their equipment. They lived entirely in the open with only small pieces of cloth two or three feet square stretched between the branches of the trees to give some shade from the sun. In winter the sun was warm but the air cool and it was cold at night. In summer it would be intensely hot, but from May to July the monsoon would blow strongly up the coast from the south-west and this, we were told, produced thick sandstorms which would blanket the place for days or even weeks at a time. The severity of these storms, the bedouin said, varied from year to year. They were the main cause of the movement of almost all the nomad inhabitants northwards to Sur during this period.

I spent the afternoon visiting the few encampments which we could find, talking, joining them over their coffee, making friends and offering the men work. We had brought some labourers with us but we naturally wanted to employ some of the people of the region if we could. However, as we had rather expected, they did not seem at all anxious for manual work in our camps and, apart from half a dozen guides whom Salim chose, we could not engage anyone.

I tasted the water at Nafun well and found it just drinkable; by itself it was pretty horrid, but as water for tea and coffee, it was just possible. However, we had the distillation units with us on which we planned to rely for drinking purposes.

Salim then showed me a remarkable thing about his people. He pointed to a large chest by one of the encampments. It had a series of concentric rings round it in the sand, made by a stick. Salim said it was the custom that if these rings were there, the chest and its contents would be safe. In the winter the sand or dust was stable enough for the rings to remain for many months and Salim said that a chest so marked and left unattended would never be tampered with. Whether the basis of this was superstition I could not find out, but such was the practice of his tribe.

We got back to camp to find tents already pitched and a meal being cooked. The distillation plant was working and the electric generator was making power. Nick Fallon, our surveyor, had been up to the escarpment towards the south-west in a Dodge Power Wagon and said that a very little work would make a track for our vehicles up on to the plateau. He confirmed reasonably firm going on top of the scarp. Percy Coriat had put up his camp near the Company one, but was prepared, when more vehicles came, to move the main body to Nafun, a place he aptly named 'No Fun'.

The general manager departed with the ships when they had been unloaded, leaving me with instructions to press on to Fahud, instructions which I knew, and he knew, I could not fulfil. The two larger ships were to return to us with the remainder of the troops and this, after a week, they accomplished.

In the following weeks Nick Fallon and the geologists went out on survey expeditions, keeping to the south of the roaming grounds of the Duru. I used to accompany them to begin with in case they met any bedouin; but we established before long that the Jiddat Al Harasis, which is a large stony plateau south and west of our camp, stretching towards Dhufar province, was almost uninhabited at that time of year and there was no need for me to be with them. We met only a handful of the Harasis themselves.

These expeditions were the first of their kind in that part of Arabia and, other than the camel treks of Wilfred Thesiger and Bertram Thomas, we knew of no other foreign explorers who had visited this region; as we had the maps of the journeys of the two who had, we could be certain that on most of our trips we were the first foreigners ever to have visited many of the areas. We navigated by sun and prismatic compass but could always find our way back without navigation, simply by following our own tracks: there were no others.

We used to spray our trucks with anti-fly spray soon after leaving Duqm and we knew we should not see another fly until we got back, although there were clouds of them at Duqm itself once our camp had been established, despite our constant efforts to kill them. On such trips we took no tents but allowed ourselves the luxury of either camp beds or air mattresses and, to pitch camp, we simply put these between the stationary vehicles. Our only discomfort was the cold at night and sometimes the mist. One would wake up to misty sunlight to find the person sleeping nearest to you was out of sight in the swirling white clouds of fog and these might not clear until the sun had been up for an hour or more.

I applied myself to the intractable tribal problem which might prevent our penetration into the interior. We had with us the two Sultanate officials whose job was to help me with any tribes, other than the Janabah, whom we might bump into. The first of these inland tribes, the Wahibah, as I have said, were on bad terms with the Janabah and we restricted our activities at the outset to Janabah and Harsusi country along the coast. I managed to make contact myself with the Wahibah whose nearest encampments were rather uncomfortably close, to our north. They accepted our presence and gave due respect to the representatives of the government, but they said if we wanted to work in their area we should have to drop Salim and our Janabi guides while in their tribal districts. This I agreed to.

This was really the limit of the possibilities until we could make contact with the Duru who lived further into the north and west of the Wahibah and were on bad terms with them, but on good terms with the Janabah.

The Sultan himself visited us by sea from Salalah in HMS *Flamingo*, a Royal Navy frigate stationed in the Gulf. He had with him Major Chauncy who was British Consul General in Muscat. He landed in a small boat and inspected the troops. He expressed himself disappointed in them. "They are only boys," he said in disgust. Percy felt he had to agree. I pointed out yet again during a long conversation which I had with the Sultan that on this coast the troops were unnecessary anyway. Fahud could only be reached by agreement of the Duru. Some of the four hundred men, I thought, might well be needed later in the Ibri area.

The Sultan would still not listen to my reasoning. He again made promises that the Duru would be contacted and in the meantime restricted us to an area of the coast and the Jiddat Al Harasis, putting this in writing in a long letter to me, which he wrote in his excellent English with his own neat and clear hand. To my thinking the letter meant an end to all our hopes.

HMS *Flamingo* at sea
18 March 1954

CONFIDENTIAL

Dear Mr Edward Henderson,

Because of several interviews I had yesterday and various subjects which I discussed with different persons, it had totally slipped out of my mind to take into consideration what the Commandant Lt Col Coriat informed me about the force and its present strength when I, Major Chauncy, the Consul General and yourself discussed the limit of the area which your geologists might explore, and that was just before the ship sailed from Ras Duggam.

The Commandant informed me that there is still quite a number of men who he considers are not fit to be retained as soldiers and might be discharged. Thus the strength of the force will still be reduced whereby it will make it impossible for your geologists to penetrate inland as I told you in the presence of Major Chauncy, and I regret very much to tell you this after reconsidering the whole matter and I am sure this is well understood by all as I have on several occasions informed everybody concerned that no penetration from the beach-head should take place unless we had the full force. Now the force has been considerably reduced and still it will be reduced before we can get replacements. I regret I do not see my way to agree to your penetration at present to the whole limit which we discussed yesterday until we have the full force at the beach-head. However, with present force in hand I still agree to your geologists exploring the following places but under no circumstances should they go beyond this limit.

1) Duggam and its immediate surroundings to Nafun, Sai and Bai but not to Saraib and up to Khaluf or Al Hugf.

2) Jiddat Al Harasis to Tarafa on the boundary between Dhufar province and Al Jaddah (Sharbatat to 55° and 20° in the north).

I must say the force has been formed in a hurry and without thinking of other problems and as we all must know that this being so things are apt to turn like this.

Really there is much to be said about the whole affair from what I have seen and heard during my very short visit to Duggam but I shall stop my pen here with a wish that things may be worked out satisfactorily.

I am informing Major Chauncy that I have written this letter to you so that there should be no misunderstanding on the subject.

Please telegraph to me just saying that you have received this letter to you by HMS *Flamingo.* I have requested the Commander of the Ship to see that this letter reaches you safely to which he very kindly agreed to do so.

Yours sincerely,
Said bin Taimor

PS I should like to urge your company to improve the water problems as there are complaints about this. They should make vigorous search for finding adequate supply of water for all purposes.

(Signed) Said

I had pointed out to him again, but in vain of course, that the geologists would not take long to complete their work on the coast and would want to get inland, but I could make no impression; and in this sorry position the Sultan had left us, and sailed back to Salalah in *Flamingo*.

We soon established an airstrip on the escarpment, our landing craft made further trips, and logistically the expedition was now firmly based.

The Imam formally complained about the Duqm landing; but he did nothing else about it. It was clear that politically we were reaching a stalemate and I advised my company in this sense. The Company, however, still believing our general manager, Heseldin, rather than me, was confident that things would soon turn out as we all wished.

There was little I could do at Duqm where the survey continued in the limited southern area, and after the first two months I returned to Bahrain. From there I revisited Muscat, by light aircraft, to try to urge the Omani authorities to make direct contact with the Duru. Saiyid Ahmad said he had no authority to do this, and the Sultan was still in far-off Dhufar and did not want to talk further about it, although he and Saiyid Ahmad were in direct daily communication by radio.

Then with the spring of 1954, I heard the news that the old Imam, Muhammad bin Abdullah Al Khalili, had died in Nizwa and that the paramount Shaikhs of the Hinawiya and Ghafiri factions had, on their own initiative, 'elected' Ghalib bin Ali Hinai as his successor. From the story that filtered through, this did not seem as if it had been a widely accepted election, more a choice by the two key shaikhs, but there had been no actual resistance so far to the new Imam. This would mean that the people of the mountain would accept him. It then became clear that Ghalib himself was little more than a front for his tougher and more ambitious and effective brother, Talib bin Ali.

Talib's policy soon became evident. He wanted to tear up the Sib Agreement and carve out a separate state for himself in the interior. As we have seen, the old Imam had complained at the Duqm landing and took no action other than this, but Talib now began to raise the tribes and recruit an army. He toured the immediate area of Nizwa with this army to consolidate his position, but our information was that this activity was unpopular among the shaikhs and tribesmen alike. His 'army' (merely armed irregulars) lived on the land and paid for nothing. I was told that the individual shaikhs of the various tribes, who resented being forced to feed his army, felt their positions were being eroded; the Sib Agreement had allowed them much authority, and they wished to keep it that way. Moreover, they liked rather than disliked the Sultan whom they had always found helpful, and who after all had never tried to impose his direct administration on them.

Talib also made his brother's faction unpopular by imposing a draconian tax on 'jewellery'. How in such an area, without an administration, it was to be collected was baffling, and I am sure it never was systematically gathered in.

All the signs pointed to a very fluid and uncertain situation in the interior and to the possibility that if Talib could get a grip on the tribal leaders of the Duru and the shaikhs of Ibri, any chance at all of our getting into Fahud would finally disappear. On the other hand chance might swing the other way.

In June the Imam threatened Ibri. This was a development of immediate major importance to us. The Duru made a living in their wide desert lands by digging and carrying salt, making and carrying charcoal and by breeding and selling their camels. Part of their wealth is invested however in trees in the date gardens of their village Tanaam, only seven miles from Ibri and in Ibri itself. They owned some property, mainly trees, in other towns that bordered the desert. For this reason, whoever held Ibri and Tanaam controlled the Duru.

Ibri was ruled by the shaikh of the sedentary Yaaqib tribe, Muhammad bin Abdullah, who was on close terms with the Duru with whom his family had intermarried. From 1925 to 1952 there had been a *wali* or governor in Ibri, paid by the Imam, but partly under the influence of the Imam; and the Duru respected the power both of the old Imam and of the Sultan.

When Talib threatened to march on Ibri, Shaikh Muhammad bin Said the paramount of the Duru, whom I had never met, went to Muscat to ask for help against him. Hearing this I also went to Muscat to meet him. There in Muscat he told us he was agreeable to the Company working anywhere in his lands, which covered most of the area which was of interest to the Company. In exchange he wanted a promise of military help from the Sultan; now at last we seemed to be closer to the position which I had always thought was essential before we could go in.

I spent several days in Muscat talking to the aged paramount, Muhammad bin Said and his son Matar. He wanted me to meet Ali bin Hilal and other Duru shaikhs, and he seemed very willing to assist us. He was prepared to send his son and other shaikhs to Duqm, and I made an agreement with him on behalf of the Company, that we should work freely on his territory, and without the

Muscat government's knowledge paid him 10,000 Rupees as an indication of intent. The Minister of Interior and I returned to Bahrain to recommend to the Company that they should mount an expedition to Fahud in September as we had the concurrence of the Duru shaikhs. I still was not very confident, but now had more reason to expect success, only provided the Sultan did not stop us.

Plans for this operation were therefore made. The camp at Duqm had been nearly forced to close in June because of sand storms and no useful work was possible in the summer. These storms were extraordinary in their severity. For example during a visit I made there in early June, early one morning I travelled the four miles from camp to the airstrip to meet an aircraft, taking a radio with me. Just as it was due to arrive and had made radio contact, the wind started and the sand came up in a blanket. The radio went dead. I never saw or heard the aircraft itself. The pilot told me later that on approaching he had made out the airstrip, but it had at once been blotted out by blowing sand and he returned to Qatar from where he had come. My companion and I meanwhile got into the Land Rover and closed it down as much as possible. By this time we could not see the front edge of the bonnet from the steering wheel and there we stayed, half suffocated in dust and heat, until the wind abated and visibility improved sufficiently to enable us to return to camp, as the sun was setting.

This kind of storm was repeated and the duration of each one grew longer, until survey work based on Duqm had to be suspended. But we were confident that conditions would be good by September, and the Fahud expedition was therefore planned in detail.

Chapter Eleven

Although I had pressed for operations in September, I was still afraid that the Duru might not come into Muscat in time for us to take them from there to Duqm to join us; and I had said to Muhammad bin Said that if things became more difficult with Talib, and if he found himself cut off from Muscat by the Imam's army, he must come up to Dubai or Sharjah, where he could always reach me through our office. However, this had been an unofficial and personal arrangement against an emergency, which I could not reveal to anyone in the Muscat government. I had, however, obtained from the Muscat government the promise of their most effective tribal official to help me on the next expedition when this proved possible. This was Sultan bin Saif Al Hawsini, the paramount of the Hawasina tribe, one of the most important tribes of the area of coast and foothills. He was perhaps the most influential tribal leader in the area which we hoped to visit, and had an excellent reputation for straight-dealing and common sense.

For various reasons the actual date of the expedition was delayed. I asked Shaikh Sultan bin Saif to come up from Sharjah, where I could pick him up in a company Dakota to take him with me to Duqm, since Dakotas could not land safely in those days at Muscat. Then we heard that Talib had marched on Silaif and Ibri and captured both, and that he had gone on and captured Tanaam, the Duru capital itself. A day later I had a cable from Dubai (I was at that moment in Bahrain) to say that all the Duru shaikhs, together with the shaikhs of Ibri, had arrived there. At my urgent request the Company sent over a Dakota to Bahrain to pick me up and I went down in it to Sharjah where I found all the shaikhs at the BOAC fort.

In those days Sharjah airfield was still very simple and rather rough, much as when I had first seen it six years before. It was still a mud-strip of rolled salt flat. The fort still did duty for offices, restaurant and sleeping accommodation for any passengers who had to stay the night on account of either bad weather or engine trouble. Aircraft were not scheduled to stay the night there, but their crews sometimes could not help it.

I walked across from our Dakota and gathered around the door of this fort I saw a large group of bedouin. From among them, the short square figure of Shaikh Sultan bin Saif came forward to greet me. As usual, he was smiling and soon he was laughing as we exchanged greetings, but when I asked him for news of Ibri, I could see from his eyes that his good humour was only a cover; serious business was in front of us, and he was really very troubled.

"Things look bad at the moment, but," he brightened again, "it may, God willing, be all for the best. Some of our people were killed at Silaif, but this has greatly angered the Duru, and all their important shaikhs are here now," and he pointed to the group about 20 yards away. "We must talk to them at once, and God willing, we will all go down to Duqm today."

Then he took me up to them and I shook hands with the old paramount, Shaikh Muhammad Said, and his son, Matar; and Shaikh Sultan bin Saif introduced me to Ali bin Hilal, Harib, Musallim and others of the leading shaikhs.

Even the aged paramount, who was usually calm and totally uninterested in his surroundings, appeared excited. Ali, who I soon found was inclined to be more excitable anyway, was quivering with the intense feeling which his words showed had mastered him. His excitable bedouin talk was not easy to follow as we made our way into the fort. As soon as the usual greetings had been exchanged, starting, I noted with some amusement, with the habitual "All is quiet in the country; praise be to God," he began attacking me with, "When are we going to Ibri?" And the others crowded close to me, taking up the chorus.

As we made our way into the fort and up the stone steps to the roof where there was an awning and which I thought would be the only place where we could sit both in the breeze and under a shade, Ali was pulling at my arm and gesticulating and protesting, behaving as if I had already refused point-blank to go to Ibri.

"Oh followers, oh people; troubles now face us! But, God willing … ." He turned, and in resonant tones began to address his fellow shaikhs and followers, stressing the urgency of the situation.

He wore the beige cotton shirt, the dark yellow headcloth and thin head-rope often affected by the true nomad; in his hand he had a camel stick (a follower carried his rifle), and at his waist, on a thin belt, was the elaborately carved silver sheath of his Omani dagger. He looked the part of the bedouin chief, thin lips, excited eyes, eloquent in the liquid dialect of the sands. He had a presence when addressing his people, and he plainly carried them with him; that all those who clustered importunately around me shared his excitement was only too clear.

Shaikh Sultan bin Saif was amused because he could see I could not get in a word, and he made much ado to get us all seated on the carpets which had been brought up on to the roof for us.

We spent the best part of the day talking under the canvas awning on the roof of the fort, and I was deeply thankful for the presence of Shaikh Sultan bin Saif. The Duru wanted our absolute guarantee that the Sultan of Muscat's forces would drive Talib out of Ibri, Silaif and Tanaam. In their minds they were justifiably confused as to what my position was. They seemed to think that I controlled the army. After all, I evidently had an aeroplane: I could, therefore, do anything. So they insisted I had to promise that I would ensure that Ibri and Tanaam would be recaptured before they would agree to come with me to Duqm. If I did not make this promise in advance, they would go back and make peace with Talib. I tried to explain my position as a company official and promised to do my best. They were not convinced that I did not actually represent the Sultan of Muscat. It was Shaikh Sultan bin Saif who finally persuaded them to accompany us to Duqm and with no absolute commitment apparently made on either side. By this time, evening was approaching, and the pilot said he had no flying hours left, could not land at Duqm after dark and so on. What with pressure from the pilot (who was quite justified) on one side, and the intransigence of the Duru on the other, it was a trying day; and at the very last there was a hitch, for the pilot would not allow the wild looking Duru on board with their rifles; and the Duru would not get into such an outlandish looking thing as an aeroplane without them. But honour was satisfied when the Duru were persuaded to put some of their ammunition (the pilot thought it was all of it) in the freight locker.

We took off, and our flight path took us right over Ibri which looked peaceful far below us on the desert's edge in the pink light of the setting sun. Well after dark we came into Duqm and landed with the aid of two or three emergency flares on the rough desert strip.

I discussed the position with Nick Fallon and the geologists, and we agreed on an early start. Angus Perks, who was in charge of the Duqm operation, had ready for us all the trucks and supplies we needed. I then went off that night with the leading shaikhs to Nafun to confirm that Percy Coriat would give us an escort.

It was there that we really came up against it. Coriat said he had specific orders by radio from the Sultan from far-off Dhufar not to go to Ibri, but said he would bend his instructions and go to Fahud if the Duru agreed. Shaikh Sultan bin Saif and I discussed it. He had a simple idea in his mind. "We (pointing to me) will go to Fahud and argue there," he said. His intention was to get the Company into the lead and then, if need be, we would all go into Ibri; the army would have to support us. Percy gave orders to that effect to his officers. I was naturally not altogether happy about this, but it seemed the only thing we could do. I felt we must be frank with the Duru shaikhs, of whom Ali bin Hilal had now become the spokesman and effective leader, despite the presence of the old paramount Muhammad Said. I told the Duru, therefore, that we could only go and see what was happening; and, although we hoped to be able to get them at least into Tanaam, we could not promise that the army would enter the village: as far as Ibri was concerned, we must wait and see how things developed. The Duru shaikhs, at length, reluctantly agreed to go on these terms: they had no alternative.

We got back to Duqm well after midnight. A start at four o'clock on 19 October, 1954, was arranged and our aim was to go to Harashif at a point out in the open desert where Angus Perks had earlier arranged a large dump of petrol and water in cans in preparation, and then to press on that same day towards the Wadi Al Amairi, just south of Fahud. The journey would be some 200 miles and we did not expect to find any water on our way. The geologists thought we might possibly find it in the Wadi

Al Amairi; the Duru reported brackish wells in that area, but we had no accurate knowledge of its quantity or potability.

The navigation for this trip was done by our surveyor, Nick; the geologists Morton and McGinty were with us and the 46 soldiers who formed our escort were under the command of Major Michael O'Kelly of the MFF. We had with us the Shaikh of Ibri, Muhammad bin Abdullah Al Yaaqubi; all the Duru shaikhs and some followers; and of course Shaikh Sultan bin Saif. As water and food were so important we took virtually no camp kit, only a roll of blankets each and the most elementary cooking equipment; this was how we were to live for several weeks. The Duru gave me a good deal of trouble since each follower insisted on sitting like their shaikhs in the front seat of a lorry or Land Rover, and there were not enough front seats to go round. These men, who had travelled hitherto only on camels, felt, justifiably in the circumstances, that it was beneath their dignity to ride on the back of a lorry with the troops. However, after much talk I sorted the problem out and we set off.

To begin with the going was good and after Harashif, where we were refuelled from the drums we had dumped, we came to a piece of open desert the like of which I have never seen before or since. It was perfectly flat and extended some 70 miles. The surface was of light sand on a gravel base, and there was not a sign of an animal or an insect or a plant upon it: the surface was smooth and flat without a mark. It seemed a shame to sully its smoothness, as we cruised over it at 50 miles an hour. The bedouin said they had never crossed it, as it lay well off all their routes, and I doubted whether any living thing had crossed it before. After crossing it we came into rough country where the winter rain water from the distant mountains ran across the broad gravel plain and then into and under the sands. Far as we were from the mountains, this produced a maze of winding, narrow, dried-up water-courses; no sooner had you crossed one than you were in another. It always looked as if some other route would be easier, but if you tried it, the alternative usually turned out worse. These twists and turns delayed us and made navigation more difficult. Nick was of course a first-class desert navigator, and each night he could fix our position exactly by stellar observation with a theodolite. This desolate area was later discovered to be one of the world's main breeding grounds for locusts. But we saw no visible sign of hoppers.

We had counted on reaching the Wadi Al Amairi on the second night and visiting Fahud on the third day, but by dusk on 20 October we were only in the Wadi Musallim and there we stayed the night. The Duru were fascinated by the route which we had taken. They had expected us to take a long circuitous trail partly through the sands of the eastern edge of the Empty Quarter where there were a few brackish wells. Since we were self-sufficient as far as water was concerned, we had taken an absolutely direct route, only veering off a straight compass line when we had to avoid particularly bad going. We had already formed some idea of the country from aerial reconnaissance, and the route which we were able to choose in consequence was unknown even to the best travelled of the Duru. When we got into the area of the *wadis* we were in country that was familiar to them, and the Duru could help us in establishing names of *wadis* and dunes and could advise us on the positions of water holes.

We set off early on 21 October after morning tea and biscuits. The Duru were finding our food very trying. Out of politeness, they wanted to eat with us, but they preferred the soldiers' food and at mealtimes would dodge from one group to the other. I remember one of the Duru being given an open tin of sardines. He smelt it and tipped it disgustedly on to the sand. He preferred his fish 'fresh', although theirs was often old, and dried in the sun on the sand; tinned fish was unnatural they thought. We did no cooking and, beyond making tea and Nescafé and heating up soup, we lived on cold tinned food and biscuits. The troops boiled rice every night, and, of course, the Duru thought this much more civilised than having to rough it on sardines and other delicacies.

As we approached the Amairi, Musallim, one of the head shaikhs of the Duru, said he expected to find some of his men there, and he wanted to warn them in advance that a large party with Europeans and troops was coming with the agreement of their tribal leaders. Otherwise, scared tribesmen would, he thought, loose off their rifles at us.

This seemed sensible, so I drove on ahead with Musallim and one of his colleagues, and they guided me successfully down into the *wadi* bed, rough gravel about 20 feet below the level of the plain, and to the well Muqbarah, an unlined, shallow water hole where there were several trees, thick bushes and clumps of grass. We got down from my Land Rover and slung a bucket down the well to try the water which proved sweet.

We heard a movement in the bushes and Musallim shouted, giving his name and asking who the person in hiding was. A very scared-looking tribesman eventually emerged, clutching his rifle by the barrel. He said he had been with a party of Duru at the well overnight. Early in the morning they had heard the sound of our engines and at first thought it was the noise of airliners which commonly fly over at a great height. But it soon became evident to them that this was something different, and at last they could see the tall plumes of dust which our trucks were throwing up. All his companions went off on their camels to warn other Duru camping further up the *wadi* to get their families out of the way and to devise some way of attacking the intruders; he had been left behind to hide and to spy upon these strange invaders. To him we might have been creatures from Mars. This was the first time that anyone had come to the Amairi on anything but a camel, and many of the Duru had never seen a car.

Musallim told him who we all were and sent him off on his camel to explain to his fellow tribesmen that there was nothing to fear. His camel was about a quarter of a mile away among the trees, hobbled with a rope between the front legs in the customary way, and he went to fetch it. Musallim told me that he wanted to meet as many of his people as he could and to send them up and down the more populated parts of the Wadi Al Amairi and Wadi Al Aswad to warn other tribesmen of what was going on and to explain that we were there with the agreement of their tribal leaders.

As all the ranging grounds of the Duru are exclusive to the one tribe, they will let no one in without permission and they seldom give such permission.

As we could now see clearly the area was a dangerous one for bedouin of other tribes. Water holes were very few, and round most of them would be Duru camping. It was therefore impossible for a party on camels to cross the area without the knowledge and agreement of the Duru. The same can be said of the tribal area of the Al Bu Shamis to the north, and Wilfred Thesiger made a remarkable journey through their district without their approval, or rather in the face of their objections, by travelling at night and lying up by day away from the water holes, and relying entirely on water carried on his camels. But Duru country is so much more extensive that no one could possibly travel over these vast wastes without the agreement of the tribe. Our cars, however, had introduced a new dimension to desert travel in this area, and only in cars could such a sudden incursion as ours have been made.

In Arabia this total exclusivity of desert ranges may be unusual. In other parts of Arabia with which I am familiar, desert ranges are recognised as belonging mainly to particular tribes, arrangements can be made for other tribes to cross them or to spend a whole season grazing over them. In the case of the Duru their lands lead nowhere and there is no point in any other tribe crossing them. The tribes of the hills do not venture far into the desert. The tribes to the north and south of the Duru travel mainly towards the north-east to the settled villages of Oman, and over to the west of the Duru's area lies the Empty Quarter. At the season of the ripening of their dates, the Duru take their families to the plantations in the settled foothills, but they tend to camp away from the larger towns. This is partly because of the strong instinct of the bedouin to stay out in the desert as long as possible; they can never be happy for long in settled areas. There is some evidence for thinking that one of their reasons for disliking staying even one night in or near Ibri is a fear of malaria which they told me they attribute to devils which inhabit date trees in the gardens. This is not an unreasonable assumption; there has been bad malarial infection in many parts of Oman, and there can be no mosquitoes except when there is irrigation or open water wells. When at a later date in the Al Ain oasis I arranged anti-malarial spraying and the administration of Paludrine, the mosquitoes were exterminated and the resultant decrease in fever among the sedentary locals was attributed by the bedouin to the noise our cars had made. This, they said, frightened the devils in the trees, and the fever had been checked.

Musallim advised us to camp at Muqbarah and the other shaikhs agreed. It would give the bedouin time to hear about us. Evidently the noise of our coming, especially that of the big six-wheeler Nubian trucks in which we carried the soldiers, would precede us for up to three hours, in those totally silent wastes, depending on the wind and, of course, our speed. In the difficult and the slower going of the *wadis,* we might be announcing ourselves many hours ahead.

The halt at Muqbarah enabled us to put all our vehicles in order. On the previous night we had to send our British mechanic back to Duqm since he had suffered severe burns in an accident with a Primus stove. He was driven back non-stop by one of our best drivers and taken to Qatar by air where, after a long stay in hospital, he recovered completely. The vehicles were suffering mostly from choked filters and suspension breakages, and the half-day in the *wadi* enabled these faults to be put right.

We went up a small hill near the camp and could see to the north the outline of Jebel Fahud and to the north-east and east the far-off mountains of Oman in which Talib and his army were sitting. What were they doing we wondered. I could not help thinking how Thesiger must have felt camping near here with his party of only four or five bedouin, reliant solely on his wits and the loyalty of his companions.

We found that the water was plentiful and drinkable, and this was a very great help since it meant that we need not send vehicles back to Duqm for water. Our main worry from now on would be the fuel for the vehicles, but we carried sufficient for the next two days. On 23 October, we expected a larger party to come up with Angus Perks, Percy Coriat, some more troops and several loads of petrol. We had a radio with us and could speak to Duqm and, as soon as we had tried the water at Muqbarah, we sent a message asking for an alteration in the loading of the next convoy. From now on, our need would be for petrol, not water, and also for empty barrels in order to exploit the water supply in the Amairi, and any other sources we might find.

As we ate our evening meal by the well in the Wadi Al Amairi and discussed the future of the expedition, we felt rather more cheerful. But on the political side I had fresh cause for misgivings.

During the late afternoon, several tribesmen had come in to see Musallim and the other shaikhs. They told us that several people had been killed in the first attack on Silaif by Talib's men, that Ibri had fallen with very little fighting, and that Talib had left a strong garrison in Ibri fort under a leader called Saifyan. Some said that Tanaam, the seat of the principal Duru shaikhs, had fallen to Talib and some said it had not.

The Duru shaikhs had now become highly excited again and insisted that we should immediately go to Tanaam with the troops to recapture it if necessary. With great difficulty I managed to persuade them that we must await the arrival of the Colonel with the main body of men. They reluctantly agreed to stay one more day in the Amairi. Next day they sent only one sleepy tribesman with us when we set off as a small party with the geologists and Nick to look at Fahud, take rock samples to assess its age, and look for and mark out an airstrip. Our little party successfully accomplished all our tasks during the morning, and we had lunch amongst the rocks of Fahud.

It was wonderful to have reached Fahud at last; although the scene was inevitably what we expected. This was because we had all flown over it so many times and had photographed Fahud from the air, that it did not leave anything much new to see. Whenever geologists were on board the aircraft, we used to circle slowly around it at a few hundred feet to get a closer look, and very uncomfortable this was on a hot bumpy day.

From the air we had seen the cirque formed by the harder strata which remained when the softer ones, particularly those near the middle, were gradually weathered over millions of years. These harder strata have, in turn, been cut off leaving the springing of the arch as ridges sticking out of the plain, the whole of the upper part of the dome being removed by weathering. As you approach it across the desert, Fahud looks like any other mountain of brown limestone in the desert. If you drive into the cirque, the nature of the formation is apparent and you can see where the strata have been broken off or worn away to leave those ridges which are all that remains above the surface of what once must have been a huge whaleback.

On the desert below the rocks on one side there was some shrub and some of those very unpleasant plants (*harm* and *arad* in Arabic) which grow in salty water, smelly useless things. Even camels cannot eat them. The bedouin warned us not to dig for water in this area. It was too salty, and this we later found was the case. We would have to rely on wells in the Amairi *wadi*-bed.

At last we were in Fahud, but would we ever get the chance to drill? Could we maintain ourselves here? The sleepy Duru guide we had with us, like all his fellows, was obviously agreeable to anything but only if we went to Ibri, the little town nestling in the pale blue mountains on our horizon. It was in Ibri that we should find the answer.

When we returned to camp we found that Angus Perks, Percy Coriat and the main party of troops had arrived from Duqm.

Chapter Twelve

Our little camp in the *wadi* bed looked larger and busier when we got back to it. The shaikhs had grouped themselves under trees by the well. The troops were established on vantage points above us on the edge of the main plateau 50 yards or so from the water, and the oil company party had grouped itself a little down the *wadi.* Still we had no tents, but there was now an adequate number of empty drums for water, there were piles of petrol drums, and a small pump was chugging away by the well.

Angus Perks had brought bad news: he said that after we had left, Coriat, who had come up with him, had received direct orders by radio at Nafun from the Sultan not to take the troops into either Tanaam or Ibri. If this was so, it looked as if the whole basis of agreement with the Duru had been cut away, and I explained to Angus the falseness of our position as it would now seem to the shaikhs; unless we took them at least into Tanaam we should be breaking our word. My assessment of the conflicting evidence available was that the Imam had probably not taken Tanaam, since we knew the village had no proper fort; and as it could not therefore be easily defended by a garrison of Talib's men against the Duru, we thought it would not have been worth their while to capture it, and thus risk a counter-attack in which they would be outnumbered.

The aged Shaikh Muhammad, his son Matar, and Shaikhs Ali bin Hilal and Musallim on every occasion I met them in the camp were all pestering me to get them into Tanaam; and I suggested to Angus that if we could take the shaikhs into Tanaam in company transport, the MFF could remain some distance short of it. The effect in Ibri would be much the same as if troops had actually reached Tanaam; and at that point we should have to think up some way of getting the Imam's men out of Ibri.

Fresh news had reached the Duru that the Imam threatened to burn all their date trees in Ibri and the other towns and villages where they had them unless the Duru submitted to him and accepted allegiance to him rather than the Sultan. This made the Duru more eager than ever to get into action, and they said that they would raise a force and capture Ibri themselves if need be, once we had taken them to Tanaam. A visit to Tanaam was clearly vital if the expedition was to continue even for a few days. The alternative was to withdraw and leave the Duru to make peace with Talib. This would mean giving up all hope of finding oil. The trees at Ibri were the key to the desert.

Angus and I went over to Percy Coriat. We found him gloomy. He now had, he said, altogether 96 troops with him. They were too young and inexperienced and all ill-trained. Many had been in the force only as long as a month, and hardly knew how to fire their rifles, let alone move into an attack as a cohesive body. Apart from rifles he had only a few Brens and two-inch mortars; and neither weapon is suitable for an attack on a solid fort. He repeated that he had direct orders not to enter Tanaam. Angus then asked him innocently, "But do you not have an overriding order to protect the Company in all circumstances?" "Of course, this is what we are here for." "Well, then, the shaikhs insist on our taking them into Tanaam. We shall have to drive them there. All we ask you to do is to come up close enough to be in support if we get into trouble."

The argument went on and on around these points. We were sitting on the sand under a tree near the Company area. In the middle of this discussion one of the Duru came over and said to me, "The shaikh wants you." I said, "I'll be over in a minute." "What," I asked Percy Coriat, "am I to say to them? They will be insisting on our going to Tanaam at once." "You must not say that I will take the troops into Tanaam or Ibri. Anything else you say about the Company is your own business, but you must not make any promise about the troops." He spoke quite angrily. It was plain how much his orders had upset him, and how much he wanted to help us.

After further discussion with Angus, who was prepared to support me in any move which seemed essential, I decided to tell the shaikhs quite plainly that the Company party would go on to Tanaam taking the Duru with us, within the next three days. The troops would, we hoped, be close to us, but more than that I could not promise.

As I expected they simply replied, "What if the Imam's men are in Tanaam already? What of the threat to burn our trees in Tanaam and Ibri? These trees are the wealth of our tribe. Whoever has our trees has a knife at our throats."

The discussion went on until midnight, and it was finally agreed that on the following morning, 24 October, Angus Perks and Nick Fallon would take some of the shaikhs up nearer Tanaam, reconnoitre the route, dump petrol, seek intelligence and return to camp at Muqbarah. On 26 October at the latest, if it proved practical, we would go with the shaikhs into Tanaam.

Ali then asked me for money to help him to collect some followers to make us look more impressive. I tried to argue that in this crisis surely we did not need to pay his men. Ali said he knew his men; they would have to abandon their families, wherever they might be, to join him; and an inducement was needed to get them to do this immediately. I had two tin trunks full of silver Maria Theresa dollars, the most acceptable currency of the interior at that time; and I agreed to pay one Maria Theresa dollar a day to each man who stayed with Ali for as long as the crisis lasted.

The following morning, 24 October, Angus and Nick and a few of the shaikhs went off to the Wadi Aswad without any troops, but with some Duru, while the geologists visited Fahud again on their own. The geologists were now confident from their first look at the fossils that the rock was of the right age and this, therefore, made the oil prospects good in the Fahud structure. Only drilling, however, could now give us the final answer; but this raised all our hopes and made me all the more desperately keen to overcome what looked insuperable political obstacles. To be thwarted now would be hard indeed.

The shaikhs left me in peace all that day. It was hot and dusty in camp, but the air was dry and by evening the desert became pleasantly cool. I spent some of the day making notes on water wells and interrogating the tribesmen who came to see us on this important topic. We also recruited some followers.

Nick and Angus returned before dusk to report comparatively good going, and that a good well lay on our route called Tawi Murri. The shaikhs had got hold of several followers in the Wadi Aswad whom we would pick up when we went forward.

My main trouble now was with the company drivers who drove the big Nubians, and who said not unreasonably that they were not soldiers and they had heard there might be fighting. We had no drivers for our Land Rovers, and drove these ourselves to save carrying more men and consequently more food and water than necessary, but the big vehicles with the troops and petrol were essential, and there were not enough of us to drive them ourselves. None of the soldiers could drive except the three British officers, who like us, had a Land Rover each. I was, therefore, forced to agree to paying double overtime to keep the drivers with us, and on this basis they served us loyally for the rest of the expedition.

News as regards Tanaam was still conflicting, but we had cheering intelligence that the Ibri garrison was small and that the Imam and his brother had gone to Rustaq with his army.

A convoy of vehicles had meanwhile gone back to Duqm and returned with a few more troops and more fuel. Percy Coriat now had 126 men in all. He reminded me again, as he had at Sur, of the unique occasion over 100 years ago when a brigade of regular British and Indian troops was cut up by a mass attack of tribesmen armed with swords and axes in the Jaalan in eastern Oman. He said his own ill-prepared, tiny force, although safe enough in vehicles in the desert, would be vulnerable to such a mass attack by tribesmen when in the close country of the foothills in Ibri. I thought this appreciation was only too realistic.

On 25 October we set off in six Land Rovers and five Nubians, taking all the MFF party except a small guard for Muqbarah camp, all the shaikhs and their followers and, from the Company, Angus, Nick, the five drivers and myself. We had an easy trip up to the Aswad, and camped there for the night. We gave Shaikh Ali a driver and a vehicle to help him round up followers, and a dozen or so were collected and joined him that evening, when I held my first pay parade for the tribesmen.

Percy Coriat, Angus and I then drew up a simple plan for the next day. The three company Land Rovers driven by Angus, Nick and myself would take the shaikhs into Tanaam, followed by a Nubian with the tribesmen. Percy would halt a mile or two short of Tanaam and we would send word back. If we were in trouble he would come up and help us, if we were not he would camp not far away. The shaikhs thought it a crazy plan to have the troops behind us, but somehow we got them to agree to it. I did not emphasise very precisely what the MFF would or would not do, I said the military are a law unto themselves, but I trusted them to protect us in whatever way they saw fit. Fortunately at no time did the shaikhs attempt to talk to Percy Coriat. Had they heard directly from him quite how closely he had been restricted by his orders, I do not believe they would have gone on with this operation.

On the following morning our little column of vehicles set off for Tanaam. It was not very far, and the going was good. Nick was in the lead, followed by Angus, myself and one Nubian with the tribesmen in it. Just before noon, coming over a rise, we saw a village with palm trees: the first sign of permanent habitation we had seen since we had left Duqm nearly a week ago. Behind the village we could see the grey and brown of the hills that surrounded Ibri on its north and, behind them, the blue of the main range of the mountains of Oman, which had been always on our horizon over the last few days. Now they were nearer and looked to me more threatening.

The village lay in front of us, peaceful and quiet, the only sounds the noise of the poultry and the creak of a well pulley, a dog barking, the usual village noises. The village consisted of a few mud houses on the edge of a palm grove, and scattered around the houses were many small huts of palm fronds. Smoke was gently rising from fires near the huts and among the houses. The shaikhs said that they thought all must be well in the village, but they were not sure. They had a discussion: "Drive on," they said, "but go slowly as it may be necessary to stop and go in finally on foot." These people were not used to seeing cars.

We drove on, in my case at any rate, with some apprehension. We could see people coming out of their huts and gathering. The shaikhs stood up on the seats, hanging on to the windscreens, shouting and waving. As we got closer we saw that everyone was friendly and there was no sign of an enemy. We pulled up and the shaikhs jumped down and were soon surrounded by their people.

Shaikh Sultan bin Saif was sitting with me. "For goodness' sake please find out what is going on," I said to him. "That may not be too easy to do quickly." He smiled and disappeared into a noisy group of tribesmen.

Angus and Nick lit cigarettes and we waited as patiently as we could. After some 15 minutes Shaikh Sultan bin Saif came back to us and said: "Talib never came to Tanaam. There was a fight at Silaif and then Ibri fell. He stayed a few days and, leaving a garrison, went back to Nizwa. He returned only a week ago with some men, but then went off to Rustaq. I cannot be sure how big the garrison is, but they are all in the fort in Ibri and do not go out much except in strong force, for fear of the townspeople; but remember Ibri fort is strong and hard to capture."

Meanwhile our Nubian had come up with the other Duru. I asked Sultan to get hold of Ali bin Hilal and Matar. When they joined us I suggested that we should bring up more vehicles and camp by the village. Ali wanted the troops to come up as well, and he formally invited them to stay near the village where there was plentiful water.

We sent off the truck to bring up more vehicles and I went to look for Percy Coriat. He was in fact only about half a mile behind us and had been anxiously watching us through binoculars, ready to come in quickly at the first sound of shooting. He laughed when I gave him the shaikh's invitation and said: "I think I have nothing to lose now. I shouldn't be here anyway."

We drove back to Tanaam together and ate our lunch sitting in the cars. It was by now very hot. The Duru told us they had prepared a big meal for the evening and after it they wanted a discussion.

Meanwhile Shaikh Sultan bin Saif had been busy. He said he had found out more about the Ibri garrison. He thought it was not so large and its morale was poor as the townspeople were obstructing them in every way. Muhammad bin Abdullah Al Yaaqubi, the Shaikh of Ibri, who was with our party, had already sent in to his people and ordered as many of his followers as possible to come out to Tanaam to meet him and join with him in an assault on the garrison. Ali bin Hilal and Matar were collecting followers as fast as they could. If they could collect several hundred, we hoped that the Ibri garrison might feel that they could surrender without losing face. If it came to a fight I did not think we could dislodge the garrison: it would have to be done by bluff if it were to be done at all. If we could not dislodge them within a day or two, Talib would be back in Ibri with reinforcements and an opportunity would be lost forever.

I went over to Percy Coriat and told him all this. He seemed a new man. Four Land Rovers were standing together in line and troops were climbing into them with Brens, rifles and the tiny two-inch mortars. "We are off to look at Ibri," he said with a laugh, waved his stick, jumped into the leading car and away they went.

Needless to say the shaikhs were overjoyed when they saw Percy Coriat drive off and heard where he had gone, but unfortunately they assumed that he had simply gone off to capture Ibri, and that nothing further would be required of them. I tried to explain what the army means by the term 'reconnaissance'.

We knew the topographical features of Ibri and its surroundings from air photography and from our own recent observation from the air. The town itself nestles right against the foot of a ridge which overlooks it from the north and east. In the centre the ridge is broken, and a narrow gorge takes the main bed of the Wadi Al Kabir through it. The cliff on the westerly edge of this gorge directly overlooks the fort which is embedded among the houses of the town and has virtually no field of fire. To the south of the town are the extensive date groves and gardens. The *wadi* winds past the date gardens and some seven miles away on its edge lies the village of Tanaam. There is another similar break in the ridge four miles east of Ibri and here is the well-sited fort on one side of a gorge, called Silaif. This had been captured by Talib, and then for some reason, presumably lack of men, had been left without any garrison. Some four or five miles to the north of Ibri lies the big fortress of Ainain which sits astride important irrigation channels of the upper *wadi.* This was held by the Shaikh of Dariz who had accepted the authority of the new Imam under duress; but the shaikh was reported to be out of sympathy with the Imam and to favour the Sultan.

It was becoming apparent how much the people of the whole area disliked Imam Ghalib and his brother Talib; and they evidently were prepared to throw in their lot with the Sultan's central government and hoped for oil and its riches as a consequence. Talib and Ghalib seemed to them to have nothing to offer: no administration, no money and no expertise in regard to oil. Talib's moves about the country with armies were unpopular as the villagers had to feed the troops. Ghalib was accused of being extremely austere and bigoted, whereas the people of Ibri and the neighbourhood, although devout practising Muslims, were markedly liberal in their attitudes in many ways.

Late in the afternoon Percy Coriat came back, looking excited and pleased. He explained that he had put patrols for a short time up on the heights to the north and east of Ibri. There had been a little shooting from the town, but none of it effectively directed, and some might even have been in greeting. He proposed repeating his patrol with nearly all his men early on the following morning; and he suggested that this would give an opportunity for the shaikhs to put men into the groves to the south, and the fort would be surrounded at least in appearance.

He calculated that although militarily such an operation made no sense at all, in view of the low morale of the garrison and their ignorance of the real weakness of the MFF detachment, success might come of it. Not only was morale of the garrison reported to be low, their supplies and ammunition were said to be insufficient and their numbers apparently somewhere between 50 and 200. The townspeople were obstructing them, and they hardly dared to go out of the fort except in large parties and armed. He said if only the Company would produce an aircraft to do a demonstration run low over the town, this should do the trick on its own.

I discussed all this with Angus. He would have asked for an aircraft to fly a demonstration, but he did not think the Company would agree; however he agreed it made sense to put the troops and the tribesmen in position round the fort and see what came of it. Nick had marked out a strip for use in an emergency near Tanaam, and we could land a Dove or Dakota there to evacuate any casualties. We had to be content with that. The whole operation hinged on persuading the shaikhs to co-operate, and after a hasty evening meal of rice and mutton with the Duru under their trees, I asked the leading shaikhs to draw aside for talks. First I had a long talk with Shaikh Sultan bin Saif, to which Ali bin Hilal listened.

Shaikh Sultan bin Saif concurred with Percy Coriat's view and said that if we could get several hundred men into the lower town, and at the same time dominate the fort, or appear to do so, with troops on the heights, and move our vehicles about ostentatiously on the open ground between the *wadi* and the hill to the east, where they could be seen from the fort, there was a very good chance that things would go as we wished. His information about the feeling in the surrounding area was that Dariz would accept the Sultan, Silaif could be easily garrisoned, as its fort was empty, and only the Baluch in Al Araqi looked like giving us any trouble once Ibri fort had fallen.

Encouraged by this advice I went with him across to where the main group of Duru shaikhs were sitting under the trees. We did not have much difficulty in persuading them to agree to the sort of action we had in mind. My only problem was that the need to give each irregular one Maria Theresa dollar a day would soon exhaust my stock of cash, and I had no means of getting more until we had established an air supply route. I made it a rule that I would only pay those who had left their families in the desert to join us; from now on people from the immediate area would have to join for the sake of the cause. Muhammad bin Abdullah Al Yaaqubi made strong objections, and said that, if any money was being given, his people would need some of it. So I said, right, no money for anyone.

Considerable wrangling ensued as a result of this remark of mine, but in the end it was agreed that if Shaikh Muhammad could have some of his people taken up by truck that night, they would assemble as many armed men as possible in the date groves by first light, and no money would be needed for them. All the Duru would be sent to join them in the Nubians: the Duru now numbered some three hundred, of whom I was paying some one hundred and fifty or so. The trucks would then return to pick up the main body of troops, the advance guard going up with the Colonel just before first light to make sure of taking the commanding positions on the heights.

It does not take long to put that on paper, but it took almost all night to arrange. I went back and arranged these plans with Percy Coriat and Angus Perks and I felt that everything possible had been covered. We had little time for sleeping, and before dawn we saw Percy's column move off, the bedouin having already been put in position during the night under the charge of Shaikh Musallim and some of his younger colleagues. Shaikh Muhammad bin Abdullah Al Yaaqubi had taken his party into the town, where he meant to raise all the able-bodied men he could. He was also intending to ensure that messages from different sources would reach the garrison to the effect that a large force had arrived, of which we were only the advance party; tanks were on their way; all the Duru had gathered in the groves and numbered many hundreds; and all the townspeople had taken up arms to eject the garrison.

Nick, Angus and I were busy in the first hours of the operation supervising the transport and, at about seven o'clock when the Nubians had been loaded and dispatched with the last batch of troops, we went up ourselves to see what was going on.

Although it was still early, the sun was well up as we drove into the narrow gravel plain made by the junction of the Wadi Al Kabir and the Wadi Al Ain. These flat gravel beds are typical of this part of Oman and like the deeper *wadis* out in the desert, are made by the flash floods in the mountains, running across the plain to disappear eventually under the sands of the Empty Quarter. Close in to the foothills as we were, the *wadi* bed is wide and level and, although bumpy enough, comparatively easy going for a Land Rover or truck and much better than the narrow channels we had encountered further south. There are ridges of larger rocks, but for the most part the gravel is even in texture. Over to our left was sandy scrub country with acacia and other desert trees, a few of the straggly, gaunt, tall *bu samra* among them. Half a mile to our right was the same sort of country, with now the first foothills closing in on us. We passed a ruined village and fort, light brown mud walls matching the soil, with a few bedraggled palm trees and the remains of a garden, which Sultan told us was Dubayshi.

Soon, in the line of the ridge to the east, we could see the break immediately beyond and above Silaif, although the village itself could not be seen for the bushy country between us was slightly raised. This was where some of the recent fighting had been; we were now in the critical area.

Leaving the Wadi Al Ain we swung slightly leftwards making towards the point where the foothills rose up beyond Ibri to its north, and immediately in front of us we could see the second break in the ridge which must, we knew, be immediately above Ibri. Some ten minutes later, turning a corner of the *wadi* bed and following the Nubians, we saw the first trees of the Ibri palm groves which stretched southwards from the town for nearly a mile by the side of the *wadi* bed. The steep bare foothills were now closing in to our right and we could see in what an interesting, rather too interesting strategic position Ibri lay, overlooked as it was by steep bluffs on two sides.

We could hear no sound of shooting but we thought it wise to climb up out of the gravel *wadi* bed on the eastern side, as the Nubians evidently had done, leaving the date groves to our left and slightly below us. The ridge of Jebel Kawas was only half a mile to our right, and beyond the palm trees on the left of the *wadi* we could now see the pale brown of the mud buildings and the larger turrets of the fortress among the houses. After crossing so many miles of desert it was moving to see this township among the groves, nestling under the bare brown and pink hillside, sprawling, silent, seemingly deserted in the warm morning air. But on this particular morning our knowledge that some 300 armed men were in the groves and Percy Coriat's men of the MFF were even now in position somewhere on the crags to the north and east above us, while the enemy sat apparently silently in the main fort, added excitement to the scene and heightened our appreciation.

One of the things I love about Oman is the sharpness of the morning scene on a clear day. The colours are very vivid and contrasting, the deep green of the palm branches, the pale smooth brown of the houses, the brightness of the rocks on the near hills with behind them the pale blue of the central Omani range.

We were again following the tracks of the Nubians and now we could see them and a few Land Rovers drawn up on the right of the *wadi,* close under the foothills, and perhaps 300 yards from the edge of the date gardens to our left.

Percy had established himself on the edge of the *wadi* to the east of the town, and his troops were in position on the heights above him. So far, he said, only one shot had been fired from the town. The town was strangely still, but people were now to be seen coming out of the edge of the town into the groves, and the Duru were walking through the trees towards fort and town. Unfortunately only those near the edge of the grove or in the *wadi* were visible, and we were not certain that the garrison in the fort could see even these, as trees tended to screen them.

We established ourselves on a small hillock near Percy's headquarters. Shaikh Sultan bin Saif was still with us, but by now we had lost touch with most of the shaikhs, who were I hoped fulfilling their part of the operation by encouraging the tribesmen in the town and groves. Nothing seemed to be happening near the fort and as time went on it began to look as if nothing would happen.

I suggested to Shaikh Sultan bin Saif that we should get hold of a reliable emissary in order to take an ultimatum to the garrison. Percy Coriat at once said he would not have anything to do with this; but Shaikh Sultan bin Saif agreed and Nick Fallon drove him to the edge of the town and was to go back and pick him up later. About an hour afterwards he appeared with two men and Nick went down and fetched them. The two men with him were prominent citizens of the town, well known and respected.

Shaikh Sultan bin Saif then wrote a note, as the representative of the Sultan. We both realised that the Sultan would never approve of such a note, and if we failed, Shaikh Sultan bin Saif would be in trouble, so would I. If we succeeded perhaps we should be forgiven. In it the commander of the garrison, who we had learned was named Saifyan, was offered a safe-conduct to come and talk to Shaikh Sultan bin Saif with a view to agreeing on terms of surrender and to saving the lives of the garrison. The military position was described in the note and the numbers of those with arms, who were gathered to attack, was given.

The two men were taken to the edge of the town and disappeared into its streets carrying the message.

It was now eleven o'clock in the morning of a very hot autumn day. The place we had chosen had no shade, but we felt we should not move, since the letter had described where Shaikh Sultan bin Saif would receive Saifyan, and we were in clear view of the fort whose garrison, as we intended, could see all that was going on around us, with troops and vehicles moving ostentatiously.

We waited an hour and I was losing patience and hope, when our two Ibri citizens reappeared at the edge of the town; two other men were with them.

Nick Fallon went across to pick them up. As they came towards us Sultan told me that he was sure one of the two men was Saifyan himself, and this proved to be the case. The second man was a follower.

Saifyan stepped slowly down from the Land Rover and walked over to where we were standing. He was a short, rather insignificant-looking man, in a dark cloak with a white turban. As was only to be expected he looked unhappy and uneasy when Sultan, whom he recognised at once, introduced him to me. Then he took Saifyan aside and sat down with him. After about half an hour's talk, by which time we were in an agony of suspense and curiosity, Sultan came over and said, "It's no good, he says we must all go away, we have no right here, and if we do not go Talib will come and destroy us."

Percy Coriat, who had joined us, fumed when he heard this. "Tell the silly idiot we have surrounded him, show him the troops and the Duru down in the grove." (Many of the latter were now plainly visible from where we were.)

"I have done that," said Sultan.

Percy looked angry and he went over and spoke to Saifyan in Arabic; his determination to keep out of politics seemed suddenly to have evaporated. He said that he guaranteed to let them go safely out of the area and back to Nizwa if they surrendered, otherwise the fort would be attacked and some might be killed. He left us snorting indignantly and went back to his troops.

I then tried my hand, and afterwards asked Sultan to have another go. I thought perhaps that things might swing our way. Percy had evidently made an impression. At length, after what seemed a long time, Sultan came over to us and said that Saifyan had agreed to instruct his men to surrender. A note was to be taken to the fort by the follower, with the instruction that the men should come out.

But still we were, however, not altogether sure if all was well and I, therefore, suggested to Sultan that it would be wise to have the note intercepted. This was done and we were not so very surprised to find that it said something very different. It told Saifyan's men that he was being held prisoner and they must not surrender. Percy was back with us again when we learnt this interesting development, and he managed to look very fierce and angry and said something very loudly to Shaikh Sultan bin Saif about the danger of double-crossing him. Saifyan seemed to take note of this and looked very sheepish.

By now it was nearly three o'clock in the afternoon and we had all been sitting in the hot sun, occasionally refreshed by coffee produced by one of the Yaaqib. I thought that our physical discomfort could only help us, as Saifyan seemed to suffer the heat worse than we did.

I said to Sultan, "Please tell him again that we know he must agree to the surrender proposal, he and his men will be safe, better for all of us that he should make his mind up quickly."

Sultan had another long talk and this ended with Saifyan writing a letter which ordered the garrison to come out and meet us at the edge of the town. This was dispatched by hand by the follower.

There was another long wait during which I think we all had made up our minds that there was another trick being played. None of us had slept much, if at all, the night before, or indeed for several nights, we were all extremely tired, and we realised that if the garrison did not come out there was nothing that we could do to force them to do so. An ignominious rebuff seemed only too likely, and we knew what the Sultan in Salalah would say if we failed. Only Angus remained cheerful and optimistic. I myself once more felt that the thing was going wrong.

Suddenly Nick shouted, "I think they are coming."

A rather sad collection of 50 men, some young, some rather elderly, all in traditional Omani headgear and Arab robes and cloaks, were filing past the corner house of the town into the open in front of us.

Percy looked most relieved, but said it was up to Shaikh Sultan bin Saif to take the surrender; he would stay where he was, he had no permission to take part in this sort of thing.

I suggested to Sultan that they should lay down their arms. These would be put in one of our trucks, and with Saifyan and a follower, they would be taken a short way up the track towards Nizwa and deposited under a tree. The garrison could walk there and pick them up. Food and water would be provided to start them off, but they must make their own way out of the area. Sultan agreed, and we went across to speak to them.

It was a scene I shall never forget. The 50 men had walked slowly out of the gap between the houses which gave on to the *wadi* bed where we now were. They made a line in the shade with their backs to a wall which enclosed a date grove. As I have said earlier, the Omani is a proud man, he walks with short quick steps holding his body stiffly upright, head back, and with a natural grace. Their very way of walking distinguishes them. These men were all Omanis, their jaunty sprightliness had gone, but yet they held their customary pose with dignity. Not surprisingly they seemed astonished. They had never seen foreigners, certainly not Europeans, before. They were surrendering technically to Shaikh Sultan bin Saif and to an

Arab force, but who were these strange people with them, what were these strange vehicles that had brought them? These were the first strangers in history to come from the south, the first vehicles of their kind to come to Ibri from anywhere. No wonder they looked amazed and frightened.

I felt that I ought to have been embarrassed at such an encounter with honourable and decent people in such an unfortunate position. We ourselves were, however, anxious and tense with the responsibility of the situation. We knew that it was in all our interests that these men should simply go away, and now that they seemed prepared to do so we thought it impossibly good luck. I myself still feared that even at this late moment something unfortunate might happen to prevent a happy solution.

They stood silently in the shade of the wall and trees. They each wore a multicoloured Kashmiri scarf wound as a turban round their heads, all had beards, some black, many orange-red with henna dye, some few were white and wispy. They were mostly tall, for Omanis tend to height. Their eyes looked down and they scarcely spoke. I suppose they thought that they would all be shot, and they could not realise that I was anxious only to get them out of the town, decently but quickly.

Sultan passed the word to them that they were to lay their arms down in the sand. Nothing happened. He spoke again and one of his men ran up the line. It was a very tense moment, and the atmosphere was brittle. For a tribesman to give up his arms was akin to giving up his life, and only in hopeless circumstances, when leadership is absent, will they do this. As the word passed a second time, the first man stepped a pace forward and put his Lee Enfield on the sand in front of us.

Shaikh Sultan bin Saif, bright and alert as ever, turned to me and said, "Do not worry, my friend, all will be well."

He looked as if a great weight of responsibility had fallen from his shoulders, he smiled and the little creases at the corners of his temples tightened. He was happy, and I knew that for the moment, at least, we had gained our immediate objective.

Soon all the rifles were laid out in front of us, roughly in a line. Some were British Lee Enfield of various vintages, some were Mauser, and one of these pieces, a remarkable one, was a muzzle loader of enormous length with a smooth bore. This would have done us no harm, but the others were serious weapons to be reckoned with.

I called to our drivers and asked them to load these weapons into one of our lorries. This they did. I then got hold of our most trusted driver, an Omani who knew the camel-caravan route to Nizwa, and arranged with him that the arms would be unloaded by a certain tree about five miles away on the camel track. Then he asked Saifyan and one of his men to get into the truck and ride as far as the tree, then they were to get down and stay with the weapons to act as guards.

They climbed into the truck and went off, and as soon as it had disappeared, I asked Sultan to tell the unhappy garrison to walk on after them, disgraced, unarmed and on foot.

After a few words the unhappy group walked off up the *wadi* in the wake of the vehicle and their arms, and their honour. It must have been a bitter moment for them.

Chapter Thirteen

Looking back, it is easier to assess the historical significance of such moments, but even at that time we were conscious that we had reached a turning point in the history of Oman. The Sultan at that moment had become the direct ruler of much of the interior, and certainly its deserts. Whether oil flowed or not, a political advance of importance had been made; and if oil were found, it would be as a result of that day's work. I could see no prospect of obtaining the necessary conditions for search and production of oil if Oman were allowed to break up into separate parts, as it had seemed to be on the point of doing.

With the knowledge of what has happened since, I think that there can be little doubt that if Talib had continued his attempt at a separatist movement and dragged the Duru with him, against their will, the modern development of the whole state of Oman which the oil revenue now makes possible, would have been delayed for very many years.

What was uppermost in my mind at that time was the miserable condition of the inhabitants of this remote area. The bedouin really lived at below subsistence level, infant mortality was very high, young men and women aged quickly and were senile in what we call middle age. They had virtually no property and for food relied almost entirely on dates. Rice and meat were a great rarity, a little fruit was available in the markets in early summer, and some vegetables in the villages; but in the desert they lived almost entirely on dates and camels' milk.

Once the shaikhs had explained the reasons for our coming, the bedouin had become extraordinarily friendly; and we found them amusing and pleasant company. Of course they saw me as a source of money, and who can blame them for making the most of an opportunity; but when the immediate crisis passed off and we had no need of an irregular force, their importunities slackened. The people of Ibri itself were slightly better off than the desert folk, and after the fort had been surrendered they showered embarrassing hospitality upon us; for these people who have so little are generous with what they do have.

The Sultan had no source of revenue sufficient to enable him to develop and administer the interior. When he succeeded his father in 1931 the state treasury was in debt. By the early 1950s the books balanced, but he had a large domain.

The coastline is over 1,000 miles in length, the population of Oman was then believed to be about 750,000, but it may have been a million. There were no roads, no developed water system, there was only one small missionary hospital in the whole country and there was no electricity outside the capital and very little in it. The highest mountains reached 10,000 feet. The villages were in separate valleys making communication both between them and the coast and between each other difficult; but even if revenues had been available, the development of such an area, with difficult climatic conditions, presented a daunting prospect. The Sultan kept assuring us he was desperately anxious to find the revenue through oil in order to develop the country. The oil, if it existed, was almost certain to be found under the desert, in the Duru's ranging grounds, but the mountainous interior stood between the coast and any potential oilfield. He needed to extend his authority and to replace influence with direct rule.

Under the Agreement of Sib in theory some arrangement might have been made to develop the oil resources by agreement with the tribes, but I had little hope in that direction. Now Talib had broken the traditional observation of the Sib Agreement by seizing Ibri and had then been driven out again by the MFF, it seemed that the way might be open for the Sultan to establish direct rule at least in the oilfield area, to give time to the Company to prospect and produce. If Talib were allowed to continue his attempt to make a separate country out of the interior, against the wish, as we know, of many of the tribes, no stability could be secured in which any oil company could work. Progress would be postponed indefinitely. The key to the whole problem lay, I knew, in the establishment of the authority of the Sultan in Ibri, and its extension after oil had been found.

After the truck had driven away with the arms, and the garrison had walked off up the *wadi* bed and disappeared, Percy Coriat had them discreetly followed and observed until after they had picked up their arms and continued some miles on their way towards Nizwa. Shaikh Sultan called me and we went into one of the neighbouring date groves and sat down on a tree trunk to talk it over.

"Oh my friend," he said, "God had willed that a good thing should happen here." But, he added with a smile, "He would wish us to make certain of it and, God willing, we can do what is needed. Those people of Talib's have now gone from here, but we must be sure that all the towns and villages of this region will reject the Imam if he tries to return; and above all we must make sure of Dariz and the valley leading from there to the Wadi Hawasini where my people are. Then we will have consolidated this area. You must at once persuade the Colonel to do what is necessary to bring this about. Patrols to the villages are essential. Will you do this?"

I did not explain that the Company headquarters, situated in the mezzanine and other higher floors of Peter Robinson's in Oxford Street, would have had a fit at such a proposal, and would fire me at once; but I said that of course I agreed, it was just what I was thinking myself.

We then discussed the problem in more detail. The fort of Ainain, the large village of Dariz, the twin villages Al Araqi, the fort and village of Silaif, and the village of Bat, all these must declare against Talib and for the Sultan if any stability were to be gained; and we in Ibri must be ready to withstand, if need be, a counter-attack from hundreds of irregular tribesmen within perhaps two weeks. If we could cover all these points the immediate future was reasonably secure. If not we would be in trouble and could as easily lose all that we had gained.

I readily agreed with Shaikh Sultan's appreciation; and with his help I put on paper an assessment of the local tribal position as he then saw it. I had come armed with all the information which I could obtain from existing written records and I had in addition been interrogating any bedouin I met over a period of some months, but Sultan's balanced appreciation of the current political position among the tribes and his assessment of the strength and reliability of the shaikhs was essential as a basis for future planning.

The success which we had achieved so far we owed to the good sense, tact and tribal knowledge of my friend Shaikh Sultan bin Saif Al Hawsini. Short, thickset, dressed in a simple white Arab shirt or robe, that reached his ankles with a black cloak, the edges piped with gold draped on his shoulders and flowing loose to the ground, he wore on his head a white headcloth with black head-rope. He had an alert, friendly and cheerful manner; nothing seemed to depress him, and in our more difficult moments surrounded by a mob of importunate bedouin, he alone was smiling and calm, while I would be on edge, maddened by the difficulties that seemed to frustrate everything we attempted.

His wisdom, calm and coolness were outstanding and one could see why the Sultan prized him above all the shaikhs of this region. He taught me to be patient with the bedouin, and when they became too difficult he would intervene, and save me much of the wear and tear of the argument. Sultan did much to explain to me the reasons why the bedouin could become so difficult and the causes of their all too common human failings, which make them so often the enemies of their own real interests.

As a companion I have never met a more sympathetic warm-hearted person than Sultan. When the bedouin clustered about us shouting and pushing, he would have ready an amusing quip. When the Duru shaikhs refused to help us over an essential operation, he would make a joke of it. His sympathetic smile bridged the gap of cultures between us, and I am sure he was quicker to learn my ways and habits, than I was to appreciate his. He spoke not a word of English, but I was beginning to count him almost as an occidentalist. He appreciated our attitude and could assess our reactions accurately.

After the garrison had left we sat talking in the shade of the trees, and one of his followers would now and then bring us bedouin coffee or sweet tea to refresh us. I said that patrols laid on systematically under his direction were the obvious solution, but I doubted if we could do it so simply. Let him arrange to visit all the leading shaikhs in each village, I would go with him and we would ask the MFF for protection. Sultan smiled at this suggestion, but readily agreed; and he added, not for the first time, "And if you bring an aeroplane, all our troubles will be over."

The afternoon of 27 October was a happy one in the history of Ibri. At about five o'clock Sultan and I broke off our talk and we met Shaikh Muhammad bin Abdullah Al Yaaqubi by the edge of the town near where the garrison had surrendered, and with the shaikhs and many of the Duru followers made our way to the fort. Our companions and the townspeople were all excited, and as we approached the fort loosed off their rifles in all directions.

The carefree way in which we all entered the fort to a fusillade of small arms was much the most dangerous part of the day's proceedings. The fort is large and rambling with very thick walls, and although its courtyards could be dominated by troops on the surrounding heights, its towers have thick walls and narrow slit windows; it was quite obvious that the garrison could easily have kept our small force out of the fort as long as their food and water lasted. But stocks of both we found were very low. It must have been partly this and partly the low morale which induced the surrender.

In the courtyard we were shown the gun, a big muzzle loader with a bore of some three or four inches, which stood ready loaded pointing roughly to the main MFF position. From the way it was sited I doubted if the large ball would have cleared the wall of the fort. The ball was then removed and the barrel packed with rubbish and the gun fired in celebration. It made a rather feeble boom, but with a great deal of smoke and flame. This was accompanied by cheers and many more shots from our Duru irregulars.

That evening, Shaikh Muhammad bin Abdullah Al Yaaqubi insisted on our staying the night in a new mosque in the grove to the north-east of the town. He apologised because he had no suitable houses to put us in; and we felt rather embarrassed at taking over a mosque, but there was no refusing his offer for a night or so at least, and it put me in mind of the ancient practice of quartering troops in churches in Europe. It also showed the natural tolerance of the Ibri people. This is how they welcomed the first really foreign and non-Muslim group of any size to come to Ibri.

The MFF took up position on the heights and built rough defensive positions, *sangars,* there. We did not expect any immediate counter-attack from Talib since he had no motor transport at all, and his main force was reported to be in Rustaq, but after a week or so we thought it likely that he would make some move against us.

Percy Coriat made a strong-point with slit-trenches by the *wadi* just north of the gap in the hills through which the *wadi* runs. After two nights spent in the date grove he said he could not guarantee our safety unless we moved into the strong-point area. He was right to move us, although I could not see that he was in a position to guarantee our safety wherever we were. However, we complied and a very uncomfortable time was had, since we still had no tents, but some camp beds had now been sent up. Angus had gone back to Duqm and among other things organised traffic along our now very lengthy supply route. Our water supply was perfectly satisfactory for as long as we stayed in Ibri where there was plenty, but all petrol and food had to come from Duqm; and the convoys took two or even three days, as many of the vehicles were by now giving trouble after the bashing the desert tracks had given them (and us!).

I suffered a brief attack of malaria, and being confined during daytime to a camp bed under the narrow shade of a palm tree, with the air temperature in the shade around 100°F in the day, was far from amusing, and to keep in the shade meant moving my bed every half an hour or so. Moreover the bedouin kept visiting me, and although I had paid off the private army of the Duru, bedouin came flocking in looking for 'help'. Our strong-point camp was very congested and I longed for the peace afforded by desert camp life, and its comparative privacy. These were trying days.

But by 31 October I felt a little better. Shaikh Sultan bin Saif was now more worried than ever that so many surrounding villages had not yet declared their allegiance to the Sultan of Muscat. They needed a little more encouragement, and if we dared not visit them they would assume we were afraid of Talib; this would prevent them showing their hand in favour of the Sultan. Shaikh Sultan thought he should call on them, but, as I had feared, we were told that the MFF would not be allowed to go with him; if I were to go, according to the curious rules of the game which we were playing, they would have to come. Percy had confirmed this rather reluctantly; but he was firm that he should not on his own initiative send out patrols. "After all I should not be here at all, and when the Sultan hears, I shall get the most fearful rocket, old boy!"

Accordingly on 31 October, Shaikh Sultan bin Saif and I set off in my Land Rover followed by the MFF platoon in trucks which was under the command of Major Mike O'Kelly.

I had heard so much of these places near Ibri that I was now excited to see them. When one has talked and talked about places, discussed the personalities and allegiance of their shaikhs, and discussed the relative strength and importance of their forts, one has a picture of them and it is fascinating to see the reality.

Our first objective was the Arab part of Al Araqi village, a group of habitations that was half-Baluch, half-Arab. We had some reason to believe the Arab shaikh had now declared his loyalty to the Sultan; but when we approached we saw no reassuring red flag flying on the north-eastern quarter.

At the end of the village we stopped our vehicles and Shaikh Sultan, myself and a few of his followers went forward on foot. As we came round the corner of the first house we could see, by the entrance to the fort, and in its courtyard, a group of armed men. Sultan said to me, "Watch out, these are the Imam's people."

He bravely held his ground while I went back to shout to Mike O'Kelly to ask him to come to our aid. This Mike very quickly did, and at once came up to the fort at the head of two sections carrying Brens and rifles. The appearance of the troops enabled Sultan to persuade the 'enemy' to withdraw. He at once called the shaikh of the village and asked him to find some friendly armed men to man the fort. He soon collected ten villagers whose loyalty he trusted and we saw them go into the fort.

The waiting period while the 'enemy' were removed and friends put in their place was filled as usual with the drinking of coffee and tea. Rugs were spread for us in the courtyard of the main fort and we were able to watch the unusual scene in comfort. It was not unlike a Shakespearean play in which the enemy are on one side of the stage, and the supposedly 'good' people of the play on the other, at one and the same time, seemingly unaware of each other's presence. But this was reality, not a scene on a stage. The atmosphere in the fort was extremely tense, and there was little conversation, but both Mike O'Kelly and Shaikh Sultan bin Saif managed to look very relaxed. I suppose the little drama took no more than 15 minutes.

I was extremely relieved when Sultan declared that we could now safely move on, as the well-disposed people were firmly established, their shaikh professing utmost loyalty to the Sultan, and the 'enemy' had just departed (having had coffee of course). Our next objective was the great fort of Ainain, which, as its name indicates, sits astride the line of two water channels. Its domination of the water channels, which are the sources of water for Ibri and Al Araqi, gives it importance and this and its size ensures for it a special significance in terms of old-fashioned tribal fighting. It would, of course, be hopelessly vulnerable to modern artillery or rocket attack, but to such weapons as were available at that time to the Omanis, it was virtually impregnable.

The fortress lies near Al Araqi in the middle of the small plain at either end of which are Ibri and Dariz. Making a circuit of the gardens of Al Araqi we took a winding path to it among the stunted trees and bushes that are typical of the area of the foothills. The plain was still and silent, and the morning air rather oppressive. Mike O'Kelly now decided to keep right up with us in case, despite Shaikh Sultan bin Saif's assurances, there were some of the enemy in Ainain as well, and we advanced roughly in line abreast.

As we drew close to the fort we could see the Sultan's red flag flying from the upper turret. We were, however, met by a fusillade of shots, and Mike and I both stopped our vehicles. "Go on, go on," said Shaikh Sultan bin Saif in genuine surprise and concern, "this is their way of welcoming us." We should have known better I suppose, but it does take some getting used to, and how is one to know they are not firing at you with rather poor aim?

Welcome indeed it was. Several men came running out of the main door with shouts and broad smiles to greet us. Their leader was the son of the Shaikh of Dariz. The shaikh had been forced to acknowledge Ghalib when the Imam's army came through, and had to quarter some of them in his village. But he had considered himself powerless to resist. He was, therefore, forced to raise the Imam's white flag on Ainain fort, and instructed his son, who usually held that place on his father's behalf, to recognise the Imam and his brother when they came here. This he had naturally been obliged to do.

When the Shaikh of Dariz heard that Ibri had fallen and heard the news of the departure on foot of the garrison, he decided that he could safely show his allegiance to the Sultan, and sent messengers to Shaikh Sultan bin Saif to this effect. The flag on Ainain had then been changed again, and his son was ordered to welcome us and accompany us to Dariz whenever we should appear.

From Ainain's ramparts we could see Dariz clearly across the plain a few miles away and we looked eagerly at its fort to see what kind of flag was flying. Through Mike's binoculars it looked much nearer to white than red, but we could not be sure. The Shaikh's son laughed when questioned on this all important point, and said, "Yes, father's flags have all faded and he gave me the reddest one as this fort would be the first you would reach."

He then assured us he would go with us to see his father. I was relieved at this since despite Shaikh Sultan bin Saif's assurances and apparent readiness to take risks, I was beginning to feel less than keen to accompany him to each new place, unless we had some of the people of the shaikh concerned with us.

After coffee we set off with the young shaikh sitting in the Land Rover between Shaikh Sultan bin Saif and myself. This time we all drove straight up to the fort in a close group. There was no firing and no excitement; very few people were about in the narrow streets between the square mud houses.

The young shaikh ran in to get his father and we waited outside. The old man came out almost at once, a dignified figure with a white beard and wrinkled smiling face, and greeted Shaikh Sultan bin Saif warmly with the bedouin embrace and touching of noses; then he asked us all in to his *majlis*. Mike first posted his soldiers and then joined us.

We were entertained with coffee, tea and hot milk with cinnamon. The room was quite a large one, furnished as is usual in that area, with Persian and Baluchi carpets. As we sat talking, more and more of the villagers came in and we stood to shake hands with each group.

The shaikh then invited us to lunch. As it was only eleven o'clock in the morning, and Shaikh Sultan bin Saif said lunch could not be prepared in less than two or three hours, as the sheep would not have been killed yet, I suggested that we should visit the Baluchi quarter at Al Araqi first and then return. This was agreed.

Sultan bin Saif's tactics with regard to the Baluch were as follows. He doubted whether they would readily accept the allegiance of the Sultan. This particular section of the Baluch have been in the area many years. Although their ancestors originated in Baluchistan, those in the interior of Oman speak Arabic and dress and live as Arabs. The village had rather a reputation for opposition to the Muscat Government. Over the last 30 years, this had meant little, and there had been no actual fighting between the Baluch and other Omanis but Shaikh Sultan bin Saif thought that the arrival of uniformed soldiers from Muscat, for the first time in history, might cause trouble. I had no reason to disagree with this assessment; and as with all our dealings with tribes, relied on his judgement.

Shaikh Sultan bin Saif thought that now that Ibri, Ainain, Dariz and the Arab quarter of Al Araqi were flying the Sultan's governmental flag, the Baluch, who were small in numbers, would have no option but to follow suit. This seemed a logical argument, and it had been for this reason that he had bypassed this village and left it to the last of this group.

We advanced in our trucks to within 200 yards of the Baluchi village. All was quiet, no flag was flying and no people were in sight. The son of the Shaikh of Dariz had come with us, and Shaikh Sultan bin Saif also had several men from Ibri with him. He calculated that the presence of the Shaikh's son would prevent any trouble, since if the Baluch fired on any party of which this man was a member, there would at once be a feud with the people of Dariz. Ainain fort was astride the main part of the village water supply and the position of the inhabitants of Al Araqi would be impossible if they were at war with whoever held Ainain. This sounded all very reasonable, but I said I did not feel like driving straight into Al Araqi without Mike and the MFF, nor did I even much like the obvious alternative of going in with the troops since this would almost certainly prove to be provocative. So we discussed what we should do.

Shaikh Sultan bin Saif was the most accommodating of men. He may have thought me a little unhelpful not to drive in with him, but he agreed at once that it was unsafe for any of us to go in; and even added, perhaps as a sop to our conscience, that the presence of Europeans in the first instance might produce the wrong effect. The Baluch might feel entitled to fire at foreigners, whoever was with them, and they were likely to resent uniforms even more.

Shaikh Sultan bin Saif said, "I will go in with my party on foot. If I do not come out within 10 minutes you are free to take what action you like, but I am sure it will be all right."

The patrol had drawn up some 200 yards from the houses. Shaikh Sultan bin Saif gathered his men and set off on foot into the village. They disappeared round the corner of a house and then there was silence. Mike deployed his men, and we sat and waited.

Although Shaikh Sultan bin Saif had seemed so confident, I was worried about him, and I wondered how

Sharjah airstrip, 1948. This point is now near the centre of downtown Sharjah. (*R. Codrai*)

Drilling at Jebel Ali, Dubai, in 1951. Shaikh Saeed bin Maktoum, Ruler of Dubai 1912-1958, with the author. (*R. Codrai*)

Jebel Fahud from the air, 1950. (*R. Codrai*)

His Excellency Saiyid Ahmed bin Ibrahim, Minister of the Interior in Muscat, Oman. (*Sultanate of Oman*)

Fort Mirani, Muscat, Oman. (*R. Codrai*)

Paramount shaikh of the Hawasinah, Shaikh Sultan bin Saif Al Hawsini, photographed in 1988. (*Rehma Studio Al Khabura*)

His Highness Shaikh Shakhbut welcomes His Highness Sultan Said bin Taimor to Al Ain in December 1955.

Colonel Eric Johnson in Buraimi after the fighting stopped.

Silaif, Oman (*R. Codrai*)

Abu Dhabi Fort with the British Agency in the foreground, 1959. (*R. Codrai*)

on earth we could rescue him if he met resistance since we had a force of merely 25 men and two Bren guns.

We waited a full ten minutes with no sounds except the common noises of an Omani village, the ever-present squeak of a well-pulley, the cries of poultry and the periodic noise of water swishing into the water channel from the leather bucket that is pulled by the ox.

Then round the corner of the house came one of Shaikh Sultan bin Saif's men. He ran over to us and said in some excitement that Shaikh Sultan bin Saif had been well received and he was trying to persuade the shaikh, Rashid bin Said of the Baluch, to come out to meet us. But he did not want us to go into the village.

We all felt better after hearing this news, but we were kept waiting another half-hour before we saw the squat figure of Shaikh Sultan bin Saif coming out from among the houses accompanied by the white-bearded Shaikh Rashid of the Baluch and several followers from each side.

The shaikhs came very slowly towards us. I thought that the Sultan's soldiers in what was their inevitably offensive looking positions behind Brens and rifles had something less than a friendly air. Perhaps this was what was upsetting the shaikh. When he finally came up to us the old shaikh looked far from pleased. We shook hands. He said very simply, with or without irony I shall never know, "I acknowledge my loyalty to His Highness the Sultan as ever before." Not much more was said, the shaikh took his leave and walked back to the village. Mike ordered his troops into the trucks and we drove back to Dariz. No flag, however, flew over the Baluch quarter of Al Araqi; "Perhaps he hasn't got one," said Shaikh Sultan bin Saif with a smile.

At Dariz we found the whole village in a festive mood. We were immediately invited into the main *majlis* of the fort where the shaikh greeted us warmly.

We all sat down and had coffee amidst a buzz of friendly conversation. We described our visit to Al Araqi and the shaikh laughed hugely when we told him how glum Shaikh Rashid had been.

Shaikh Sultan bin Saif warned me that lunch was still not ready and recommended a walk round the village to look at the farms. This was agreed and we were made very welcome and given coffee and tea and yet more hot camel's milk and cinnamon by several villagers in their houses.

Then we were summoned back to the fort where a large meal was spread out on rugs and sheets in the open under the trees.

I was placed between Shaikh Sultan bin Saif and the old Shaikh of Dariz. We talked of tribal matters, and, knowing that his tribe, originally Bani Ghafir, was commonly known as the Miyayaha, I said in all innocence, *"Inta Miyahi"*, meaning, "You are a Miyahi" (or a tribesman from the Miyayaha). This produced guffaws of laughter, but the shaikh looked very embarrassed, and I changed the subject.

Shaikh Sultan bin Saif afterwards explained to me that the word Miyayaha (adjective Miyahi) means changing of sides and was used as a name for this section of the Bani Ghafir because it changed its faction. Thus to say what I said really meant, "You are a changer of sides." As he had changed the colour of his flag only that day, this was felt to be much too apt, and accounted for the way in which his followers had dissolved in laughter. Shaikh Sultan bin Saif had guessed that I had not meant it that way, and that I did not understand the meaning of the name, but doubtless the others thought I had done it on purpose; and if ever afterwards I wanted to make Shaikh Sultan bin Saif laugh I had only to remind him of this gaffe of mine. We returned to Ibri well satisfied with a good day's work.

My opinion of Sultan bin Saif's judgement and ability had already been high, and now it was looking as if he was nearly infallible on tribal affairs. I also thought he had shown great courage in going into Al Araqi on his own.

We were still worried about Silaif. Our information was that the fort was unoccupied, and the villagers loyal to the Sultan. It was said that some six people had been killed in the original attack on Silaif, and although it did not look likely that there would be another attack on the place immediately, it did seem only prudent to make sure of it, as later the Imam might try to seize it as a prelude to an attack on Ibri. This seemed to be a standard practice for anyone wishing to take Ibri, and it would prove very embarrassing to us if he did this again.

Percy Coriat did not altogether agree on its military importance, but I pointed out that, in these tribal affairs, it is only what seems to be of importance to the tribes that matters, never mind orthodox military principles. They usually run their tribal affairs by accepted rules, rather like a game of chess, and casualties are kept to a minimum if the rules are observed. If a large force presents itself before a village, the village usually surrenders, since it can do so without loss of face. This is really the secret of such skirmishing. If certain forts are captured the allegiance of a whole region can be changed. It is, however, vital to capture all the right forts. Therefore, we should anticipate Talib's moves and make moves to counter them; and when he heard of the action we had taken it would, I hoped, discourage him altogether from attacking in this area. If we left key forts empty it would be an open invitation. This was the very mistake Talib had made and which enabled us to come in.

However, Percy was quite right in refusing to put any of his own men into Silaif. It is a good military principle to keep a small force concentrated, and he still had only 126 men.

I tried therefore to persuade Shaikh Sultan bin Saif to collect loyal irregulars to garrison Silaif. He had no authority from his master to do anything, except to assist the Company; he still had no government money, but I could lend him cash, hoping we would be repaid by the Muscat Government later. He was, therefore, in a delicate position, not knowing for certain the wishes of the Sultan of Muscat 500 miles away, but guessing disapproval of such tactics. Yet he agreed at length to my proposal.

The following day, again with Mike O'Kelly and a platoon, we went to Silaif. The villagers streamed out to greet us and assured us that the fort was without a garrison. The door of the fort was in fact wide open and there was no one in it.

Silaif fort is in a commanding position some four miles south-east of Ibri on the same ridge that skirts the north of the latter town. The fort is built at another break in the ridge similar to the gorge at Ibri. It is partly built on a low cliff and with curtain walls which straggle up the hill and reminded me of those at Antioch, but on a much smaller scale. Our ten men, whom we had taken up for the purpose, could not hope to hold it against a force of any size, but they might prevent a small force from getting into it, and this was all Shaikh Sultan could manage for a time. Percy Coriat promised to send patrols to it periodically in order to encourage its defenders.

The valley system of which Ibri and Dariz form the centre, had now become a bloc in which all the people with the exception of those in a village called Bat, had acknowledged the Sultan. Shaikh Rashid of the Baluch controlled all the other Baluch villages to the west. We counted on Ainain fort and its commanding position over the water channels to keep him in line.

Bat village was at a point which commanded an important valley on one of the routes to the east and, to complete the job of assuring allegiance of the shaikhs of the key places, it was essential to visit this village and persuade its shaikh to show his hand.

On 3 November Shaikh Sultan bin Saif, Mike O'Kelly and I went to Bat with this aim, accompanied by a patrol of MFF. Shaikh Sultan wanted all of us to stay outside the village to begin with as the situation might become delicate, he thought; therefore, we halted on a prominent little hill near the village and sent in on foot an emissary to explain our presence and our aims. He returned some time later with a village notable called Salim who was under instructions from the elderly, indeed senile, village shaikh, to discuss the question of allegiance with Shaikh Sultan bin Saif, and go with us to Ibri for the purpose. They seemed prepared to accept the Sultan as their Ruler, but he wished for an adequate force to overawe the village in order to make his submission appear not too readily given. As they correctly considered they were unable to defend themselves from the Imam's army, they had ample justification for seeking an insurance policy to protect themselves from Talib's wrath.

In the event, by delaying a day, they lost their chance of appearing to submit to a sizeable force. The patrol that went with us on 3 November had consisted of some 20 men. By the time we got back to Ibri we discovered that Percy Coriat had received fresh orders by radio from Salalah reiterating that he was to send no patrols at all. I explained to him how serious it would be politically if Bat did not acknowledge the Sultan and at least by implication disavow the Imam; but the best I could get from him was the promise of an escort of two soldiers for myself and Shaikh Sultan bin Saif, if we were unwise enough to visit Bat again contrary to his advice. Percy now had his radio working, connecting him with Duqm and thus in turn Salalah, and he could get in touch with the Sultan again; but the Sultan, who had disapproved very strongly of our entry into Ibri, could not be persuaded by radio messages that the policy we were following was not only right but was proving a great success. Direct contact with his master now tied Percy's hands completely.

The interdiction on patrolling not only put an end to moves designed to secure the extension of the Sultanate's direct authority in the whole Ibri area, but it also brought to an end a plan we had formulated for obtaining the allegiance of the shaikhs of Dhank, a place some 40 miles to the north. We had already been in touch with some of the leaders from Dhank who had come into Ibri. Dhank is an important communications centre, only a little less significant politically than Ibri itself; and it was a pity we could not do anything there. As it turned out, its shaikhs did not formally acknowledge the direct rule of the Sultan for two further years, after the Saudis had left the Buraimi area.

To revert to the problem of Bat, Salim turned out to be an extremely reasonable and intelligent man; sent by his shaikh with instructions to negotiate for a larger force than the 20 which had first come to the village on 3 November, he in the end found himself being talked into accepting a ridiculous 'force' of only two soldiers.

At first he would of course have none of it, but the irony of the situation must have so fascinated him, he started to laugh and then decided to agree. "But," he said, "it must be first thing tomorrow, since I shall have to convince my shaikh that I was given no alternative. If I were to tell him this in advance, he would start to argue and then we should never get anywhere; and what is more, we shall have to enter Bat together."

Shaikh Sultan bin Saif and I discussed the wisdom of this after Salim had agreed to our proposal. He thought it would be all right. I reluctantly agreed. "Moreover," said Shaikh Sultan bin Saif, "if it works it could prove a great gain, as it will show that in fact no pressure is needed to induce admission of allegiance to the Sultan." This was an important point, but was the risk worth taking?

We parted for the night chuckling at the ironical turns which this little affair seemed to be taking and, having arranged for our 'escort' to parade at sunrise, we went to sleep on it.

We set out the following morning in three vehicles (one would have carried us all, but three looked so much better) and we reached the neighbourhood of Bat still in the cool of the morning. On this occasion, as we had previously agreed, we all drove in together.

From the very first, as soon as we reached the houses, we were welcomed with the greatest possible warmth and friendliness. The old shaikh, too decrepit to walk, could barely stand to greet us; but he received us in front of his unpretentious mud-brick house, surrounded by all the men of the village.

We were invited to lunch, but excused ourselves and instead were entertained with tea, coffee, fruit and cheese, dishes on as lavish a scale as the place could provide; and it was after mid-day before we could get away. Salim seemed to have great influence over the shaikh and his elders, and his first words had been sufficient to persuade them to accept the *fait accompli* with as brave a face as possible, despite the disadvantage that this proclaimed to the country at large, and the Imam in particular, how genuine was their loyalty to the Sultan. By strong contrast, when they had earlier submitted to Ghalib and Talib, the Imam had with him a force reputed to be of 400 men.

Salim came back with us to Ibri to stay another night as the guest of Shaikh Muhammad of the Yaaqib, who arranged a celebration dinner for us all that evening.

Shaikh Sultan bin Saif and I felt rather pleased with ourselves, and we all had a good time that evening with considerable laughter and fun, and perhaps too much mutual congratulation.

These days of patrols up the valley were interspersed with much feasting in Ibri. The villagers vied with one another to have Shaikh Sultan to meals in their houses. We continued to live in the palm-grove to the north of the town, but at meal times, when I was not out on patrol, we would find ourselves in one or other of the houses. As the weather was still hot, meals would usually be spread out under an awning in the courtyard. We would sit on rugs, with cushions between each guest and his neighbour. Twenty or thirty, sometimes many more, would sit round each meal, which invariably consisted of mounds of beautifully cooked rice surmounted by whole sheep or goats. Little dishes of cheese, tomatoes and fruit would be round the main dish.

Some excursions into Ibri houses gave me the chance to see the way of life of the inhabitants. Ibri's market was narrow and rather dark, but the cooler for its darkness. Only the simplest daily needs were available, and I noticed very little tinned food at all. As far as I could discover, a little battery set with dry batteries in the shaikh's house was the only one in all Ibri. This meant that people were ill-informed, or perhaps not informed at all about anything that went on outside their immediate neighbourhood. They would know about happenings in Dubai or Muscat, and in Zanzibar where all the main Omani tribes were then well represented, but they knew little of Kuwait or Bahrain, nothing of Persia and almost nothing of Saudi Arabia, except when some of their number went on pilgrimage, and this seemed rather uncommon because of the distance and lack of money.

Men and women would work in the little fields and vegetable gardens. There would be work for the men cleaning and repairing the underground water channels, and the older boys spent much of their day with herds of goats on the little hills around, or in the main valley. The women spent a lot of time at the water basin. The water ran first in a tunnel then a channel from a source up the valley. Where it came out of its tunnel was the large basin, lined with large blocks of stone, used for drawing drinking water. Immediately below it, the stream divided and in each channel were basins for washing clothes, again lined with stones. Next below these were the bathing places, one for men and one for women, discreetly screened with wattle fencing. We were permitted to use the men's bathing area, and sitting in the strong stream I once let my Lux soap slip and thought this a serious loss. I need not have worried, ten minutes later a small boy brought it back: it had been intercepted in the women's section below.

Ibri had a great beauty, in those days when almost nothing in the modern industrial world was yet visible. Everything was locally made: houses of local clay bricks, walls of brown clay, huts of palm fronds, pathways of clay beaten smooth by the feet of passers-by, the market's roof was of wood and palm frond, and around the houses pressing on them from all sides the rich green gardens of date palms with lush patches of vegetables and lucerne among them. In the tiny shops in the *souq* almost everything was locally made and there were very few manufactured goods from abroad available.

In that month it was still hot, but dry by day and warm and it was pleasant by night: and the most noticeable thing about Ibri, if you once got away from the market or the watering places where people assembled, was its stillness. Looking out across the narrow valley from the palm groves to the steep hills and crags the scene was quite still, with scarcely anything moving. The heat at midday seemed to drip from the brown and reddish crags on the north and east. When there was no wind the hot air seemed to be draped like folds of cloth on the scene, perhaps the only movement was the distant figure of a peasant walking along a track at the edge of the palm grove, footsteps silent in the soft sandy earth. The few sounds that came to one seemed almost detached from what was basically a silent, apparently uninhabited, scene, the occasional crowing of cocks, the creaking of the wooden wheel of a water pulley drawn by an ox, a sound which is such a feature of Oman, perhaps the call of a shepherd boy from across the valley, or the distant, barking of a saluki dog.

The villages had enough water for drinking, enough very simple food to eat, they were simply clothed and their housing was almost primitive, but they had the appearance and atmosphere of content. In the greetings exchanged it was the peace they talked of: "Peace be unto you," "And unto you peace." "What news from your countr?" "No news, the land is quiet, the land is untroubled." "Praise be to God."

It was a society devoid of officialdom. There was the shaikh, friendly, paternal, helpful and accessible always to his people. The *qadi,* the religious magistrate, distinguished by a white headcloth, bound with another cloth close to his temples and close about his ears and with no black head rope such as the others wore. He was a simple, devout, quiet person, respected, but not feared, and a personal friend to most people apparently. There was the *areef* or controller of the water channel and the collector of water tax, a very important person. He ordered the opening and closing of the little wooden and mud sluices in the water channels; so and so's little field had so many hours' water on so many days: everyone had his appointed share and everyone paid his appointed tax. It was all known and remembered and nothing written, but the *areef* had to supervise, to regulate, in order to prevent this most important matter from producing discord. Many fights and disputes started from differences over water rights.

No peaked caps, no police, no official forms to fill in: it was a community that governed itself internally, almost invisibly, and the better for that.

All the Ibri townspeople showed an immediate and open friendliness to us. If we wanted anything done which was within their capability we had to do no more than mention it, and in return they wanted nothing. To be honest, I could not say quite the same of the bedouin, and knowing I had money they were inclined to cadge; but a laughing response and a tiny sum of money would send most of them away cheerful; and as they had virtually no money I could not find it in my heart to blame them.

We talked about the local politics, we talked about the chances of oil and the blessings that would bring, we talked about agriculture, cows and camels. They wanted to show me things and taught me the tribal *wasms*, the brands by which each tribe and each section, recognise their beasts.

They asked me about my country, our ways and religion. In answer to the last, "We are people of the Book," I would say, "We are Christians," and that contented them. Christians, I had been warned, would be unpopular; they were hitherto unknown in this area, but I found we were not disliked for being foreign Christians, or so it seemed, and I only once noticed animosity on that score, on the part of one individual. The embarrassment he caused was covered up as well as possible by his comrades.

When I was ill with malaria, they all thought it necessary to call on me and talk: this is their habit when someone is ill, however serious. I explained to Shaikh Sultan bin Saif it might perhaps be a very good and comforting habit, but when you have a temperature of 104°F and a splitting head, and are living in the simplest possible way in the open in the heat, you crave only a bit of peace; and he did his best to keep them away, but he only partly succeeded.

As on other occasions when I came upon a people who did not know our ways, and found them living their life as they had done for thousands of years, I felt a responsibility I could never discharge satisfactorily to introduce them sensibly to the things our world had to offer. I wondered what they really thought of us, and I am sure that unwittingly we began a process of change, and from the day we arrived life in Ibri has never been quite the same, and by now it will have taken on an altogether new quality. They were still a strongly tribalised community, and the fact that we had come with their shaikhs was undoubtedly a point in our favour. If we were acceptable to their shaikhs and their shaikhs thought fit to come with us, we must be all right. But although we were accepted for this specific and good reason, their warm and generous hospitality was the spontaneous habit of the country, their instinctive response to the arrival of any stranger.

In Arabia a shaikh is chosen by common consent, and although he lives with his people as an equal and in the same manner as they do, he is accepted completely as their representative for as long as he remains their shaikh. Both shaikhs and people naturally spoke a great deal about developments in local politics. It was evident that their expression of dislike for the Imam's government was not just dished up for my benefit. But their professed preference for the Sultan was not built up on practical experience. It was built on hope, hope that he would bring peace, hope that he would hasten the finding of oil, hope that this would bring material development. I felt sympathy with them and prayed that they might not be disappointed.

The situation was now such that in this important area which was both a geographical and strategic entity, all the people accepted the Sultan alone as their direct ruler and seemed glad to take orders from his representative Shaikh Sultan bin Saif.

I now saw two further desirable purely political aims. The first was to go through to the Wadi Hawasini where, naturally, all the tribesmen owed direct loyalty to Shaikh Sultan bin Saif, their paramount, and therefore to the Sultan of Muscat himself; this would join up a good slice of the country and above all give direct access through the mountain chain to the sea from the potential oilfield area. It would get round the difficulty that Talib could probably control all the outer mountain passes between the likely oil area and the sea. The second was to make sure of Dhank in order to give the Sultan complete and direct control again of the whole of the area of the Dhahirah plain up to Buraimi. Buraimi itself was then subject to the Arbitration Agreement.

These were obvious things to do. However, the new orders received by Coriat made any further move by us impossible. I therefore arranged, through the Company, that Shaikh Sultan bin Saif would fly to Dhufar in order to explain to the Sultan in person how things had gone with us and explain what he, Shaikh Sultan bin Saif, thought needed to be done now.

Nick Fallon had meanwhile chosen an airstrip near Ibri to the east, and measured it; and I, rather light-heartedly, at his suggestion marked it out by the simple expedient of towing the trunk of a palm tree behind a Land Rover along each of its sides. The tree made a clear yellow cut in the grey gravel surface, and showed from the air as a yellow line. I believe our strip is still in use as the airfield. We were, therefore, able to ask the Company for an aeroplane, and in due course, a Dove came. I took the opportunity of its arrival to give Shaikh Sultan bin Saif, Shaikh Muhammad bin Abdullah Al Yaaqubi and some of the Duru shaikhs a ride in it, and persuaded the very co-operative pilot, on the excuse that our guests wished to see their own villages, to give them a tour round a very much larger area than the one which had given allegiance to the Sultan. Shaikh Sultan bin Saif, quite unknown to me, arranged for it to be put about as local gossip that our innocent little ten-seater De Havilland Dove was both a bomber and a fighter of great power and speed.

At a luncheon party given afterwards by the Shaikh of Ibri, in honour of his colleagues and our pilot, one of the elderly bedouin shaikhs who had been for a ride in the Dove said, "I want a machine like that for myself." It took quite a bit of questioning to discover that he was not referring to the aircraft at all, but to the Land Rover which had taken him to it. It transpired that he thought the aircraft rather ordinary, since he had already seen them flying overhead; and he also thought aircraft would be too complicated; whereas the motor vehicles, which were really new to him, he thought more wonderful, and more suitable. Like some of the others, his first ride in a car took place on the same day as his first ride in the air.

Regretfully we began to unravel the arrangements we had made in regard to Dhank, while awaiting news of Shaikh Sultan bin Saif's important trip to Salalah. Meanwhile Shaikh Zayed, who had been hunting in the Wadi Al Amairi, visited us and his arrival was the occasion for great rejoicing and much feasting, for he was very popular and the biggest personality throughout the Dhahirah and with all the bedouin of this area and indeed of all the eastern fringes of what we called the Empty Quarter. I had been in touch with him as much as was feasible over the whole of the operation, and I now found out that it was he who had arranged for Talib to be told that the MFF would attack Rustaq, and had thus prompted Talib to withdraw his main force in that direction at the crucial point. I had given Shaikh Zayed our plans as accurately as I could, and I had said that when we got to Ibri, we counted on seeing him.

As I have explained, although Shaikh Zayed had no responsibility himself at all in the Ibri area, the Sultan had welcomed his co-operation in the Dhahirah, and I thought that his appearance now would have a stabilising effect. This proved to be the case.

It was a great pleasure to see Shaikh Zayed and his brother Shaikh Hazza in Ibri, and all the town rejoiced. Lunch and dinner were occasions for entertaining them for three days, and they in return entertained at their desert camp just outside the town.

There was one particular party given by the townsmen, in which the warmth and friendliness of our hosts were as great as usual, but in which I had a curious experience.

Our hosts had over-extended themselves in the interests of hospitality, a worthy motive. They offered us a camel, sheep and chickens all served, it seemed to me, on top of ton upon ton of rice. This was a sort of 'brunch', served at about ten o'clock in the open; just before the feast a wind came up which served both to cool the meal and to spread over it a layer of fine sand. As we squatted round it, my neighbour advised me to dig deep into the pile with my right hand, sound advice, since only thus could rice be found that was still warm and free of sand. I was getting on well, but in the process came upon the fingers of the man opposite who was doing the same. It was a little unnerving to find something moving amidst the rice.

These meals were fine ones, the meat and rice being beautifully cooked. Hosts and guests were able to enjoy themselves, and after a cup of coffee the party would split up into groups. It was an easy and pleasant form of entertainment for the guests; but it must call for very hard work from the hosts, and for the tribesmen and shaikhs it meant a great expenditure. The cordiality of these meetings underlines the notion that to break bread or partake of salt is a very real expression of friendship and a ritual to celebrate the forgetting of any differences. These desert scenes were part of an age-old tradition which is now unfortunately beginning to change.

Shaikh Sultan bin Saif, and a little later Percy Coriat, made their visits to Dhufar and saw the Sultan who, when he had heard the full story, reluctantly, and with bad grace, accepted what had happened so far. Although he said he disagreed with our methods he never attempted to explain how he thought we could have done otherwise if we had hoped to achieve our objectives. But he maintained his veto on any further adventures. In this I am sure he was badly mistaken, and he missed the opportunity for gaining control over all Oman.

I remained in Ibri for several more days unable to get about much because of fresh attacks of malaria, and dysentery. I was helped over this period by Stewart Watt, who joined us, and when I finally left, took over responsibility for the political side for me.

While I was in Ibri preoccupied with tribal affairs the geologists established a camp near Fahud. Between bouts of illness I went to Fahud, the journey was now easy as tracks were well-established and the weather was cooler. We each must have covered considerable distances and we still had no drivers for our Land Rovers. Mine was usually fairly full, two shaikhs in front and followers behind. Almost all the tracks were rough, and when they had been used a few times became corrugated. Ten hours' driving in one day, which was quite common, in very considerable heat and incessant bumping was very tiring indeed. Land Rovers are wonderful over bad country, but I sometimes regretted the Chevrolet and Ford trucks I had used in 1948-49, as they gave a much better ride even if they did often stick in the softer places. In the Dhahirah a Land Rover would never get stuck, except in the one smooth stretch south of the Wadi Amairi where there must be a sizeable bump at just about every quarter of a minute on the way. But it was still exciting and we all enjoyed it: it was not until the situation in Ibri became stabilised and there was less to think about that I began to notice how tedious some of these lengthy journeys were now becoming. During this time I made one trip up to Dubai and back and thus could claim to be the first to drive a motor vehicle from Dhufar to the Arabian Gulf.

Chapter Fourteen

For a time my health was not up to desert life. I went on leave and was then posted to Kirkuk in Iraq, to do work which did not interest me and in the spring of 1955 I was contemplating looking for something different when the Company suddenly posted me back to Bahrain to look after concessionary matters again.

I found myself once again, among other things, studying the familiar old 'Buraimi' problem.

To recapitulate, when the Saudis entered Hamasah in 1952, Her Majesty's Government intervened to prevent bloodshed. Then followed a Standstill Agreement in October 1952, and in 1954 an Arbitration Agreement. By the latter, the Saudis and the British-officered Trucial Oman Levies, later to be called the Trucial Oman Scouts, were each to maintain one officer and 15 men in the oasis. The Saudis had the right to supply their small force by air, since no other means was practical. Each little force set up its camp near Al Ain; and the arbitration procedure, with judges chosen by each side to meet in Geneva, was set in motion.

Her Majesty's Government, however, said that they had received clear proof of attempts to bribe officials of the Tribunal. Two of the three judges resigned because they had similar evidence of this.

It was then decided, secretly in October 1955 by HMG to abrogate the Arbitration Agreement unilaterally because HMG claimed that the Saudis has breached it by their behaviour in regard to one of the judges. The Trucial Oman Levies were to go into the Buraimi zone that day.

They would ask the Saudi contingent of 15 police and the Saudi Emir to leave, and a plane would be there to take them away. They would be joined in the operation by the Omani army.

Since I knew the area and all the shaikhs involved, Sir Bernard Burroughs asked me if I would be prepared to go into the Buraimi zone with the troops as his representative to persuade the inhabitants not to resist the entry either of the Trucial Levies or the Omani Army, and should they have done so before I could get there, to intervene and stop any fighting. The aim would be to persuade the shaikhs of Buraimi and Hamasah to go to Muscat and make their peace with the Sultan's government. The Sultan was still in Salalah. Sir Bernard said he would inform Colonel Johnson, Commander of the Levies, that I would be representing him and would be responsible for all political issues, thus in effect, for peace or war.

Her Majesty's Government was most anxious to accomplish all this without any bloodshed, and two squadrons of Levies, about 220 men, were to go in by vehicle from Sharjah to do the operation. They planned to surround the Saudi contingent at first light, and then fly them out. This part of the operation would not present much difficulty, it was thought. A contingent was also expected to come from the Omani Army, but it would not be there for the first few hours.

The real problem was that an unknown number of bedouin were in and around Hamasah. These were mainly Kaabis from Mahadah in the Sultanate (from just outside the Buraimi zone). They were all Sultanate subjects, but they supported Shaikh Rashid bin Hamad of Hamasah. It was feared that even after the Saudi contingent had left, these bedouin might remain in Hamasah and resist the entry of the Sultanate forces or the Levies.

I foresaw two difficulties. First, the force we deployed did not look to me big enough to achieve our aim, but I was told no more troops were available. Second, I could not see the shaikhs, Saqr Al Naimi, Rashid bin Hamad, Obaid bin Juma and Mana bin Ali surrendering to the Sultan. Unless they were heavily outnumbered it looked as if they might fight.

We had no time to consider the finer points, since the day I was told of the plan, in secrecy, was the day before the operation was to take place.

My brief was to prevent bloodshed if I could; and I was flown at once from Bahrain to Sharjah from where I went to Dubai to spend the night in the Company house there.

I was to take off from Sharjah before first light in the Dakota which was to fly the Saudi contingent out. In order to allay suspicion I ordered my usual morning tea at seven o'clock in the Company house in Dubai. But by four o'clock I was driving the company Humber over to Sharjah. There I was given an excellent breakfast at the airfield, cooked by the OC personally.

On the airfield was the solitary Dakota, and in the chill morning darkness I climbed aboard with a small suitcase.

What I missed most was the presence of Shaikh Sultan bin Saif. Had he been with me I felt I should not have had much to worry about. I was the only passenger. We lumbered into the air and in just under an hour, as the sun was rising over the oasis, we came down towards the landing strip.

I was standing behind the Captain in the cockpit and we could see the airstrip marked with a line of oil drums, showing as a streak of light brown on the gravel plain. At the corner of Hamasah village there was a pall of white smoke and we could see a small group of vehicles by the palm trees of Al Jimi village. By the side of the airstrip stood a single Land Rover which I hoped belonged to the Levies. The pilot asked me, "What do you make of it? Is it OK to land do you think?"

"It looks all right to me," I said. "I think we can go in but I should keep the engines running after we get down."

With that he banked steeply; turned and came down on to the strip. We taxied up to the solitary vehicle with the engines popping in typical Dakota fashion. He braked gently, for fear of sticking in the soft ground, and pulled up near the Land Rover.

I was relieved to see the tall and bulky figure of Major Norman Smith, the second-in-command of the Levies, who came over to us, and, as I jumped down, shouted a hearty, "Good morning." In the open vehicle an Arab was sitting with what seemed to me a rather fixed look on his face.

"That's the Emir Bin Nami. I have just shot him," said Norman.

"Oh really. Why?"

"Resisting arrest, silly coot," he replied.

I walked over to Bin Nami who was the Emir in charge of the Saudi contingent and who looked distinctly uncomfortable; but he maintained a dignified pose, and we exchanged greetings.

"It's all right," said Norman, "it's only a flesh wound in his leg. We've patched him up. He was struggling to keep hold of that," and he tapped a big steel chest which was in the back of the Land Rover.

I had a little further talk with the Emir Bin Nami, but the atmosphere was distinctly cool, and in the distance I could hear the crackle of small-arms fire from the direction of Hamasah.

As we stood there by the Land Rover the remaining Saudis walked up to us. There were 15 of them, all dressed in the customary long white robes or shirts, and most of them had black cloaks decorated with gold braid.

They all looked rather gloomy, but in the circumstances that was only to be expected.

Norman and I helped Bin Nami into the aircraft and settled him down as comfortably as possible. The other Saudis got in as well.

It was not until we were waving the aircraft goodbye that I realised that, in my excitement at this curious encounter, I had left my suitcase in the aircraft, and that for some time to come I would have with me only the clothes I stood up in.

"Come and look at the Saudi camp," said Norman.

I jumped into the Land Rover with him, and we went the half-mile or so across the plain to the group of tents in which the Saudis had been living. We walked around them, but there was not much to be seen, and the only thing of interest to us was the metal chest which was in the back of Norman's Land Rover. We forced the lock and found in it stacks of currency notes, which when we later counted them, amounted to over 175,000 rupees.

"That's all yours," said Norman.

"All very well," said I, "but where can I put it? Can you give me a car?"

"Sorry, none to spare."

I went walking on through the camp, and round the corner of the tented area I came across a wooden shelter in which I saw a blue Chevrolet saloon car. I got in, found the key was in the ignition switch, and it started. I backed it out and drove it over to Norman's Land Rover.

"Give me a hand with that chest," I said, and we put it in the boot of the Chevrolet and locked it up.

"Now tell me what's going on."

"We came in before first light. Tony Steggles got into Hamasah outskirts with his squadron without any difficulty, but he came under fire almost at once from the big new square house we call Bait Ageel. While this was going on I came over here with the other squadron. The Saudis were just getting up for morning prayer. They could see at once that we were a hundred odd to only fifteen of them, and there was consequently no resistance until I went into that large tent and found Bin Nami struggling to get away with that great chest. God knows where he thought he could hide it."

"Anyway I went for him, he dropped the chest and got hold of me, pinning my arms. I had my hand on my pistol and I shouted, 'Let me go or I'll shoot you.' He didn't let go so I shot him through the leg. That fixed it. We bandaged him up and that was that. Now I must get back to headquarters. The Colonel is over at Al Jimi village."

So saying Norman smiled and walked away followed by his men. They climbed into their Land Rovers and trucks and went off in the direction of Al Jimi.

I got back into the Chevrolet and finding that its tank was half full of petrol followed in the tracks of Norman's squadron.

As I came close to Al Jimi I could hear intermittent small-arms fire from the direction of Hamasah, and a cloud of white smoke was hanging by the houses of the village.

The small group of vehicles which were those of the tactical headquarters of the Levies were tucked away behind a sand dune, about 400 yards from the scene of the fighting. Standing on the dune, and looking at the village through his binoculars, was their commander, Lieutenant Colonel Eric Johnson.

I got out of the car and went up to him, and we exchanged greetings while he went on looking intently at the scene.

In front of us there were two or three hundred yards of open, almost flat sand, at the other side of which there were a few very low, lumpy dunes and behind them the walls of the first mud houses of Hamasah village. Slightly to the left of these was the new square house which was called Bait Ageel. In this the Saudi Emir, Turki bin Ataishan, had lived for much of the time between 1952 and 1954. A little further to its right was another house which the Saudis had also occupied up to 1954, when they had moved out of the village in accordance with the Arbitration Agreement, to the tented camp. Again to the right and behind this house were the buildings of the village itself and in the midst of them the squat mud tower of Shaikh Rashid bin Hamad's fort.

Eric Johnson was well known for his silent manner and at first said nothing, but before long he began to explain what was happening. He told me that the Levies had arrived before sunrise, one squadron going at once to the tented camp and the other entering Hamasah, where they were fired on. Captain Tony Steggles with another British officer had got into the smaller of the two houses without opposition, surprising a few bedouin who had immediately run away. But almost at once they had come under fire from Bait Ageel. Soon after this they came under more intense fire from the village itself and also from the bedouin who had taken cover behind the wall of the neighbouring date garden.

Tony Steggles got all his men into defensive positions behind reasonable cover in and around this one house, and a small one next to it, but he had had to leave his transport in the open where it had already been damaged by small-arms fire. Both sides were therefore in good defensive positions and, we discovered afterwards, at one point the two sides were only 20 feet apart.

Eric told me an attempt had already been made to reach this squadron but they had been driven back by heavy crossfire from positions on the other side of the open ground. It seemed that this squadron was cut off from any support in daylight.

The squadron which had come back with Norman Smith had been put into position on the edge of Al Jimi village but for the time being they were unable to play a positive role. They were not able even to give effective covering fire.

Eric told me that the village of Buraimi itself was reported to be quiet, and as usual its shaikh, Saqr bin Sultan Al Naimi, was trying to keep out of any trouble. He had for some time ceased to take orders from the Sultan. His position with the Naim and Al Bu Shamis tribes was no longer effective, and he sat almost besieged in the fort of Buraimi with only two or three of his followers and his pile of silver. His influence in the desert areas and particularly in Dhank some 40 miles to the south, where he owned the main fort and much of the gardens, had, it was thought, largely evaporated. In normal times a tribe would get rid of a shaikh who had lost effective control. Shaikh Saqr had so far managed to survive but this could not have lasted had not the Saudi presence and the Arbitration Agreement temporarily frozen tribal politics.

Eric's information was that his troops were up against a hard-core of some two hundred local bedouin, under the leadership of Shaikh Rashid of the Al Bu Shamis and Shaikh Obaid bin Juma of the Bani Kaab. The tribesmen themselves were all Kaabis and Shamisis, all therefore subjects of the Sultan of Muscat.

Eric said that shortly he would make another attempt to get a party across to the squadron in Hamasah, under cover of a smokescreen, to take in ammunition and evacuate a badly wounded soldier. It would be a hazardous operation because the extent of open country which had to be crossed was too wide to cover effectively with two-inch mortar-bomb smoke, which was all he had; and his own fire power was not adequate to keep the heads of the opponents down all the time. He did not have much hope that they would get through.

A Lincoln bomber had been flying over our heads for the past ten minutes, and I asked Eric what it was doing. He said he had a call on it for support from its machine guns, but in the present circumstances he could not use it, as the fighting was going on in the village, and it was vital to avoid any risk to non-combatants. Air power could have finished this skirmish in minutes, but Eric would not even consider it, rightly, for fear of the casualties to civilians.

He was naturally unwilling to commit himself any further as to what he could do militarily; but without using the air support the military situation at least in daytime did not look very hopeful to my lay eye.

He said that just before they had set off on this operation, he had been told that I would be joining them, and that I would be responsible for any action necessary on the political side; and he asked me what I intended to do.

I said that it was too early to give him much idea. It happened that the principal 'enemy' leaders were very well known to me personally, and I hoped to make what use I could of this, and to get them talking before long. It might be possible at least to arrange a truce, if not a surrender. Eric said he was not interested in a truce, but if the enemy could be encouraged to surrender that would be fine, as far as he was concerned. He was anxious to avoid heavy fighting within the village, but he would have to do whatever was necessary to support and maintain contact with the squadron which was in the houses. He was in touch by radio with Steggles who reported so far one man dead and one severely wounded. Steggles also reported that he could hold his position without any difficulty; but unless he could be further supported, movement was impossible.

I said that I would do all I could to get in touch with the shaikhs. I told him that I intended to establish myself by a prominent tree just to the north of Al Ain village. Unless he heard to the contrary he could contact me there; and I would in turn keep in touch with him as soon as I had something to report.

There seemed nothing more for us to discuss, so I got back into my Chevrolet and drove off in search of the Abu Dhabi shaikhs.

I did not have far to go. Half-way across to Al Muwaiqi fort, the headquarters of Shaikh Zayed bin Sultan, the Ruler of Abu Dhabi's brother, I met Duda Al Amiri, a colourful character, riding his horse over the small dunes with his usual panache. I stopped the car, jumped out and waved. He waved back with his rifle, and galloped up to me shouting: "Oh bin Hender, what are you doing driving Bin Nami's car? I almost shot you."

I did not take this too seriously but the car was familiar in the area as that which belonged to the Saudi Emir: I hoped this was all part of Duda's flamboyant humour.

I explained that I was looking for Shaikh Zayed and his brother Shaikh Hazza; and, bearing in mind his comment, I asked Duda to warn his villagers that if they saw the car it would be bin Hender and not bin Nami driving in it.

He laughed and asked me to follow him, galloping off back towards the Levy headquarters as he spoke.

We had almost got back to where I had left the Colonel when he jumped off his horse and led it up a steep dune. I stopped the car and followed him on foot. We soon came to a point among the trees where we had a good view of the fighting; and there I saw Shaikh Zayed and his brother, looking at the scene through their binoculars, with a group of their men standing near by.

I was greeted with a broad smile.

"What's going on?" asked Shaikh Hazza. "Can't your troops get those Kaabis and Shamsis out of it?"

I explained the small numbers of the Levy force; and our unwillingness to use air support right in the village.

Shaikh Zayed laughed.

"Why don't you do what you did at Ibri? Go and talk to them!"

"I should love to but I can't get near them. Can't you help me?"

By this time we had walked down the dune, and Shaikhs Zayed and Hazza sat under a tree, and coffee was immediately produced by one of their followers.

"This is the Sultan's business and nothing to do with me," said Shaikh Zayed. "Hasn't he sent up a representative and where are his troops? He cannot trust Shaikh Saqr: no one can do anything with that man now."

"I am expecting the Sultan to send someone up, and some troops, not many, are on their way I believe. But I am not in touch with them, and all I can hope to do is to send across to the shaikhs over there, and try to get them to come over to talk. Couldn't you help me to do this?"

Shaikh Zayed turned to his brother, and had a long talk, at the end of which Shaikh Hazza turned to me.

"This is not our affair, as you know. Our people and our villagers are not directly involved; but I will stay with you and do all I can to help. You must do the talking."

I could not have hoped for anything more than this, and I thanked him, and suggested that we should go over to Al Ain to the place where I had promised the Colonel I would be.

Shaikh Hazza agreed at once and waving goodbye to his brother, we got into the blue Chevrolet.

Hazza laughed to find himself riding in the Saudi car.

"Who is the Amir now?"

We drove across to Al Ain and stopped under the tree, just by the tall new fort. A rug was brought out from one of the houses for us to sit on, and Shaikh Hazza's followers produced for us tea or coffee by turns, it seemed, almost after every quarter of an hour.

The noise of small-arms fire continued throughout the morning from the direction of Hamasah; the Lincoln bomber circled endlessly over our heads; every now and then one of the villagers would come out and say something to Shaikh Hazza. At one time we saw clouds of smoke in the direction of Hamasah, and then the noise of firearms increased for five minutes or so. We agreed that it was essential to make contact with the three shaikhs and Shaikh Hazza sent for three of his followers in order to make the first attempt.

He told his three men that each must go to one of the shaikhs to inform them that bin Hender was in Al Ain and was willing to speak to them. They could come across quite safely, and they had Shaikh Zayed's assurance that they could come freely into Al Ain and leave it again. Alternatively they could send emissaries. He then got hold of his driver, and instructed him to take the three men to within a short distance of Buraimi in the Saudi car, from where they could continue on foot. The car was to come back to us.

After he had put these moves into operation, he called two others of his followers, Muhammad bin Shaiban and Sultan bin Jazi; and he instructed them to stay with me, and do whatever I wanted. Then he stood up and said:

"There are some people I need to see. I shall be in the village and if you need me all you have to do is to send word."

I spent the rest of the morning with Muhammad and Sultan, and we were given dishes of fruit and dates; and other refreshments followed in their turn. We had a long wait in front of us; and during this time I turned over in my mind the good and bad points of the situation which faced us.

Among the bad points I counted the following:

– The number of men involved in the fighting and their arms seemed to be nearly equal on each side. This meant that, although the superior training of the Levies gave them an advantage, with the enemy behind good cover a successful attack against them might be costly.

– The enemy numbers might possibly increase a little, but, apart from the small detachment expected from the Muscat Army, ours could not.

– Fighting in the village endangered civilian life.

– I had no help yet from the Sultan's side, politically.

Among the good points I counted the following:

– Shaikh Rashid bin Hamad and Obaid and their immediate retainers alone were likely to hold out. Their followers might start deserting.

– Although the shaikhs in Hamasah could, in theory, call up more followers, I thought this unlikely.

– The shaikhs who were resisting probably did not realise how comparatively weak the Levy forces were; and they would probably assume that we should make use of an aircraft.

Comparing the situation which had faced us in Ibri I was not very hopeful that we could achieve a surrender without more bloodshed. By midday none of the emissaries had come back, and, becoming rather anxious, I asked Muhammad if he would get in touch with Shaikh Hazza.

About ten minutes later Shaikh Hazza came over to us and suggested that, as there was no fighting in Buraimi village itself, he saw no reason why we should not go over and find out at least what Shaikh Saqr thought. I did not much like the idea of this, as Buraimi and Hamasah are only a few hundred yards apart, however I agreed to go part of the way.

Five of us got into Bin Nami's car.

"They won't fire at this," said Shaikh Hazza with a laugh, and we drove within 200 yards of the great fort called 'The Fort of the Moat' which belonged to Shaikh Saqr.

"Go on further," said Shaikh Hazza.

"This is quite close enough."

"Perhaps you are right," he said, and we all got out.

Then he told two of his men to go in, to find out what happened to the original three, while we sat and waited as patiently as we could.

All seemed to be peaceful in Buraimi village and some of the inhabitants appeared to be going about their daily business much as usual: Women were filling pitchers at the *falaj*, and boys were guarding their herds of goats along the streets. Smoke was rising as usual from the huts in the village, but the centre was deserted and quiet, and I could see through my binoculars that the little market was shut up, and its shops shuttered.

We sat for nearly an hour before all five of Shaikh Hazza's men came back to us. First they talked to their shaikh, and then Hazza turned to me and explained what they had to report.

"They say that Rashid and Obaid insist that your troops go away. They will not accept the Sultan's government, and they will not meet his representatives. They would not object to talking to you if you go over to them; but they do not see that there is anything to talk about. They just say 'Send the troops away'."

"Not much good," I said.

But Shaikh Hazza smiled. "I think this means they are afraid; and I am sure that they would do anything to stop this shooting."

"Well, what do we do now?" I said.

"This must seem to come from you, not from me," he replied. "Tell them the fighting will go on until they surrender. You have aeroplanes and other arms, and other troops will come. They cannot keep on against this opposition; and they must come over and talk to you about it. They have your promise for their safety while the talks last." Then he added, "And repeat Shaikh Zayed's guarantee of their safety while they are on our territory."

"That seems to me sensible," I replied. "Can you get one of your men to put that over as if it is coming from me?"

"Certainly," said Shaikh Hazza; and he turned and spoke at length to his men, three of whom then walked on into the village to pass this to the shaikhs.

We waited where we were for nearly two hours, until Shaikh Hazza's men returned, together with a young Shamsi, whom I recognised as a cousin of Rashid.

He sat down and was given coffee. Then he asked to speak to me alone and we went aside a little.

"Oh, bin Hender. My uncle and Shaikh Obaid are willing to talk to you, but they will not accept the Sultan's government and they will not go to Muscat to be imprisoned. What can you offer them?"

I then explained to him at length that they should surrender, and try to make terms with the Sultan. The Sultan's troops were already on their way (this was true and I had just had news that the first small body had already arrived). The Sultan's government was here to stay: they must make their peace with them.

The young man said there was no question of his uncle accepting the Sultan; and I said that he had no other choice.

"I must go and talk to my uncle again."

One of Shaikh Hazza's men drove him into the village, and then came back on his own.

I talked again to Shaikh Hazza, who said he was convinced that both Rashid and Obaid would give in, if they knew they would be allowed to leave the country in safety. As for Shaikh Saqr, he was an unknown quantity.

After some time the nephew came back, and we had another long talk. The upshot of this was that the two shaikhs would only agree to stop the fighting if they were taken by air to Saudi Arabia, and if the same terms were given to any of their followers whom they nominated. No reply had yet been received from Shaikh Saqr; but the nephew reported that Shaikh Hazza's man was still with him.

I replied that the shaikhs must come themselves. They would be safe as Shaikh Zayed also guaranteed their safety, and I would arrange for them to go by air to Saudi Arabia. I told them that it was essential that Shaikh Saqr of Buraimi, whose men were not involved in the fighting, should either join them or submit to the Sultan, otherwise the fighting might continue. If the fighting went on, the Levies would be free to take full military action, and to this there could only be one end.

I sent him back in the car to talk to his uncle and the driver was instructed to bring back our emissary who had been sent to talk to Shaikh Saqr. When he came back to us this emissary was with them; but he reported that Shaikh Saqr had nothing to say.

Shaikh Hazza and I drove back to Al Ain, where he got down, and I drove on to see Eric.

The Colonel explained that an earlier attempt to relieve the beleaguered squadron had been made (this was the increased firing we had noticed), but they had not got through. However, the badly wounded man had been evacuated, thanks to the great bravery of one of the

Levies, who had simply driven him across the open country as fast as he could in a Land Rover, through heavy fire, and had brought him out safely.

He therefore planned to do nothing more at the moment; but after dark he would have to put in an attack which would clear up the whole position.

I explained how things had been going with me; and I said that I counted on a surrender before very long, but I could not be sure when this would be.

Eric said that if the surrender took place, of course that would be satisfactory, but unless all the enemy surrendered he could not agree to a cease-fire, and a night attack would be unavoidable.

I pointed out the dangers that such an attack would involve with possibly heavy casualties on each side, as well as among the civilians. Furthermore, I saw a danger that even if his small force could get into the village, the enemy could withdraw through the gardens, and it did not seem to me that we had anything like sufficient forces on our side to surround them.

My object was to try to persuade the Colonel to give more time to allow a surrender to take place, but without appearing to question his military assessment of the chances of capturing the villages. Of course I understood that he had no alternative but to relieve his squadron at night by an attack, if surrender seemed unlikely on the part of the shaikhs.

It was finally agreed that we should continue to keep in touch; and Eric promised not to put in his night attack without giving me plenty of notice.

I then went back to Al Ain where I found Shaikh Zayed and Shaikh Hazza.

I described the position as I saw it and Shaikh Hazza said that, although he himself thought that the best solution was for all the shaikhs to give up fighting and to be taken to Saudi Arabia, he could not see the Sultan ever agreeing to such a decision. I said that since he had not sent up a political representative, I was in no position to consult him. At this Shaikh Hazza laughed, slapped me on the shoulder and said: "You are lucky."

Shaikh Hazza readily agreed that once more his men should go in to Buraimi and Hamasah to try to press the shaikhs to come over quickly. I could not be explicit about the plan of the night attack, but I stressed that the Levies would have to take suitable military action, if the surrender did not take place soon.

Shaikh Zayed and Shaikh Hazza went back to Al Muwaiqi, and I remained under the tree with my two companions, Muhammad and Sultan, waiting as patiently as possible. Fortunately the weather was not too hot, and we were constantly supplied with traditional refreshments from the shaikh's house.

Just after sunset I was visited by Norman Smith, who told me that the night attack was now planned for eleven o'clock. He was instructed to tell me that, although the actual time was secret, I could say to the shaikhs that an attack would take place if the surrender were delayed.

I said to Norman that I recommended putting back the time of the attack, since, although I now felt confident that the shaikhs would surrender during the night, we might need more time. Promising to pass this to the Colonel, Norman went away once more.

Later I was joined again by Shaikh Zayed and Shaikh Hazza. More carpets were spread out, lamps were brought, and a sumptuous dinner of sheep and rice was spread before us. During and after the meal more people kept coming and going and news began to filter through from Buraimi and Hamasah. Varying reports came in about Shaikh Saqr, but it seemed to be established that he and Rashid had only just now met for the first time for a considerable period. It was believed that Shaikh Rashid would surrender, but most people thought that Shaikh Saqr would do nothing. This of course might produce an extremely confused position and we should not know whether we were still at war or not.

Towards ten o'clock, a very tired Norman Smith came over to say that the night attack was now timed for midnight; but he was instructed to stay with me in case at the last minute the enemy shaikhs actually turned up and the night attack could be called off.

I told him I thought a surrender was imminent, not enough time was being given to our negotiations, and I strongly recommended a further postponement. Back went Norman to return 15 minutes later with the news that he was to stay with me to see how things were going: the attack would not go in unless it became clear that surrender was out of the question. He was to report back to his headquarters by midnight in any case.

After reporting to me on these lines Norman went over to a nearby tree, lay down on the sand and went to sleep. I told his driver on no account to wake him, and Shaikh Hazza also asked his people to keep away from him lest he were woken by accident.

We waited until after eleven o'clock and I sent a car to a point just short of Buraimi with yet another emissary. He got back to us at quarter to twelve with the news that Shaikhs Rashid and Obaid were together with Shaikh Saqr and they were doing their best to try to persuade him to join them in coming to see me. They had with them a battered old Ford truck and they could come in that. They asked us to wait and to make sure that the troops would not attack.

Shortly after half-past midnight we heard the noise of a car on the Buraimi track and out of the darkness came the old Ford pick-up with no lights; and as it drew up in front of us I could see the figures of the three shaikhs and the driver crammed in the front, and a large group of their followers were in the back.

They got down slowly and walked rather stiffly to where Shaikh Zayed was standing. They rubbed noses and spoke the greetings softly. Shaikh Zayed answered as quietly. Then they greeted Shaikh Hazza in the same way. Shaikh Hazza took Shaikh Saqr by the hand, and led him the two or three paces to where I stood. I gave him the usual greeting and said: "I will now take you to the commander of troops."

I called to Norman's driver and asked him to awaken him. Rubbing his eyes Norman came over protesting, "Why didn't you wake me, this is awful, it's half-past twelve, what will the Colonel say?"

"Don't worry. I think the Colonel will be very pleased. Allow me to introduce you to the enemy. The night attack will not be wanted."

Norman smiled happily. "I'll tell him. Wonderful!" He jumped into his Land Rover and drove off.

The shaikhs remained standing looking utterly tired and dejected. Tired indeed we all were. Coffee was handed around and nothing was said until from behind the shaikhs two men appeared. They were dressed in the usual long white robes and they wore dark cloaks; but I saw that their black head-ropes were round their necks like halters and their black and white headcloths were draped round their shoulders.

As they approached Shaikh Zayed they went down on their knees in the sand and started to crawl towards him. Shaikh Hazza who was next to me whispered their names and I then realised that they were the two heads of families who alone of all the people of Abu Dhabi had joined the Saudis during the three years of their presence in Hamasah.

It was a dramatic moment and I was full of curiosity as to Shaikh Zayed's reaction. As the first one reached him, and seemed to be trying to kiss his feet, Shaikh Zayed with the natural dignity which is especially his, stooped, took him by the shoulders, raised him and said:

"Peace be unto you. You are forgiven and you may return to your house in peace."

He did the like with the second.

Both of them made for Shaikh Hazza who said with dignity in a soft voice.

"You heard the brother's word. Go to your homes. He has forgiven you."

This dignified and decisive act of the shaikhs made a great impression on all of us, and there was a silence which was first broken by Shaikh Hazza, who said to Shaikh Saqr:

"Bin Hender will take you to the Colonel. You should go with him."

The group of shaikhs who had surrendered looked rather doubtfully at one another but they climbed in Bin Nami's car. I got into the driving seat and took them across the mile or so of sand to the Levy headquarters.

There I found the Colonel, whom I thought looked somewhat impatient and perplexed. Apparently Norman had only half convinced him that the surrender was really taking place; and he was not unnaturally somewhat short with him for being so late. When I got out of the car the Colonel turned sharply to me and said:

"What is going on, the attack will be starting in a few minutes."

I smiled and said, "Wait a minute, let me introduce you to the 'enemy'." Then more seriously, "Eric, would you please formally accept the surrender of these shaikhs. It is all over."

Then I presented Shaikhs Saqr, Rashid, Obaid, and Mana bin Ali.

Shaikh Rashid acted as their spokesman and said in a very low voice that they put themselves in the hands of the Colonel and trusted his honour. I made what I felt was a suitable translation.

Eric looked rather surprised, and turning to me said in English: "Please assure them that they will be safe. But tell me what shall we do with them now?"

I gave the shaikh Eric's assurance, and suggested to Eric that we should find somewhere for them to rest under guard.

We found a nearby hut whose owner was agreeable to their staying in it; a guard was put upon them and I suggested that they should be given some coffee. Meanwhile we walked over to the wireless truck to send off suitable signals, reporting what had happened, and asking for a Dakota at first light to take the shaikhs out of the oasis, and then on their way to Saudi Arabia through Bahrain.

Eric and I then discussed the need of some formality to mark the surrender of the villagers of Hamasah; and we agreed to meet at eight o'clock that same morning for this purpose. I told him that from the information that had reached me it seemed unlikely that we would now have any more trouble; and the relief of the soldiers who were in the houses could probably go ahead right away but I recommended that no big movements of troops should take place until daylight.

I drove back to Al Ain where I found the Abu Dhabi shaikhs sitting in one of their houses discussing the events of the night. Tired but happy, Shaikh Hazza was already making jokes about what had gone on.

By this time it was nearly three o'clock in the morning and we had been on the go for 24 hours. The shaikhs offered me a room for the rest of the night and some blankets; but before I went to sleep I arranged for a guard to be put on Bin Nami's car, having in mind the safety of the steel box locked in its boot.

The discomfort of a rather hard floor and the buzz of early morning flies woke me at six o'clock; and I drove over with Muhammad and Sultan to the Levy headquarters. The Levies had spent the night in the open, since their tents had not yet arrived from Sharjah. By the time I reached them the shaikhs and their main group of followers had already been taken to the airstrip to await the Dakota which was to carry them to Bahrain.

I suggested to Eric that he should send an officer, together with Sultan and Muhammad, to warn the headman, if such a person there now was, of Hamasah that he would be coming in with a party of troops to make a formal entry at about eight o'clock.

Then I borrowed a razor and washed and shaved in the *falaj* stream. Eric invited me to join him for breakfast, and by the time this was over, his officers were getting the troops ready to drive across to Hamasah.

We discussed the curious question as to quite what we ought to do in the villages which after all were nothing really to do with us. We decided on a fairly formal entry into Hamasah with the small Muscat force, and a whole squadron of Levies, after which the Colonel should talk to the leading people. He would reassure them and say that all fighting had stopped and that officials from the Muscat Government would be coming to Buraimi very soon. Then we thought we should inspect the forts of both Hamasah and Buraimi. I was particularly anxious to make adequate arrangements to secure Shaikh Saqr's reputed treasure, which of course was the property of the Muscat Government; and I wanted to enquire at once into a horror story that Shaikh Saqr had kept a prisoner at the bottom of a deep hole in the ground for many months in the castle called 'The Castle of the Moat'.

Eric drove off at the head of the column while I came behind in one of his vehicles.

Eric got down by the door of the Hamasah fort, where he met the headman of the village, and we were shown round the fort by him. Not so very long ago I had been in that building for a dinner party as the guest of Shaikh Rashid; but the courtyard we now saw behind the fort with its iron rings in the walls to which prisoners had been tied, I had never seen, although I had heard stories about this notorious place.

After we had looked round the village and spoken to some of the people, the column moved on to Buraimi where Eric sent off an officer and some men to find and set free the miserable prisoner, while we went straight to the small fort in which Shaikh Saqr had lived. We found this deserted except for the shaikh's bailiff, Saiyid Kamil, who was well-known to me. We asked him where the famous treasure was stored; and he pointed to a long low building across the courtyard. The double doors were locked but they gave way to the combined weight of Norman Smith and one of his soldiers. We filed in to find a long room lined with large wooden, brass-bound, Kuwaiti chests. Ten of these stood round the wall.

From earlier visits I knew where the shaikh's private apartments must be, and hoped we might find the key to the boxes there. The bailiff had the key to the main entrance of the private apartments and to the inner keep. Here on the first floor was the small concrete room in which the shaikh used to live alone. As he was always in fear of his life, at night he would lock himself in there against all comers. As his predecessor had been murdered he was always thought to be in fear himself of a similar fate.

We searched the room but could not find any keys. I asked the bailiff to send at once for a locksmith.

While this was going on we heard that the prisoner had been found and the soldiers had pulled him out of the hole in which he had been incarcerated for eight months, without ever coming up. The hole was some 40 feet deep and the floor at the bottom measured some ten by four feet.

The poor man was far from well and the skin of his face was a horrible yellow. We saw he was well looked after, and I later heard that he had made a good recovery. We looked down into the pit and tried to imagine what the heat would be at the bottom at midday in the summer when the sun would shine directly on it. The outside temperature would be over 120°F in the shade, but down the hole there would not be a breath of wind, and for several hours at each midday, no shade.

The Colonel went on with his tour of inspection while Norman Smith and I examined the treasure.

When we had the boxes open we found them filled almost to overflowing with silver rupee coins dating well back into the last century; it was the 'Thousand and One Nights' over again.

As an immediate precaution we had the bolt of the door mended, secured it with two large army padlocks and put a strong guard on the building. Eric and I kept the key of one lock each to demonstrate that neither of us separately had access to the treasure while we awaited the arrival of the Muscat Government official. As yet, only a junior officer had arrived with a small troop of infantry, and it was they who had been with us when we entered the village. A *wali* (governor) had been promised.

All the bedouin who had been engaged in the fighting against the Levies appeared to have left, but the majority of the villagers in both places were still there. In Buraimi the villagers clustered around us in a very friendly way. They took pains to point out that the treasure in Shaikh Saqr's fort represented the taxes which the shaikh had taken from the poor villagers of Buraimi and Dhank over the years. It was really their money, they said.

We spent some time talking to the villagers and then went over to the Levy camp which had now been set up in the Abu Dhabi sector. There we were joined by Brigadier Baird, the senior British officer in the Gulf, who had come over by air from Bahrain to see what was going on.

I showed him the box which had been the cause of the trouble between Norman Smith and Bin Nami. He thumbed the notes: they amounted to 175,000 rupees; and curiously the silver in Shaikh Saqr's treasury, when it was later counted, came to almost the same figure.

I was quite glad to hand over responsibility for this chestful of money and also the documents which were all returned to the Saudis.

The same plane had brought my suitcase and, later in the day, Sabir bin Muhammad drove in from Dubai with my Company Land Rover and a camp bed so that once again I felt equipped and mobile. Bin Nami's car I handed over to the Colonel.

I had a long talk with Robert Baird and discussed the need to do something for the inhabitants who for various reasons were in rather a poor way. Robert promised to support any proposal which I might make towards helping them.

That evening Shaikh Zayed asked us over to dinner in Al Muwaiqi; and after the meal we had a long talk over the events of the past days.

The Saudis had never occupied any part of Abu Dhabi territory; but their presence had naturally had an effect on the whole area. It was only the quality of Shaikh Zayed's leadership, and his hold over the bedouin and the villagers alike that held Abu Dhabi together under the stress of this constant temptation.

Whatever Shaikh Zayed achieved as Ruler of Abu Dhabi (which he has been since 1966) with all the money which he now has, it can hardly exceed his wonderful achievement in holding his people's loyalty over the years when he had virtually no money.

Chapter Fifteen

I stayed on in Al Ain as Political Officer for HMG for another six months, on a temporary secondment from the Company. In due course a Governor arrived from Ibri to be in charge of the Sultanate sector. His first sight of Shaikh Saqr's silver seemed to astonish him; and he asked for my help in counting it.

I asked for a tailor from the village and set him making canvas bags each big enough to hold 1,000 rupees. We borrowed a set of heavy scales from the market and by counting out 1,000 coins and sewing them up we were able to use the bag as a measure to weigh against the rest. Nevertheless it took the best part of the morning before we had the whole treasure counted and securely sewn up. Eric and I then handed over both keys to the Governor in front of several witnesses; but he took them over, I thought, with some reluctance.

The new Governor of Buraimi was the son of the Governor of Ibri, and I had already met him. He seemed a capable young man. We soon struck up a friendly relationship, and I explained that, although I had no responsibilities on his side of the border, I was only too ready to help him in any way I could. With him had come a detachment of troops under the command of my old friend Mike O'Kelly and I said to the Governor that we thought that the position in Buraimi and Hamasah itself would be secure, but we could not be certain of some of the areas to the south.

I had already collected some information about the political developments in the area. The bedouin and settled tribes who had been involved in the fighting had either gone back into the desert or, in the case of the Bani Kaab, to their villages in the mountain valleys, and the latter having now lost their leader, Shaikh Obaid, who had chosen to go to Dammam, were already grouping round another shaikh who was loyal to the Sultan. The Al Bu Shamis had likewise lost their paramount, Shaikh Rashid, and were said to be grouping mainly behind Bin Rahmah who had a long history of loyalty to the Sultan (and incidentally a close relationship with Shaikh Zayed).

Away down to the south all seemed to be well in Ibri; but in the foothills between us lay the town of Dhank which had a mixed community, some of which had owed allegiance to Shaikh Saqr who had maintained a representative there and some to smaller shaikhs of little tribes or tribal splinter groups. I felt, as I had done in 1954 when we first entered Ibri, that until Dhank declared for the Sultan there would still be a dangerous situation in the Dhahirah district.

I suggested to the Governor that he and his father in Ibri should make enquiries about the loyalty of the people in Dhank, and do something to ensure that they declared publicly their allegiance to the Sultan. Later I had a visit from Colonel Cheeseman who had succeeded Percy Coriat as Commander of the MFF in Ibri. He agreed in principle to sending a squadron to Dhank as a demonstration of the Sultan's power, if he could be sure that this would be politically expedient.

The Governor of Buraimi made immediate enquiries about the position in Dhank, and in due course began to make contact directly with the leaders there.

Meanwhile Shaikh Zayed had given me a three-storey tower, the most northerly fort in Al Ain, to live in. I took the room on the upper floor and Sabir, Muhammad and Sultan made use of the rest of the building.

On the days subsequent to the arrival of the Governor in Buraimi he and I again exchanged visits; and it soon became clear from the information we each were getting that the majority of the shaikhs of Dhank were only too anxious to show themselves to be loyal to the Sultan; but I was not surprised also to hear that they felt that it would be good to have this declaration of loyalty made at the same time as a visit of a strong squadron from the MFF. This seemed in keeping with local practice.

Colonel Cheeseman paid us another visit and it was agreed between him and the Governor that they would meet at a point where the main track from Buraimi to Ibri branched up the *wadi* towards Dhank, at nine o'clock on the following Thursday. Having now got the assurance of all the shaikhs that they could welcome a visit in force from the MFF, it was agreed that a squadron would then enter the town and would be entertained in the usual way by the leading shaikhs as their demonstration of loyalty to the Sultan. The Governor suggested that although I had no official position on his side of the border, it would be helpful if I would agree to accompany him.

Accordingly, early in the morning on the appointed day I called at the Governor's fort and, together with Sabir and three of the Governor's personal staff, we set off in my Land Rover for the rendezvous. We reached it at about half-past eight and made ourselves coffee and had a breakfast of dates. We waited there until nearly eleven o'clock in the shade of a thorn tree, but no troops came; and by this time I was becoming very anxious and thought that I should go to look for Cheeseman. The Governor said he would wait where he was since there was a considerable risk that I might miss the troops by taking a different track; there were a dozen different tracks between Ibri and Dhank. Someone must be there at the rendezvous in case the troops arrived without my seeing them.

Sabir and I set off alone over the bumpy gravel to Ibri, and we got there at about half-past one. I went straight over to the mess tent where I found the Colonel and several of his officers finishing lunch. I was tired and rather exasperated and I am afraid walked into the tent in a testy mood.

"What are you all doing?" I asked. "The Governor is waiting for you and he is very upset."

"Good Lord, old boy," said the amiable but scarcely perturbed Cheeseman, "Didn't you know it's all off." The fall of Dhank has been cancelled. Orders from HQ. They said you would have been told."

"As far as we are concerned, it isn't," I replied, "it should be falling right now: all it needs is a show of force. We simply must not let the Governor down, he has arranged it and is waiting for you."

It did not take much more than three or four minutes to persuade the excellent Cheeseman that he ought to do something right away. He ordered his signal officer to raise Muscat on radio and having failed to get through, cheerfully agreed to come with me to Dhank, bringing a squadron of his men.

Then he turned to me and said: "What about a spot of lunch?"

While I was having lunch troops were got ready and the vehicles marshalled together. Meanwhile I had sent Sabir back to cheer up the Governor and tell him we were coming.

When his troops were ready Cheeseman asked me to join him in the leading vehicle, and we bumped our way in convoy in clouds of dust towards Dhank, necessarily rather more slowly than I had come down the same track in the morning.

It was nearly evening before we reached our rendezvous. The Governor was still where I had left him, but he had taken advantage of Sabir's return to send him into Dhank in my Land Rover to bring out some of the leading shaikhs. When we arrived they were sitting round him in a ring on the sand and seemed amiable and friendly enough.

He was overjoyed to see Cheeseman and the troops and the three of us drew aside to discuss the situation.

"It seems to be all right, except possibly for one small fort, and one quarter of the town, at the far end, but the shaikhs do not want anything to happen tonight. They would like us to come in tomorrow morning when all the forts will fly the Sultan's flag. I have given them one each. I am confident that it will go off smoothly," said the Governor.

This was agreed and after a cup of coffee with the shaikhs we sent them back into the town in my Land Rover driven by Sabir. I remarked to Cheeseman and the Governor:

"Sabir seems to have captured the place on his own, do we really need to bother?"

They laughed a little wryly.

We spent a quiet night by the tree; and on the following morning we set out in what I now had learned was the traditional order in this area. The Governor and one of his staff came with me in the front car, while the army was close behind. It was a peaceful warm morning as we drove down into the *wadi*-bed and up the rough watercourse towards the town which is set in a deep valley with steep bare rocky cliffs on either side. Water was running in the bed and driving was not easy: I therefore kept up a good speed to avoid sticking in this soft ground.

A number of the townsmen came out to watch and I drove straight up to the main fort, the Governor directing me, bumping over the rocks and gravel.

On this occasion there was really no cause for anxiety, but for some reason I was a bit nervous, and misjudging my speed I skidded to a halt in the gravel, the back wheels locked and we struck the main doors of the fort hard enough to break the door hinges on one side. The door collapsed inwards and I felt we had captured this castle. Fortunately this was taken as being rather amusing, and we all climbed out laughing. We were at once invited in for coffee and fruit, and warmly pressed to stay for lunch.

While waiting for the meal we made a tour of the fort and the town. It had small but attractive gardens between the rocky cliffs, but there was something sinister and forbidding about such a rocky and overshadowed setting. Inside the main fort we were shown the stocks which were made out of a massive tree trunk, split in two, with pairs of holes for legs – enough of them for half a dozen people to be fastened into it at a time.

After lunch we said goodbye to Cheeseman and thanked him for his spirited reaction; and the Governor and I went back to Buraimi.

With Dhank declared loyal the whole Dhahirah was one again.

Chapter Sixteen

When the episode of Dhank had reached a successful conclusion, I made my report on what I thought needed to be done to rehabilitate the Buraimi area.

One curious effect of the recent problems had been to hold up repair work and cleaning of the irrigation channels throughout the oasis area. Quite why this should happen was not easy to see, but I suppose that with a general feeling of insecurity, some of the customary work simply was not done. Traditionally they were accustomed to inspect the tunnels each autumn and allocate clearance of the silt to separate parties. The channels were thus maintained over the years. As one drove around the three villages which made up the Sultanate's portion of the oasis one could see that many of the trees were dying and the fields were bare of cultivation although the season for ploughing was already nearly over. The situation was not so bad on the Abu Dhabi side but here again something needed to be done: it was bad enough and, I was warned, would become progressively worse.

Until very recent years all the villages of the oasis depended entirely for their agriculture on the *falaj* system; and it is only in the last few years with the introduction of modern drilling methods that the other water resources of the area can be reached and exploited.

I do not think anyone knows how old the *aflaj* of Oman are but almost all the towns and villages in the foothills must have depended on them from earliest historical times. Some have been found that may be as much as 3,000 years old. On the edge of the desert, villages can be seen which have died whether as a result of the encroachment of sand over their fields or from some disaster within the *falaj* or the drying up of its springs. From the air one can pick out many such villages, and the series of circular depressions which mark the line of the *falaj* which used to supply this water.

Quite how the early settlers managed the construction of a *falaj* I cannot imagine; but local experts still exist who are capable of building a *falaj* from the start, and we therefore know how they set about it today.

The spring is sought by common-sense deduction from the surface geology; and water diviners are sometimes also used and with success. Wells have to be dug at the most likely sites until a suitable spring, with sweet water in sufficient quantity, has been found.

In the Buraimi area most of the *falaj* springs are found at a depth of nearly 80 feet; and the shafts of the wells are dug very wide to begin with through the soft earth and sand, and when firm rock is reached below there are narrow holes just big enough for a man to go down. Almost unbelievably these upper shafts are dug without any shoring, using the most rudimentary implements; hammers, chisels, baskets and ropes; and in this area usually some 30 feet of loose material surrounds the upper part of the deeper shafts, a perpetual threat to those working below.

If the spring is judged sufficiently plentiful, the experts then find by 'survey' (but without using any recognisable modern instruments) a place somewhere on the surface of the ground which is slightly lower than the spring, and this area must be a suitable one in which to excavate flat fields for agriculture. A tunnel then has to be dug underground back from this point on the surface to the spring; and in the Buraimi area this tunnel will be anything from two to five miles in length. This is done by digging vertical shafts at intervals of something like 30 to 50 feet and joining up the tunnels underground horizontally. The last tunnel to be dug is the one between the spring itself and the nearest vertical shaft in the line. This last is obviously a very dangerous operation; finally they must open up the tunnel to the full force of the spring which immediately fills the tunnel with water. The opening up of the last two or three feet is therefore the work of a specialist, who is working down in a rope harness with men above to pull him clear, hopefully before the tunnel fills and it is too late.

After the *falaj* has been completed, stone flags are placed over the necks of the rock shaft (that is at the bottom of the loose excavation and at the top of the rock shaft); and the loose soil round the upper part of the open shafts is pushed back to seal it, leaving a saucer-like depression on the surface. This is done to prevent people or animals from falling into it; and from the air a line of such circular depressions indicates that a *falaj* is, or has been, underneath.

In the course of time, with the action of the running water, the tunnel changes shape and there is a tendency for the bottom to silt up and there may be falls from the roof. When this happens and the flow of water is reduced, an expert has to be called in: the nearest shafts to the point where the trouble has occurred are opened and the expert climbs down to inspect the tunnel and to organise repairs and cleaning.

Depending on the nature of the work, shafts will be opened every hundred yards or so. Digging out the shafts, and going down to remove the flagstones at the neck of each rockshaft, and then going on down into the water channel are difficult and dangerous tasks. The skill for the initial building of a *falaj* is vested with a single tribe: but repairs and cleaning are done by specialists from many tribes.

At the outflow of the *falaj*, fields must be excavated and levelled off, and small surface channels, controlled with sluices of mud or stone, must be built to irrigate the land. The large mounds of earth which are often to be seen around the edges of the many villages are from the spoil taken perhaps hundreds of years ago, when the levelling was first done.

It is the nature of the *falaj* which gives the local village its characteristic form; and seen from the air the village looks almost like a fruit bulging out on either side from a stem at the point where the water runs out of the ground: from above it is seen as a green mass with the light brown of the mud houses along its edge.

Most of the villages have dates as their chief crop, despite the fact that nowadays this is by no means the most valuable crop which could be grown from this very sweet water. Shaikh Zayed has, since the time of which I write, done much to correct this, to introduce new crops and increase the water supply by digging wells and fitting pumps and pipes.

Each village is a compact distinct group separated from its neighbour by its desert steppe. Around the northern villages of the Buraimi group there are small forests of thorns and acacia; and on the west are rolling pink and red sand dunes and to the east the cliffs of the foothills of the Omani mountains.

The point where the *falaj* water comes out is in many cases a focal point for the community. There is often a mosque there, since water is needed for ablutions before prayer, and there are also shelters for bathing places at such a point.

A favourite place in Al Ain was to sit on a hot summer's evening in the water in a small aqueduct about 10 feet above ground level in the shade of a tree and in what breeze there was. Sitting there dressed in a loin cloth with the minnows tickling your toes, watching the world go by was a pleasant way to get cool in the evening.

Sultan and Muhammad were both experts on *aflaj*; and Shaikh Zayed instructed them to teach me something about the subject. Shaikh Zayed himself was a great expert and had done a great deal to open up new *aflaj* and mend old ones.

We first did a survey of the gardens and I made notes as to the length of time between each opening of the sluice in the various parts of the gardens. In some gardens the water could reach the trees as often as it was required, in others once in 15 or 20 days or even longer. At the extremities of many of the gardens no water was coming through at all; and palm trees were dying and none of the customary crops could be sown. As the trees die their fronds first hang drooping, then fall off, leaving a tree trunk sticking up foolishly to the sky. It was a heart-breaking sight to see the trees dying and the decaying mud houses around them, with the realisation that it was still the date which was the main source of livelihood for these people.

Shaikh Zayed was fully alive to this difficulty and had begun to drill wells and fit pumps. But the water from these wells was not so sweet as the water from the *aflaj*; and the *falaj* water had the additional advantage that when the channel was clean, and would allow the water to run satisfactorily, it required no machinery.

Having found out how serious the position was, I put up a case to the British Government for systematic repairs, and I was offered engineers and machinery. My reply was that all I needed was cash to encourage the people to work for themselves.

I was given a small sum to start with, and decided on Shaikh Zayed's advice to begin on Al Ain village. I did a rough survey of the lines of the channel and adapted this to a sketch map on the sand; and then I gathered experts and got them to mark where the trouble-spots underground were likely to be. Based on this information we chose the shafts to be opened and when this had been done, sent the experts down to inspect the tunnel. They came back and reported the depth of silt to be cleared.

I then made notes of what work needed to be done and asked my advisers how we were to get the people to do it.

Sultan's answer was immediate:

"Hold an auction. Tomorrow at three o'clock Arabic time, or nine *firanji* (European time) I will have a dozen or so men and we can auction the work out. Give me the Land Rover and I will go and tell them."

The following morning Sabir drove us to the appointed place; and there were perhaps a dozen villagers standing by an open shaft.

"These are the 'contractors'," said Sultan.

We all followed Sultan who made a mark on the ground with his stick.

"From here to that tree is the first section: who will do it for one thousand rupees?"

No one spoke up and to encourage them Sultan strode with his long paces to the other end of the work.

"This is no distance, my brothers! It's not worth six hundred, I am only saying a thousand to start the bidding." And he turned to me:

"Much too expensive," I said.

Then one of his contractors shouted: "I'll do it."

Sultan turned to the others:

"Will you let him get away with that? Who will do it for nine hundred?"

So it went on until we got it down to 700 rupees.

"What do you really think?" I asked in a whisper to Sultan.

"Much too expensive," he whispered back. "You say that to me loudly and get into your car."

"Much too expensive," I said in a firm voice, shaking my head and got into the Land Rover. Sabir started the engine but before we had begun to move there was a shout for us to stop. Sabir switched the engine off and we saw two men waving.

"Six hundred and eighty," said one.

"Six fifty," said another.

"Six fifty it is," I replied.

I got down and went over to the man who had clinched the deal, and together with Sultan and the neutral inspector went into the details.

The contractor promised to complete the work within three weeks, and was paid half the money in advance.

He proved as good as his word and completed the task only two days late. One of the experts acceptable to the contractor was sent down to inspect the channel, and only when I received his approval was the remainder of the fee paid.

The reader may criticise my attempts to keep the price down, but I had difficulty in getting agreement to even small sums and I wanted to do the best I could with it. The more work done the better for the village people.

We were lucky with our first cleaning, since the section was known to be the worst in the whole *falaj* system (this is why I chose it) and cleaning it alone increased the waterflow very dramatically. I made notes of the number of days each section of the garden was watered; and after each cleaning and a test period for several days I was able to evaluate the results. Where the gardens had water only once in 20 days before cleaning, after it had been done, their turn might be as frequent as once in ten days. Alternatively in gardens in which the water had not previously reached as far as the fields on the outer edge, these outer areas could now be watered and the number of waterings in the inner areas kept the same until the *falaj* was fully clean, when it could be made more frequent, without starving the outer fields.

I reported my first successes and was given more money in small sums until in the end at the cost of nearly £5,000 all the *aflaj* in the Abu Dhabi sector had been adequately cleaned.

I had no means to measure the increase in the water flow scientifically, but the area properly irrigated had nearly doubled and most of the dying trees revived. This sight cheered us as much as the sight of the dying fronds at the crowns of hundreds of trees had depressed us before we had started.

I had to take great care in cleaning the *aflaj*: it is as easy to wreck them as it is to save them. It is essential to clean systematically upwards from the outflow towards the spring since otherwise if the flow were to be increased upstream first the extra water would fill the lower tunnel completely, and at any place where the roof were at all loose it would bring it down. This would block the *falaj* which would continue to fill until perhaps the whole roof was brought down.

If this damage was done to a long and deep *falaj* it would be beyond recovery: it would die and a village would die with it. Apart from Al Ain village itself (where there are two) each village had only one *falaj* and it therefore depended entirely upon it until at a later date wells were dug. If the *falaj* ceased to flow the villagers would have to leave their houses and seek a new home somewhere else.

This was therefore work of vital importance. I roughly surveyed all the *aflaj*, and inspected one or two myself, but I found the descent into a *falaj* hazardous and difficult, and after one or two attempts I decided this was better left to the experts. After all I would be useless down at the bottom anyway.

Our various contractors never forgot a contract. I being literate and therefore without a perfect memory, had to make a note of each agreement. They, being illiterate and with apparently perfectly good memories, did not. Although on several occasions they did not finish on time, and on many occasions pleaded for more money because they claimed the experts had underestimated the work, no contractor ever disagreed as to either the cost or the completion time, which had been originally negotiated. Their memories were always exact.

When they complained that there was more silt in the *falaj* than had been expected, or that the roof was loose and gave trouble, I would ask for second opinions of other accepted experts, who would go down and make their own inspections. We could then agree on an addition to the price if it seemed justifiable.

The work was not quite completed when I had to leave, but by that time all the gardens on the Abu Dhabi side were receiving water regularly and all were safe. The last to be done was that of Shaikh Zayed, Al Muwaiqi garden itself.

Chapter Seventeen

I shall always feel glad that I had the privilege of playing a part, however modest, in the rather unusual means by which this formerly almost unknown part of the world came to be introduced to modern life, and thus to so many entirely new things both intellectual and material.

As I have described earlier, the Trucial States and Oman had until now a standard of living as low as could be found anywhere, and in which the local inhabitants' ignorance of the modern world was virtually total.

From the beginning I had felt that the people of the area deserved to have the opportunity, if oil was found, of living their lives in the ways they wanted, and of adapting themselves to modern life in their own fashion, rather than surrendering what is quite literally their birthright to a distant neighbour, who could not be expected to put their interests first. There is now a good chance that this will come about. There is, I am sure, a bright future ahead.

Reverting to the entry of the MFF into Ibri, and to the consequent exploration for oil in the desert, as is usually so often the case, nothing turned out as badly as the worst I had feared, nor quite so well as the best I had hoped for. But at least Oman did not break up in a series of smaller tribal units, nor was any part of the country taken over by a neighbour.

My company was granted a sufficient opportunity to search for oil, but experienced delay in finding it. Oil was later found, but there was further delay in applying the fruits of discovery to the welfare of the Omanis under whose land it lay.

The reader may be familiar with the broad outline of the way oil development continued in Oman, and I need only say a few words on this now. My company drilled Fahud, but failed to find any oil in the structure. The Company had also been drilling for some years up and down the Trucial Coast, spending many millions in the process, without finding oil there either at that time. The Company surrendered its concession in Oman. In due course another company was formed from three of the participants of the first company, the major shareholder now being Shell. The new version of Petroleum Development Oman drilled Fahud and found oil in commercial quantities, both there and later in other neighbouring structures, all of which were on Duru territory.

It was then realised that ironically the original Petroleum Development Oman drilling rig had only missed the oil by a matter of a few hundred yards, laterally; but this is the sort of thing that happens in the oil business and often, as in this case, it is really no-one's fault.

This unavoidable delay of a few years in finding the oil after the area had been opened up for access by the Company was further compounded by what seemed to many people a sadly unnecessary delay on the part of the Government of Oman in exploiting the discovery of oil from the outset.

In all fairness to the Omani Government I must stress, as I have done earlier, that Oman is a large country. Moreover, it must be remembered that the oil production from the fields which have been found and proved so far in Oman, although they may be described as 'major' are fairly modest by Middle East standards. Furthermore, having regard to the internal economic position in Oman and her population, which may number as much as one million, unless considerable further discoveries are made, Oman is unlikely to see the extraordinarily high per capita revenue from oil alone, such as is enjoyed by Kuwait, Qatar, Abu Dhabi or Saudi Arabia. However, even though these considerations are less favourable in Oman than in some neighbouring countries, as soon as oil had been proved to exist in commercial quantities, and as soon as the Company had announced its intention to produce it, the Government of Oman could have made some sort of beginning by borrowing against the certain expectation of oil revenues. It could then have set in train some of the moves for development in the fields of education and health at least. We have seen the desperate need in other oil-producing countries at this same take-off period, when the whole country may not be able to produce a single person with a good enough education to administer in any field of government. A modest crash programme aimed at training a small cadre of Omanis was surely essential, and provision of some medical service was a minimum human requirement.

At this point it was not that the Omani Government did anything wrong. It was that they just did nothing. Some years were thus wasted. Happily things have undergone change and since then a lot has been done.

Turning now from the oil and development picture to the purely political one, the events which followed the end of my story, and in which I played no further part can be summarised very briefly.

First, life in Buraimi simply returned to what it had been before.

In Oman Sultan Said came up by motor vehicle from Salalah in 1956 with a tiny force and entered Nizwa. He went on to Ibri and to Buraimi and Al Ain where I was privileged to attend a large breakfast on the sand dune near Al Ain, given in his honour by Shaikh Shakhbut.

James Morris has written an interesting record of this journey on which he accompanied the Sultan from Salalah to Muscat.

All Oman was once more under the direct rule of a single Sultan of the Al Bu Said dynasty.

Talib and Ghalib did not make any attempt in 1954-5 to capture Ibri despite the fact that for a long time the MFF only numbered a little over 100 men in Ibri, and never, so far as I know, anything like the mythical 400. I am sure now, that Talib and Ghalib did not have the capability, and subsequent history showed that they had no popular support. Sitting in Ibri in October and November 1954 we felt exposed, but with hindsight, I can now see that our position although militarily poor was politically stronger than I had thought at the time, and it would have been wise and very easy to have consolidated a larger area.

There are some aspects of the Ibri episode on which I should like to touch briefly.

Percy Coriat by bringing up his few soldiers was doing in Oman what most other Middle Eastern security forces had to do earlier in this century. This was to use a show of force to bring the tribes under the control of central government in order to develop the country and improve the lot of tribesmen themselves. It could be argued that in Oman the procedure differed rather curiously from that which followed in some of the other countries. In the case of Oman, the troops came in from the desert with the help of the bedouin, and stabilised the position among the more settled tribes. But much more remarkable, the vital Ibri operation was achieved with only two officers and just over 100 men, and the men were untrained. As my record of it shows, the whole operation was carried out without firing a shot.

The reader must be amused that my fears for the worst possible case, which are recorded quite frankly earlier in the book, were never fulfilled. This is not I think because they were unfounded, but largely because we were lucky.

The reader may also be even more amused to see that both the Sultan and the general manager were proved by events quite correct when they had told me that it would all turn out well for us. But I do not think, with great respect to both of them, that they could have seen quite how this would come about. From previous experience the Sultan may have been able to estimate, but the general manager obviously could not do so, how wonderfully Shaikh Sultan bin Saif would steer us through the many obstacles. But did either of them realise that when it came to the critical point Percy Coriat would bend the rules slightly? Everything depended on that.

Chapter Eighteen

In the narrative I gave some idea as to how the Duru and other bedouin lived when we first came into their desert fortresses with mechanical transport. They had lived in the open all their lives and their only form of modern equipment was their rifles, and some of them were museum pieces. True, the arrival of the gun had made major modifications to the tactics they employed in war, but otherwise nothing had affected their way of life for hundreds of years, until our cars broke rudely into this scene.

Since that time there have been many changes in their circumstances and the life of the bedouin in consequence has been changing. Some tribes have already become, as it were, mechanised, and the lorry, the Land Rover and the saloon car replace the camel as transport. Tribes living between ports and the populous areas of the interior have always been engaged in carrying goods and people across the intervening deserts. When motor vehicles came into the area, these slowly replaced the camel.

Some of these almost mechanised bedouin still live out in the desert by their wells, perhaps now in huts instead of in the open, and at night the vehicles park by their camps; but they still breed camels and keep large herds.

It is not easy to see how the situation will develop but a drift to villages and towns by bedouin is only to be expected.

For all the roughness of the old bedouin life, it has an attraction, a kind of simple beauty. In these days, when the most advanced nations are just beginning to wonder what they are themselves doing to the human race and to the world, what perils they are preparing for the next generation, it is perhaps refreshing, possibly in a way therapeutic, for us to consider for a moment a people of a different culture, who have not yet given themselves any reason to worry over such matters as too much progress. This is not to say they have no worries, but their worries are different in kind and in quality. I envy for example their capacity not to worry about time, to set out on a journey and not care when they will arrive, perhaps not whether they will arrive.

(Even in the circumstances of a much more simple form of life there are causes of worry which in turn create a mentality and dictate attitudes. For example, the slightest negligence over water on a long desert trip in summer means death. The traditional bedouin have always lived close to death, whether from disease or from a bullet.)

Another influence must be the habit of loneliness. I used to pass quite frequently by an area of good grazing where there would always be large camel herds. I would meet the same groups of young men or boys in ones, or twos, or threes, living completely alone in the open.

I used to stop sometimes to make coffee and talk to them. We would always carry food and we were able to give them something, and of course we gave them water and coffee. They would say this was the first water they had tasted since last time we stopped here.

Ingenuously rather, because I should have known the answer, I said, "But what do you drink?" "Camel's milk," they said, surprised at my stupidity. I knew better than to ask what the camels drank. The nearest well might be 15 or more miles away, and they would take camels for watering every few weeks. Camels can travel for as long as perhaps two weeks without drinking, but only provided they are trained to it; and if they are at pasture, and the grazing is good they can go for long periods without drinking water.

These bedouin boys would themselves eat nothing much but dates. If they were lucky they had a little dried meat. And as I say they were living quite alone out there in the desert.

In their code the killing of an enemy of the tribe, because the security of the tribe depends on it, becomes an automatic art. If you have to do it you do it. And lest we become critical and talk of callousness it is hardly necessary to remind ourselves with what alacrity, when the most advanced nations go to war, its citizens rush to join the forces. Modern weapons kill women, children and soldiers together without distinction. The bedouin code spares women and children, their casualties are extraordinarily light, and they are put to shame by the road casualty figures of any advanced country.

This way of living naturally breeds a wariness of the stranger, but once found worthy of trust, trust is complete. I believe that their idea of loyalty to a companion, to a fellow tribesman and to their whole tribe is of a nature and has a strength which people with a more sophisticated background would not find easy to comprehend.

Naturally in tough circumstances people are driven to help one another. In easy conditions they are not. A traveller is seen approaching from a distance; before he arrives you will prepare your best food to give him something to eat. You may have even less than him, but in any case you must give whatever you have. This is not the habit of the city, and it never could be.

Bedouin reliance on each other is absolute; and they are individually self-reliant.

Individuals vary greatly as in any society in their intellectual capacity; but I have noticed a remarkable thing about the bedouin which must come from this tough life and from the necessarily close companionship of those who are sharing it with them. This is the very high capability of intelligent bedouin as conversationalists.

They are interesting to listen to; and I have tried to analyse the reason for this. I think it is something along these lines. Conversation is their only form of relaxation. In the past, they could not read, listen to music, go to films or do anything we are used to doing. They deliberately set out to entertain one another by telling stories or discussing things together. They will follow a discussion and introduce lively, original, intellectual ideas into it. Some of them are, in consequence, marvellous raconteurs. Since their aim is to please and amuse the listener, they talk of the good things that may happen and have happened and generally speak less of the bad. If you do not look at something which is unpleasant or speak of it, after all it might as well not be there. This is not, as people sometimes say, insincerity, it is a philosophy. They indulge in gentle flattery, which is not flattery because it is pleasing. Flattery is surely a distasteful thing; and therefore if you find conversation pleasing it cannot be flattery. But they love to pull your leg: they laugh at and with you, at each other and particularly at themselves. And as I have said, the nomad talks in a strange dialect with its liquid syllables, which is very hard to follow at first because he uses strange words, but the beauty of the speech repays the effort. For these reasons I value them above all as a group of companions talking round the evening camp-fire.

It is now the fashion among the most sophisticated and developed nations to find ever tougher ways to travel, such as sailing round the world; and I think possibly both this and the craze for more ordinary sailing (but there should surely not be a helicopter waiting nearby to rescue you) may stem from the fact that we are over-mechanised, over-sophisticated and we crave a return to lost values. This is a healthy sign surely. Back to the self-reliance of the bedouin and the reliance on each other of companions in an adventure.

In due course one must assume changes in Arabia will inevitably destroy the values of the bedouin, but the resistance of the bedouin to change has been strong, particularly among the older ones; and perhaps any bedouin who has lived fully as a complete nomad up to the age of 25 or so finds change difficult or impossible.

I have a bedouin friend, who about three years ago, on advice from some of his settled friends, deliberately set himself to become a settled inhabitant of an oasis, having been an active shaikh of one of the most far-ranging wholly nomadic bedouin tribes. He must have been about 50 at this time. He was persuaded that this was for the good of his family and his tribe. Some of this tribe are, moreover, becoming semi-settled alongside him. He has built a house, runs a rather weedy looking vegetable garden at which he laughs because he recognises he is an inefficient gardener. He has plenty of money and his eldest son owns a car.

He is always cheerfully laughing at himself and he tells me he thinks he is in some ways, ridiculous. For a bedouin to take to the plough used to be regarded as almost shameful. But he has settled quite deliberately and I think he has succeeded. However, even my friend finds it essential to go off into the desert from time to time, as if to get his breath back. His sons doubtless will become fairly sophisticated modern young men, and the next generation will hardly know what desert life was like; nor is it probable I think that they will crave to return to it.

None of us, I believe, can doubt that the more advanced countries of the world in accepting the speed of material progress, and in tirelessly exerting themselves to accelerate the process more and more, are unwittingly throwing away some important human values. I do not think they pause often enough to reflect and perhaps identify them and consider if they cannot be saved.

I do not advocate halting progress, and certainly not for a moment delaying the introduction of new amenities to underdeveloped countries. I suppose just by working for an oil company I have in any case done my little bit to 'spoil' acres of beautiful desert and the old life. I am not one to put the brakes on; although I am not so sure that I have made up my mind about such things as space travel and supersonic travel. I think we may be progressing faster materially than is safe; since we cannot be sure that we are not destroying the very basis of life. But that is another thing.

Might we not, however, pause a moment to look first at our own values, and then at someone else's, to try to estimate what we are throwing away and whether we need to do so?

Epilogue

The rest of my own story can be briefly told. In the spring of 1956 the Foreign Office and the oil company arranged to extend and formalise my secondment for three years, during which time I was in Bahrain but travelling a great deal round the Gulf. I made many trips to the Trucial Coast and some to Oman itself, especially to Ibri. I saw something of the way in which the Trucial Oman Scouts, as the Levies were now called, and the SAS helped to end the revolt which took place under the leadership of Talib and Ghalib in central Oman in June 1957. A small body of SAS gave the *coup de grâce* to the revolt by storming the rebel strongholds on the heights of Jebel Akhdar with the Scouts in support and the Omani forces. All this time Ibri remained loyal to the Sultan and our airstrip was used to bring supplies to the interior. Talib and Ghalib fled in January 1959 and the Muscat Government established its own governors and officials in the main centres of the interior. Oil was not to be found until 1964 and even then no real development by the government took place until 1970 when the present Sultan took over from his father, after deposing him in Salalah.

In February 1959 instead of returning to the oil company at the end of my three-year secondment, I was lucky enough to compete successfully in one of those rare over-age competitions for special entry as First Secretary into the Foreign Service. My new role took me back very happily to Abu Dhabi as Political Officer, representing HMG. Things were much the same with only the first stirrings of change evident. The arrival of a few cars and trucks did not make much difference, but a few houses had now been built (some with their own electricity generators) and the British Government had built a small office for the Political Officer, and a flat above it for him to live in. This made daily life easier and increased the possibilities of office work. I received no more letters like the one I had once had from the oil company to ask why my (handwritten) accounts were so smudged, and to ask for clean copies. I had replied, 'The smudging is caused by sweat, please send a generator.' That had silenced them.

This pleasant stay in Abu Dhabi was cut short by illness which took me home. In October 1960, shortly after I left, oil was found in commercial quantities. For me there followed a posting to Jerusalem as Consul for Jerusalem and the West Bank; the latter was then not under Israeli occupation. It was an interesting but saddening experience. The tragedy of Palestine had further unfolded.

In 1964 I was posted to the Foreign Office for two years, partly to learn how the machine worked, an essential experience for a newcomer. After this I was in Bahrain from 1966-9 dealing Gulf-wide with our information effort. In 1969 I was appointed Her Majesty's Political Agent, the last in Qatar, and I was made Ambassador there in 1971 on the declaration of independence.

In November 1974 I retired early from the Diplomatic Service at my own request as my short service had earned only a small pension and I felt that unless I found a new career soon I would be too old for anything. Shaikh Zayed generously invited me to live in Abu Dhabi and gave me a house there. After a short time spent on consultancy work, I was very glad to be invited by Shaikh Zayed to help with the collection of historical archive material for the Abu Dhabi Government. The object was to obtain copies of material from all those countries which had political and trade links with the Gulf, starting with the Portuguese and

Dutch. Naturally a large part of the more recent written material comes from London and New Delhi, especially in the 19th and 20th centuries, and this is what concerns me. The work has taken me on visits to India and London where we arrange for material to be microfilmed and sent to Abu Dhabi where it is enlarged on to paper again, indexed and bound. This work takes place in the Old Palace in Abu Dhabi in which I first met Shaikh Shakhbut so many years ago.

In 1981 I had a year in London with the Council for the Advancement of Arab British Understanding (CAABU). One of my Arab friends said to me one day in his good, but not flawless, English, "Edward, in CAABU you only preach to the convicted." In fact we spread our net wider, but doing the job reminded me always of that penetrating remark.

After this I had a year and a half in the United States doing similar work. I thought the USA was fascinating, its people friendly and very hospitable, until it came to talking about Arabia. Then the majority listened politely but would not be persuaded to alter their views. The Zionist line is believed almost everywhere. There seems to me to be a gap, a fundamental misunderstanding between the West, especially the USA, and the Arabs. The West refuses even to recognise the existence of this gap and therefore sees no need to attempt to study it. It seems impossible to persuade the US Government that almost every act of theirs in the Middle East is based on this misunderstanding.

In Oman development was not remarkable until Sultan Qaboos assumed the rulership. Then it was very impressive, particularly when one remembers that the country is extensive and largely mountainous, and further that the amount of oil found so far is very modest by Gulf standards. The way in which the country has been reunited for the first time for a century is of the greatest value to the progress of Oman as a modern state.

The later history of the Trucial States is common knowledge. Economic depression continued until oil was found there in 1960. Production followed and, at long last, the hoped-for income. In Abu Dhabi major development did not start until 1966 when, under the leadership of Shaikh Zayed, something approaching a miracle took place. The money coming in to Abu Dhabi was also used to help development in other separate Trucial States; until then only Dubai, by the exertions of its Ruler and merchants, had been able to expand at all before oil was found there.

From 1966 Shaikh Zayed as Ruler directed the growth and development of Abu Dhabi, and within two years had to face the crisis caused by Britain's sudden decision to withdraw in 1971. The UAE did not then exist, and not only were its constituent parts divided, but they lacked nearly all the institutions of modern government. Most important of all was the almost total absence of educational establishments, which meant that there were very few people with the necessary training for government posts, and the people needed to teach and train nationals were wanting. Persuasion would not change the minds of the British, and Shaikh Zayed's statesmanlike decision to invite Shaikh Rashid and then the other rulers to join in making the UAE one state, involving for all of them the sacrifice of that most jealously treasured possession, sovereignty, saved the day; a new state was created. It advanced and grew at breathtaking speed, not without the difficulties which accompany all human endeavour. The exciting acquisition of new wealth created new expectations immediately, thereby pressuring those in charge to advance very quickly, often taking risks, experimenting much of the way, but always going forward. The fact that these great expectations have been so largely met in so short a time is a triumph.

When I look at the modern cities in the UAE and Oman I think of the pioneers, both nationals and expatriates. But for their work in those harsh days, living in tents in the desert with no electricity, working hard and under difficult conditions for years, none of this stupendous change could have happened. The UAE owes a great debt to these people. The leaders and the workforce together achieved marvels. Now that I am back once more, writing this in Abu Dhabi, I can say how exciting it is to see and live amidst all the new developments. In the days when I would visit Shaikh Zayed in his desert fort at Al Muwaiqi in the Al Ain oasis, I never dreamt that he would create this modern state. It is to him that the unity of these shaikhdoms is due. Such a success in joining separate communities into a whole has been a rare achievement.

Edward Henderson 1988.

Index